Witty Wordplays:
Laughing Out Loud
with Chinese Characters

"字"得其乐
——汉字笑话500篇

马长山 著
Written by Ma Changshan

李国斌 赵金基 英译
Translated by Li Guobin and Zhao Jinji

刘宏 图
Illustrated by Liu Hong

美国南方出版社
Dixie W Publishing Corporation U.S.A.

"字"得其乐——汉字笑话 500 篇

Witty Wordplays: Laughing Out Loud with Chinese Characters

Author: Ma Changshan

Translators: Li Guobin and Zhao Jinji

Illustrator: Liu Hong

作　　者：马长山

英　　译：李国斌、赵金基

插　　图：刘　宏

封面设计：刘　宏

版面设计：张龙道

Published by

Dixie W Publishing Corporation

Montgomery, Alabama, U.S.A.

http://www.dixiewpublishing.com

本书由美国南方出版社出版

▪ 版权所有　侵权必究 ▪

2023 年 6 月 DWPC 第一版

开本：229mm × 152mm

字数：95 千字

Library of Congress Control Number: 2023937764

美国国会图书馆编目号码：2023937764

国际标准书号 ISBN-13: 978-1-68372-544-2

序　言

马长山

　　大约八九年前的一个下午，我突发奇想：可否以我们中国人每天使用的汉字作为幽默对象，写出一本笑话集？

　　说干就干。我开始琢磨眼前的常用字，试图利用它们的偏旁部首、组织结构和读音的异同，寻找和制造一些笑料。写了几十段以后，脑袋空了，实在写不动了。这时我在网上搜索到一些"汉字搞笑对话"之类的段子，感到同道不少，于是又硬着头皮写了下去。后来我还邀请了李国斌、赵金基两位英语高手和漫画家刘宏加入到这个阵营中来，想让全世界更多的人——即使他们一个汉字也不认识——了解到汉字不仅是神圣伟大实用之创造，而且是幽默、欢乐、诙谐之源泉。就这样我们互相鼓励，反复切磋，终于创作出了这本世界出版史上第一部以汉字为幽默对象的笑话集——而且还是中英双语版。

　　但是在联系本书的出版时却很不顺利。整整五年时间，我在中国大陆找了无数家出版社，都没有找到合适的出版单位。好在出版是无国界的。感谢美国南方出版社让此书得以面世。 希望本书为全球的读者，特别是喜欢汉语的读者带来欢乐！

2023.4.15. 于中国北京

Preface

Ma Changshan

Approximately eight or nine years ago, on one afternoon, I had a sudden inspiration: Could Chinese characters in everyday use be utilized as objects of humor to create a comprehensive joke book?

Immediately I delved into the exploration, utilizing the radical components, organizational structures, and distinctions in pronunciation of commonplace characters to conjure amusing contents. After crafting several dozen short anecdotes, my well of inspiration temporarily depleted, impeding further progress. Nonetheless, my curiosity persisted, and I discovered some "funny Chinese character dialogues" online, a serene reminder that others shared my interests. Encouraged, I persevered and even invited two proficient English experts, Li Guobin and Zhao Jinji, as well as the skilled cartoonist Liu Hong, to join me in a collaborative effort. I aspired to create a work that would allow more people from all over the world, including those who did not perceive a single Chinese character, to recognize that Chinese characters are not only exceptional and practical creations, but also a source of wit, glee, and satire. We spurred one another on, continuously revising and refining the contents until we ultimately created the world's first collections of jokes with Chinese characters as objects of humor - presented in both Chinese and English.

Nonetheless, publishing the book was a trying endeavor. For an arduous five years, I searched across mainland China for myriad potential publishers with no success. Fortunately, publishing knows no boundaries, and I am grateful to the Dixie W Publishing Corporation in the United States for affording me the opportunity to materialize my vision. Ultimately, it is my sincere aspiration that this literary work shall impart a sense of delight to readers across the globe, particularly those who have developed an affinity towards the Chinese language.

Beijing, China.
April 15, 2023.

目　录
Table of Contents

第一章　差点把姐认成牛
Chapter 1　Almost Mistaken for a Cow

乱了辈分

出场角色：儿（ér）；母（mǔ）；充（chōng）。

儿去南方读书已经半年多了。母每日苦苦思念着儿。

一天，母的一个远房亲戚充来家里串门。精神有些恍惚的母把充当成了自己的儿，高兴地说："儿啊，你戴了博士帽啦！"

充皱着眉头说："嫂子，我是充啊，你连我都认不出来啦？"

A Relative Mixed Up with Son

Characters: 儿"son"; 母"mother"; 充"full".

Mom misses 儿 terribly who has been away from home for half a year studying in the south.

One day a distant relative 充 comes around. Mom, somewhat in a trance, mistakes him for her son.

"Oh, my boy!" she exclaims with delight. "You're wearing a mortarboard."

"Can't you recognise me?" replies the man with a frown. "I'm 充, not your son."

Note: 充 is composed of 儿 with a component on top representing a mortarboard.

差点把姐认成牛

出场角色：午（wǔ）；干（gān）。

午在商厦里见到了干。

午对干说:"妹子,我这个纱巾还不错吧?"

干撇着嘴对午说:"姐,我眼神儿不好。你披上这玩意,我差点把你看成一头牛了。"

Almost Mistaken for a Cow

Characters: 午"horse"; 干"dry".

午 runs into 干 at a mall.

"Hi, sis," says 午 to 干. "The veil looks good on me, doesn't it?"

"Excuse my poor eyesight, " replies the other, curling her lips. "But I almost mistake you for a cow."

Note: 午 has a left-falling stroke on the top left resembling a veil; 午 is graphically similar to 牛"cow".

出言不逊

出场角色:妻(qī);衮(gǔn)。

妻在商厦里见到了衮,惊讶道:"老公啊,你啥时候买了件衣服啊?"

衮笑道:"妹子,你认错人了。我可不是你老公啊。"

妻问:"那你是谁呀?"

衮:"gǔn!"

妻怒道:"我和和气气地问你,你咋让我'滚'呢?"

注释:衮,古代君王等的礼服。

Putting Foot in Mouth

Characters: 妻"wife"; 袞"ancient robe".

妻 runs across 袞 at a mall. "Hubby, when did you get the coat?" she asks in surprise.

"Sorry, madam, but you've got the wrong person," smiles the other. "I'm not your husband."

"Who are you, then?" asks the woman.

"袞," comes the reply.

"I've been courteous, but why are you being so rude to me?" says the lady crossly.

Note: 袞 is structured like 公 "husband" in the middle of 衣 "coat"; "袞" is mistaken for its homophone "滾" meaning "Get out".

家的味道

出场角色：口（kǒu）；囚（qiú）；家（jiā）。

口、囚和家在一次聚会上问其他人，他们仨谁的相貌更像一个家。

"你们仨先做个自我评价吧！"众人建议道。

口抢先说："我最像家了，虽然空空如也，只有四面大墙，可有句成语叫'家徒四壁'，这说明我最像家啊！"

囚摇了摇头，反驳道："光有几面墙，一个人没有，那算什么家呀。我是既有房又有人，看来我更像个家。"

家清了清嗓子，最后出场："口兄确实没有一点家的味道。可是囚兄，你虽然有房有人，可是人在密不透风的四面大墙之内，没有一点自由。这算什么家呀！你俩看看我，虽然没有人，没有墙，只有一个顶棚加一头猪。可是多温馨啊。不信你俩问问大伙谁更像家。"

The Essence of Home

Characters: 口"mouth"; 囚"prisoner"; 家"family".

At a party, 口, 囚 and 家 ask the other guests to identify who of them best embodies the essence of a home.

"You three start with a self-evaluation!" the others suggest.

"I am the best picture of a home," 口 asserts promptly. "Though I may seem empty, the idiom 'a home with nothing but four bare walls' indicates that I resemble a home perfectly."

"Four walls alone don't make a home," retorts 囚, shaking his head. "With a person within a house, I look more like a home."

Finally, 家 clears his throat and remarks, "Brother 口 certainly fails to evoke any sense of homeliness, and as for brother 囚, a confined space of four tight walls with a person shut in cannot be deemed as a home."

"Look at me. A pig under a roof with no wall or person lives in the real comfort of home, " 家 continues. "So you two can seek the opinion of others to determine who is the best image of a home."

Note: 口 is shaped like an enclosure of four walls; 囚 is composed of 人 "person" fully enclosed by 口; 家 is composed of 豕 "pig" with a semantic radical 宀 "roof" on top.

没大没小

出场角色：人（rén）；大（dà）。

人问大："兄弟，玩上单杠了？"

大怒道："这么没礼貌。我是大，你咋跟我称兄道弟呀！"

注释："大"，在汉语某些方言中指父亲。

A Mannerless Son

Characters: 人"man"; 大"dad".

"Hey, bro," 人 says to 大. "Having fun on the high bar?"

"How rude you are to address father as bro!" responds the other angrily.

Note: 大 resembles 人 playing a horizontal bar.

不孝之子

出场角色：克（kè）；古（gǔ）。

克问古："兄弟，你儿子跑啦？他这一跑，你岂不是作古了吗？"

注释：作古，指死亡。

The Black Sheep of the Family

Characters: 克"gram"; 古"ancient".

"Old chap, your son has run away?" 克 asks 古. "Deserted by him, you've become ancient, right?"

Note: 克 is composed of 古 at the top and 儿 "son" at the bottom; the Chinese expression "become ancient" is a euphemism for "die".

惨遭毒手

出场角色：羊（yáng）；羔（gāo）。

羊望着羔，悲痛欲绝地大哭道："孩儿啊，谁把你的尾巴切成四截啦？"

The Victim of a Cruel Hand

Characters: 羊"sheep"; 羔"lamb".

"Oh, kid. Who cut your tail into four pieces?" wails 羊, staring at 羔 with desperation.

Note: The bottom extended part of the vertical line in 羊 resembles a tail while the radical ⺗ at the bottom of 羔 resembles a tail cut into four segments.

爱心无价

出场角色：茧（jiǎn）；萤（yíng）。

茧望着天上飞翔的萤，羡慕地问："朋友，为啥你能在空中漫舞，我只能匍匐在地上呢？"

萤看了看茧，笑道："因为我比你多一颗爱心啊！"

A Love Heart

Characters: 茧"cocoon"; 萤"firefly".

"Hey, buddy. Why are you capable of dancing in the air while I can only lie on the ground?" asks 虽 admiringly as he looks up at 萤.

Sizing the other up, 萤 replies with a smile, "Because I've got a love heart that gives me the strength to fly!"

Note: Compared with 虽, 萤 has one more radical ⼍, which lies in the middle of the character 爱 "love" representing "a love heart".

冷战夫妻

出场角色：比（bǐ）；北（běi）。

比见到了北。他反复端详着北，自言自语道："夫妻一旦陷入冷战，连睡觉也要背靠背了。真爱就是两个人要永远朝着一个方向。"

The Silent Treatment

Characters: 比"comparison"; 北"north".

比 comes across 北. Looking the other up and down, 比 mutters under his breath, "Once involved in the silent treatment, a couple give each other the cold shoulder even in bed. True love means looking in the same direction now and forever."

Note: 比 is structured left to right with a pair of graphically similar components resembling two persons looking in the same direction while 北 representing a couple facing opposite directions.

儿在村里找他大

出场角色：儿（ér）；天（tiān）；因（yīn）。

大出门多半天了，到吃饭时间了还没有回家。娘让儿出去找找。

儿在村里转了好久，也没有遇见他的大。

突然，儿遇见了天。

"大，你咋让人吊天花板上啦？"儿害怕地问。

"我不是你大。我是你天叔啊！"天微笑着摸了摸儿。

儿继续找他的大。又见了因。

儿大哭道："大，你被关起来啦？娘让你回家吃饭哩！"

因笑道："傻孩子，别哭啦。我是你因叔，不是你大。"

Nowhere to Be Found

Characters: 儿"son"; 天"sky"; 因"cause".

Dad is out for long and still not back for meal, so Mum sends 儿 to look for him.

儿 is searching here and there around the village when suddenly he catches sight of 天.

"How come you're hanging from the ceiling, da?" asks the boy in panic.

"Kid," smiles the other, giving the child a reassuring pat, "I'm your uncle 天, not your father."

Then 儿 picks up his search till he comes across 因.

"How come you are locked up, da?" wails the boy. "Ma asks you to come home for dinner."

"Don't cry, dumb bunny," the man laughs. "I'm your uncle 因, not your father."

Note: 天 is composed of 大 "dad" with a horizontal stroke on top resembling a ceiling; 因 is composed of 大 fully enclosed by a radical 口.

珠联璧合

出场角色：丰（fēng）；色（sè）。

丰是一个单身小伙子。经人介绍，他认识了美女色。

丰为色的美貌所倾倒。一天，丰情不自禁地对色说："小姐，嫁给我吧，咱俩共铸多彩人生。"

Side by Side

Characters: 丰"plentiful"; 色"colour".

丰, a single young man, is introduced to 色, who is such a stunning beauty that he is completely swept off his feet.

One day, unable to contain his emotions, 丰 pops the question. "Will you marry me, miss?" he says. "Let us build a colourful life side by side."

Note: 丰 joined by 色 on the right forms the character 艳 "colourful".

寡妇的难处

出场角色：禾（hé）；季（jì）。

禾对季说："季姐，你老公去世多年。你也该找个合适的人成家了。"

"我拖个油瓶，没人待见啦。"季无可奈何地说。

A Widow's Trouble

Characters: 禾"grass"; 季"season".

"Sis, it's been years since you were widowed," says 禾 to 季. "It is time that you got remarried."

"Nobody has a crush on a woman with a son of tender age," replies the other with a heavy sigh.

Note: 季 is structured top to bottom with 禾 and 子 "son".

小巫见大巫

出场角色：句（jù）；旬（xún）。

妇产医院门口，句巧遇了旬。

旬告知自己怀了双胞胎。

句对旬说："姐姐真厉害，一下子怀了两个。"

旬笑道："现在双胞胎不算个啥。人家旬姐才有本事，一下子就是四胞胎。"

A Giant in the Presence of a Super-Giant

Characters: 句"sentence"; 旬"ten days".

句 bumps into 旬 at the gate of a maternity hospital.

Learning that the other is pregnant with twins, 句 says, "You are really something, sis, expecting two at a time."

"It's no big deal compared to 旬," 旬 laughs, "who is carrying four babies at once."

Note: 句, 旬 and 甸 are respectively composed of 口, 日 and 田, all enclosed by the same radical 勹 (from upper and right sides); 句 represents a woman pregnant with one baby, 旬 with twins and 甸 with quadruplets.

恍然大悟

出场角色：几（jī）；朵（duǒ）。

几对朵说："妹子，你一上树就显得仪态万方。我知道为什么姐妹们都要攀高枝儿了！"

Seeing the Light

Characters: 几"small table"; 朵"flower".

"Sis, you appear in all your glory on top of the tree," says 几 to 朵. "Now I see why all girls like climbing high branches."

Note: 朵 is composed of 几 at the top and 木 "tree" at the bottom; the Chinese expression "climb high branches" means marrying someone from a higher economic or social class.

顶上开花

出场角色：开（kai）；卉（huì）。

开对卉说："姐，你啥时候长出一根小辫儿啊？"

A Floret on Top

Characters: 开"open"; 卉"grass".

"Sis, since when have you sprouted that little pigtail?" 开 asks 卉.

Note: The vertical stroke running across the top horizontal line in 卉 resembles a pigtail.

少说为佳

出场角色：口（kǒu）；田（tián）。

经人介绍，口小姐和田先生在星巴克咖啡厅约会了。

楚楚可人的口小姐滔滔不绝地介绍了个人情况，包括学历、职业、收入、爱好和父母。

衣冠楚楚、气宇轩昂的田先生则一直保持沉默。

口小姐望着田先生说："你为什么不说话呀？难道你是哑巴？"

田先生拿出一支笔，在餐巾纸上默默写了一行字："我这是第一次跟女孩子约会，妈怕我言多语失，给我嘴吧上贴了十字封条。"

Silence Is Golden

Characters: 口"mouth", 田"field".

Miss 口 and Mr. 田 meet on a blind date at Starbucks.

The charming young lady introduces herself, going into details about her education experiences, job, income, interests and her folks, while the gentleman, who is neatly-dressed and distinguished-looking, simply keeps quiet all the time.

"Why don't you talk?" finally she asks, looking him in the face. "You aren't a mute, are you?"

Then silently, Mr. 田 takes out a pen and writes down his reply on a napkin, "This is my first time on a date, and Mum seals my mouth for fear that I might put my foot in it."

Note: 田 is composed of 口 with 十 enclosed, resembling a sealed mouth.

骗子是怎样诞生的？

出场角色：马（mǎ）；扁（biǎn）；骗（piàn）。

马先生和扁小姐结婚了。不久，他们有了一个儿子。

夫妻俩为孩子应该随谁的姓发生了争执。

"孩子随父姓，自古皆然。"马理直气壮。

"现在男女平等。《婚姻法》没有规定孩子必须姓你的姓。"扁据理力争。

夫妻俩找到了一个解决办法：他们用双方的姓氏组成了一个新姓——骗，并且给儿子起了一个独到的名字："骗子。"

How a Swindler Is Born

Characters: 马"horse"; 扁"flat".

"Mr. 马 and Miss 扁 get married, and soon they have a son.

The couple have a dispute over whose surname the child should take.

"The kid should take the father's family name, as it has been like that since ancient times," 马 insists confidently.

"Nowadays, men and women are equal. The Marriage Law does not stipulate that the child must take your last name," 扁 argues.

The couple find a solution: they combine their surnames to create a new one - "骗", and give their son a unique name: "骗子".

Note: 马 joined by 扁 on the right forms the character 骗"swindle"; the Chinese "骗子" means "swindler".

从头做起

出场角色：兰（lán）；三（sān）。

兰对三说："妹子，咱们女孩子有没有小辫儿，气质就是不同啊。"

三笑嘻嘻地说："长了小辫儿的小三儿还是小三儿。"

兰正色道："妹妹你错了，我现在已经是一个兰质蕙心的淑女了。"

Starting Anew from the Top

Characters: 兰"orchid"; 三"three".

"Sis," says 兰 to 三, " little braids add special charms to us girls."

"A mistress with braids is still a mistress," grins the other.

"That's not the case," states 兰 with a severe look. "Now I am a bright and beautiful lady."

Note: 兰 is composed of 三 with a radical ˅ on top resembling two braids; 三 dialectally means "mistress".

帽美如花

出场角色：木（mù）；朵（duǒ）。

木对朵说："姐，你的小帽子真漂亮。"

A Lovely Hat

Characters: 木"tree"; 朵"a flower or a cloud".

"Sis, that little hat looks really good on you," says 木 to 朵.

Note: 朵 is composed of 木 with 几 on top representing a hat.

刚刚买了马

出场角色：姜（jiāng）。幕后角色：缰（jiāng）。

妻子："亲爱的，家里没姜了。你去买点。"

丈夫："没钱了。咱们刚刚买了一匹马。"

妻子："你真是买得起马备不起姜啊。"

注释：本文中的"买得起马备不起姜"是"买得起马备不起缰"的戏仿，后者是从谚语"买得起马备不起鞍"演化而来的。言外之意是有钱买主要的物品，却没钱买相关配套的物品了。"缰"与"姜"同音。

A Horse Just Bought

Onstage Character: 姜"ginger". Offstage Character: 缰"rein".

Wife: "We've run out of ginger. Go to buy some, darling."

Husband: "We are broke, as we just bought a horse."

Wife: "It's really funny you could afford a horse but not any ginger."

Note: "One can afford a horse but not any ginger" is a parody of the Chinese proverb "One can afford a horse but not the saddle (or the rein)" which implies it is ridiculous for someone to be able to afford the main item but not the related accessories. In Mandarin Chinese, "ginger" and "rein" are homophones.

妈妈眼中的小天使

出场角色：母（mǔ）；兆（zhào）。

母见到了兆，开心地说："我儿，你咋长出四只翅膀,变成外国的小天使啦？你翅膀硬了，别不认妈了！"

兆无可奈何地苦笑道："夫人，我今天已经被好几个母亲认作儿子了！"

In the Eyes of Mother

Characters: 母"mother"; 兆"sign".

母 becomes overjoyed to see 兆. "Oh, my son, you've grown into an angel with wings," exclaims the mother. "Now you've come of age, but don't forget your mom!"

"Sorry, madam, but I'm not your son," the other replies with a bitter smile. "You are not the only one who has mistaken me for her boy today!"

Note: 兆 is composed of 儿 "son" with a radical 冫 on the left resembling the left wing, and a left-falling stroke together with a dot on the right resembling the right wing.

乖乖妙语

出场角色：母（mǔ）；乖（guāi）；乘（chéng）。

母见到自己的女儿乖正在和乘一起玩。她对乖说："乖乖，你怎么不穿裙子呢？你看乘穿着裙子多漂啊！"

乖撅着嘴答道："我要是穿了裙子，还是你的乖乖吗？"

A Witty Reply

Characters: 母"mother"; 乖"lovely"; 乘"ride".

母 sees her daughter 乖 hanging out with 乘. "Babe," says the mother, "why don't you have your skirt on? How nice 乘 looks in hers!"

"If in a skirt, would I still be your baby?" replies 乖, pursing her lips.

Note: Without the left-falling and right-falling strokes at the bottom resembling a skirt, 乖 differs in composition from 乘.

有眼不识金镶玉

出场角色：母（mǔ）；宝（bǎo）；玉（yù）。

母到幼儿园接她的宝宝。

母见到了玉，大惊道："宝宝，谁把你的帽子摘下来啦？"

玉笑着说："阿姨，我不是你的宝宝。您仔细看看我是谁。"

母揉了揉眼睛，盯着玉看了好大一会儿，笑道："你不是张姐的女儿小玉嘛！我真是有眼不识金镶玉呀！"

No Eye for Jade

Characters: 母"mother"; 宝"treasure"; 玉"jade".

母 comes to the kindergarten to pick up her kid 宝, surprised to see 玉.

"Babe, where's your cap?" exclaims the mother.

"Auntie, I'm not your 宝," giggles 玉. "Just take a closer look at me."

Rubbing her eyes, the woman stares at the little girl for quite a while. "Oh, you are sister Zhang's daughter 玉," she laughs. "I've got no eye for jade, indeed."

Note: 宝 is composed of 玉 with a radical 宀 on top representing a hat.

母不识子

出场角色：母 (mǔ)；子 (zǐ)；字 (zì)。

母来到学校门口接孩子，见到了从校门里匆匆走出来的字。母高兴地说："儿子，你咋戴上帽子啦，差点让妈认不出来。"

字看了看母，不悦道："阿姨，您不认识字吗？您仔细看看，我是您的儿子吗？"

Mom Not Knowing Son

Characters: 母"mother"; 子"son"; 字"word".

母 comes to the school gate to pick up her son. Seeing 字 hurrying out, the mother gets delighted and calls out to him, "Honey, I can hardly recognise you. Why are you wearing a cap?"

"Sorry, aunt, but you've got the wrong person," replies 字 as he throws her an irritated glance. "Take a closer look. Am I your son?"

Note: 字 is composed of 子 "son" with a radical 宀 on top representing a cap.

谁将我儿吊起来？

出场角色：母（mǔ）；兀（wù）。

母见到兀，大惊失色道："儿啊，谁把你吊天花板上啦！"

Son Hung Up

Characters: 母"mother"; 兀"towering".

母 turns terribly pale at the sight of 兀. "Oh, dear," she exclaims. "How did you end up hung under the ceiling?"

Note: 兀 is composed of 儿 "son" with a horizontal stroke on top resembling a ceiling.

父子俩

出场角色：丫（yā）。幕后角色：鸭（yā）。

春天来了，父亲带着七岁的儿子到河边玩耍。

儿子兴高采烈地坐在河边的草地上，飞快地把鞋袜脱掉，然后把脚丫子伸进了河水里。

"孩子，你这淘气的样子让爸爸想起了一句古诗啊！"爸爸兴致盎然地说。

"什么古诗啊？"儿子问。

"春江水暖丫先知。"爸爸说完，哈哈大笑起来。

注释：本文中的"春江水暖丫先知"是中国宋代著名诗人苏东坡的诗句"春江水暖鸭先知"的戏仿。

Father and Son

Onstage Character: 丫"toe". Offstage Character: 鸭"duck".

Spring arrived. A father took his seven-year-old son to the riverside for fun.

Cheerfully sitting on the grass by the river, the boy swiftly pulled off his shoes and socks, and dipped his feet into the water.

"Son, you remind me of an old line, " the father said in high spirits.

"What is it?" asked the son.

"Toes first feel spring water getting warm," answered the man with a loud laugh.

Note: "Toes first feel spring water getting warm" is a parody of "Ducks first feel spring water getting warm", a popular line from a verse composed by Su Dongpo, a great poet in Song Dynasty, which means the ducks paddling in rivers are the very first to perceive the water growing warmer in early spring. The spoof and the original line sound exactly the same.

单身汉娶妻

出场角色：得（dé）。幕后角色：德（dé）。

有个单身汉找到媒婆，请她帮忙物色一个妻子。

"不知先生中意什么样的女子？"媒婆热情地问。

"古人云，'娶妻在得不在色'，请给我介绍一个陪嫁多一点的女子吧。相貌如何倒不是太要紧。"

媒婆给单身汉介绍了一个有万贯陪嫁但奇丑无比的女子。单身汉重谢了媒婆，欢天喜地地把该女子娶进了家门。

注释：本文中的"娶妻在得不在色"是汉语谚语"娶妻在德不在色"的戏仿。

A Bachelor's Surrender

Onstage Character: 得"gain". Offstage Character: 德"virtue".

Once a bachelor came to a matchmaker and asked her to find him a wife. "Do you have a particular type in mind?" inquired the woman in a warm tone.

"As the old saying goes, 'Wive for gains rather than for looks,' " replied the man. "Just introduce me a woman with a large dowry, please. It doesn't matter what she looks like."

So the matchmaker recommended a girl who was ugly as sin but would bring a substantial dowry. Fairly satisfied, the man rewarded the matchmaker generously and led the girl to the altar happily.

Note: "Wive for gains rather than for looks" is a parody of the Chinese proverb "Wive for virtues rather than for looks" meaning when choosing a wife a man should consider her good moral qualities rather than her physical appearance. "Gains" and "virtues" are homophones in Mandarin. With one character changed, the spoof differs greatly in meaning from the original proverb.

飘柔秀发不可抛

出场角色：幺（yāo）；厶（sī）。

幺对厶说："姐姐，你把披肩发剪掉啦？"

注释：厶，同私。

Beauty Is in the Hair

Characters: 幺"youngest"; 厶"private".

"You had your shoulder-length hair cut down, sis?" 幺 asks 厶.

Note: 幺 is composed of 厶 with a left-falling stroke on the upper left resembling the shoulder-length hair.

不可装嫩

出场角色：木（mù）；禾（hé）。

木对禾说："戴个纱巾想装嫩？"

Mutton Dressed Up as Lamb

Characters: 木"tree"; 禾"grass".

"Wearing a veil, are you trying to act young?" says 木 to 禾.

Note: 禾 is composed of 木 with a left-falling stroke on top resembling a veil.

多一道不如少一道

出场角色：内（nèi）；丙（bǐng）。

内和丙是无话不谈的闺蜜。

一天，内故作神秘地对丙说："虽然我俩的名字只差一道，可却有着天壤之别呀！"

"是吗？"丙疑惑地等待着下文。

"我是明媒正娶的内人，你是横刀夺爱的小三。"内和盘托出了谜底。

丙笑着与内抱成了一团。

注释：丙，天干的第三位，用作顺序第三的代称。"小三儿"，是通过互联网流行起来的一个词，是对"第三者"的贬称。

More Is Not Better

Characters: 内"wife"; 丙"third".

内 and 丙 are ladybros who are straightforward with each other.

One day 内 whispers to 丙 with an air of mystery, "A single line makes a sharp distinction between you and me."

"Really?" responds 丙, curious to hear more.

"I am the legally wedded wife while you are the third party, a home wrecker," 内 speaks her mind straight out.

Then they two cuddle up together, giggling.

Note: With an extra horizontal line on top, 丙 differs from 内 in composition.

不要随便认夫君

出场角色：妻（qī）；天（tiān）。

妻在街上见到了天，惊呼道："天啊——不，我的夫啊，你的头哪去了？"

天不紧不慢地对妻说："你开始叫对了，后来叫错了。我就是天，不是你的夫。"

A Wrong Husband

Characters: 妻"wife"; 天"heaven".

妻 gets shocked to see 天 on the street. "Heavens!" she exclaims. "Where's your head, my man?"

"Madam, you were first right and then wrong," replies 天 calmly. "I'm heaven, but not your husband."

Note: 天 is shaped similar to 夫 "husband"; the left-falling stroke in 天 touches the top horizontal line while the left-falling stroke in 夫 runs across the top line with the extended part resembling the head.

两个钱包

出场角色：全（quán）；金（jīn）。

全对金说："姐姐发财了？一下子买了两个包包。"

A Purse Lover

Characters: 全"complete"; 金"gold".

"Wow, sis. You bought two purses at once," says 全 to 金. "Did you strike it rich or something?"

Note: Compared with 全, 金 has two extra dot strokes at the lower bottom representing two purses.

乖乖要飞啦

出场角色：千（qiān）； 乖（guāi）。

千对乖说："宝贝儿，你啥时候长了一对翅膀啊？"

About to Take Wing

Characters: 千"thousand"; 乖"cute".

"Dearest Babe," says 千 to 乖. "Since when have you sprouted a pair of wings?"

Note: Compared with 千, 乖 has two additional components representing a pair of wings.

莫名奇妙

出场角色：妻（qī）；夫（fu）；关（guān）。

妻看见了关，大哭道：“夫啊，谁把你的头砍下了，又给你安了俩犄角啊？”

关摸了摸自己的头，迷惑不解地对妻说：“我从生下来就是这个模样。再说了，我也不认识你呀，怎么会是你的夫呢？”

Not with It

Characters: 妻"wife"; 夫"husband"; 关"a surname".

"My man," seeing 关, 妻 wails, "Who chopped off your head and fixed you a pair of horns?"

Confused, 关 gives himself a touch on the head. "Sorry, madam, but I was born this way," he says to the lady. "Besides, not knowing you at all, how can I be your husband?"

Note: 关 is mistaken for 夫 "husband"; 关 has a radical ⌣ at the top resembling a pair of horns, and the top extended part of the left-falling stroke in 夫 resembles the head.

“我比你先生厉害！”

出场角色：妻（qī）；夹（jiā）。

妻问夹：“夫啊，你为朋友两肋插刀啦！”

夹道：“别随便认夫君。我不是你先生。我比他多两下子。”

Superior to Your Old Man

Characters: 妻"wife"; 夹"clip".

"Oh, hubby," 妻 calls out to 夹. "You've got your chest pierced for your friends!"

"Don't be so reckless," replies the other. "I'm not your husband, and I have a couple of skills that he lacks."

Note: With two more dot strokes (resembling two knives or representing a couple of skills), 夹 differs from 夫 "husband" in composition.

单身狗的羡慕

出场角色：人（rén）；从（cóng）。
人羡慕地对从说："有伴儿的感觉真好。"

Green with Envy

Characters: 人"person"; 从"follow".

"You must be feeling ecstatic to have a companion," says 人 to 从, brimming with envy.

Note: 从 is composed of two 人 left to right.

老哥娶了铁扇公主？

出场角色：兄（xiōng）；兑（duì）。
兄对兑说："几天不见，老兄就变成牛魔王了？"

注释：牛魔王，中国古典小说《西游记》里的一个角色，头上有两个犄角。其妻子为《西游记》中的铁扇公主。

You Married Princess Iron Fan?

Characters: 兄"elder brother"; 兑"change".

"Bro, it's only been a few days," says 兄 to 兑. "You've transformed into Bull Demon King?"

Note: 兑 is composed of 兄 with a radical ˇ on top resembling a pair of horns; Bull Demon King and his wife Princess Iron Fan are characters in an ancient Chinese novel Journey to the West.

哭泣的小牛

出场角色：谈（tán）。幕后角色：弹（tán）。

斑马看见一头小牛在田野里放声大哭，连忙上前询问原因。

可是，不论斑马怎么盘问，小牛只是大哭，一句话也不说。

斑马默默地站在小牛旁边，有些不知所措。

"朋友，谢谢你一直陪着我。可是我不能告诉你哭泣的原因。"小牛红着眼圈对斑马说。

"为什么呢？"斑马不解地问。

"因为家父经常告诫我，'男儿有泪不轻谈。'"小牛说完，又嚎啕大哭起来。

注释：本文中的"男儿有泪不轻谈"是谚语"男儿有泪不轻弹"的戏仿。

A Wailing Calf

Onstage Character: 谈"confide". Offstage Character: 弹"shed".

A zebra saw a calf wailing in the field and hurried over to ask what was wrong.

However, no matter how he questioned, the calf did not utter a word but simply kept crying.

The zebra stood there in silence, somewhat at a loss.

'It's nice of you to stay so long keeping me company," sobbed the calf finally with red eyes. "Still I cannot tell you what made me cry."

"But why?" asked the zebra in confusion.

"As my father always warns me, 'A man never easily confides tears.' " With these words the calf picked up his loud wail.

Note: "A man never easily confides tears" is a parody of the Chinese proverb "A man never easily sheds tears" meaning a man of strong character never reduces himself to tears in the face of difficulties or hardships. "Confide" and "shed" have the same speech sound in Mandarin.

没穿裙子

出场角色：桌（zhuō）；卓（zhuō）。

桌对卓说："妹子，你裙子都没穿还自我感觉良好？"

Not Dressed in a Skirt

Characters: 桌"desk"; 卓"excellent".

"Sis, do you feel confident even without wearing a skirt?" 桌 asks 卓.

Note: Compared with 卓, 桌 has an additional 八 at the bottom resembling a skirt.

我家的表叔看不清

出场角色：侄（zhí）；寂（jì）。
侄看了半天寂，说："叔，你一戴上帽子，我差点没认出你来。"
寂笑道："侄啊，你好好看看，我可不是你叔啊。"

A Wrong Uncle

Characters: 侄"nephew"; 寂"quiet".
"Uncle, I almost did not recognise you with that cap on," remarks 侄 while staring at 寂.
"Take a closer look, 侄. I am not a member of your family," chuckles the other.

Note: 寂 is composed of 叔"uncle" with a radical 宀 on top resembling a cap.

不花冤枉钱

出场角色：哀（āi）；口（kǒu）。
哀对口道："'人靠衣裳马靠鞍'，妹子，你也买件衣裳穿起来吧！"
口看了一眼哀，抿着嘴笑道："我可不想花钱买伤心。"

Budget Brilliance

Characters: 哀"sorrow"; 口"mouth".

"Hi, sis. Why not treat yourself to a dress?" says 哀 to 口. "As the saying goes, 'Fine feathers make fine birds.' "

Casting an eye over the other, 口 smiles, "I don't want to pay money for grief."

Note: 哀 is structured like 口 in the middle of 衣"garment".

错认邻居为夫君

出场角色：娘（niáng）；大（dà）；奈（nài）。

娘让二小去找他的大。二小他大是煤矿工人，昨天下班后没有回家。娘有些不放心。

二小走了很久也没有回来。娘站在门口守望。突然，她看见自己的儿子扛着丈夫往家走。娘急急地迎了过去："二小，你大受伤啦？"

"大婶，你看错人了，我是你的邻居奈呀！"

Hubby or Neighbour

Characters: 娘"mom"; 大"dad"; 奈"bear".

Mom sends 二小 (èr xiǎo) to look for his dad, a coal miner, who has not come home since the day before.

The boy is gone for long. Ill at ease, Mom stands at the door waiting.

Suddenly she sees 二小 coming back with 大 on the shoulders.

"Oh, my boy." Mom rushes forward and asks, "Is your dad hurt?"

"Sorry, ma'am, but you've mistaken me for someone else," replies the man. "I'm your neighbour 奈."

Note: 奈 is structured top to bottom with 大 and 示 (composed of 二 above and 小 below representing "二小").

三个母亲

出场角色：羌（qiāng）；先（xiān）；兑（duì）。

三个母亲坐在一起，等着她们的儿子下班回家。

第一个母亲远远看见了羌。"看，那可能是我儿子，他扛了大半只羊回来。"

第二个母亲看见了先。"看，那多半是我儿子，他扛了大半头牛回来。"

第三个母亲看见了兑。"看，那肯定是我儿子，他扛了一台彩电回来，还带着天线呢！"

Three Mothers

Characters: 羌"an ancient nationality in China"; 先"ancestor"; 兑"exchange".

Three women are sitting together, each expecting her son to return from work.

"Look. That might be my kid, who is carrying half a sheep," says one woman as she notices 羌 coming from a distance.

"Look. That could be my child, who is carrying half a cow," says the second when she sees 先.

"Look. That must be my boy, who is carrying a television set, with aerials," says the third catching sight of 兑.

Note: 羌 is graphically structured with 儿 "son" with 䒑 on top representing half of 羊 "sheep"; 先 is structured with 儿 with 𠂉 on top representing half of 牛 "cow"; 兑 is composed of 儿 with 口 on top resembling a television and with a radical 丷 on top of 口 resembling a pair of aerials.

寻父记

出场角色: 禹 (yǔ) ; 属 (shǔ) 。

大禹带领百姓治水时, 废寝忘食, 甚至一连几个月都不回家。

大禹的妻子叫儿子启到工地走一趟: "看看你爹咋样了。要是他有空, 就让他回家吃碗热饭。"

启在工地转了很久, 连父亲的影子也没看见。

正当启准备打道回府时, 他看见了属。他使劲揉了揉眼睛, 感觉属很像自己的父亲, 只是头上顶着一具尸体。

启急急地跑到属的面前, 大喊道: "父亲, 您咋扛着一具尸体呀? 是不是工地又塌方了?"

属认出眼前的小伙子是禹的儿子, 笑道: "我可没有福气当你的父亲。你快回家吧。你父亲正领着我们筑坝呢! "

A Lad Looking for Dad

Characters: 禹"Yu the Great"; 属"subordinate".

Yu the Great has been away from home for months, working tirelessly with his people to tame the floods.

Yu's wife sends their son Qi to the work site. "Go to see how things are with your dad and tell him to come back for a hot meal if he has the time," says the mother.

Yet nowhere around the site can Qi find his father. Just about to leave for home, he suddenly sees 属, and rubbing his eyes hard, he finds the man looks just like his dad, except that he is carrying a corpse on his head.

Qi rushes over and exclaims, "Dad, why are you carrying a dead body? Was there another landslide?"

"I'm not fortunate enough to be your dad," smiles 属, recognising the boy as Yu's son. "Go back home. Your father is leading us in building the dam!"

Note: 属 is composed of 禹 with 尸 "corpse" on top.

母猴分桃

出场角色：洁 (jié) 。幕后角色：捷 (jié) 。

母猴拿出五只桃子，准备给五个儿子每猴一只。

五只猴子争先恐后地伸出爪子争抢个头大的桃子。

"慢！"母猴大吼一声，"洁足者先得。都伸出你们的脚丫子，谁的干净谁先挑。"

注释：本文中的"洁足者先得"是谚语"捷足者先得"的戏仿。

Mother Monkey Distributing Peaches

Onstage Character: 洁"clean". Offstage Character: 捷"swift".

Mother Monkey took out five peaches, ready to give one to each of her five sons. The young monkeys immediately stretched out their paws to grab the biggest one.

"Wait!" ordered the mother. "The clean-footed one gets it first. Now, exhibit your feet, and whoever has the the cleanest toes is to pick first."

Note: "The clean-footed one gets it first" is a parody of the Chinese proverb "The swift-footed one gets it first" meaning he who is quick to act tends to be the first one to reach the goal. In Chinese, "clean" and "swift" are homophones.

爷爷找孙子

出场角色：孙（sūn）；逊（xùn）；荪（sūn）；猻（sūn）。

爷爷带着孙子去游乐园玩，一不小心把孙子弄丢了。

爷爷急得满头大汗，四处寻找自己的小孙子。

爷爷看见了逊。爷爷高兴地说："孙子，我到处找你，你在躺椅上玩呐！"

逊大怒道："你才是孙子哪！"

"对不起，我没看清楚。"爷爷自知理亏，赶快道歉。

爷爷又见到了荪，他以为荪是他的孙子。

　　"你这孩子，还顶着一把草跟爷爷捉迷藏。"爷爷气喘吁吁地说。

　　"老爷爷，你认错人了，我不是你孙子，我是荪。"荪是个知书达礼的人。

　　老爷爷又往前走，见到了猢。

　　"孩子，你跟小狗玩上啦！爷爷终于找到你啦！"爷爷一把抓住猢，上气不接下气地说。

　　"老爷爷，我不是您的孙子。"猢朝老爷爷眨着眼睛，"我是人类的祖先猴子呀。我帮您一起找孙子吧。找到以后，您也认祖归宗，喊我一声爷爷得了！"

　　爷爷气得大叫一声，从床上滚了下来。

　　原来爷爷做了一个梦。

A Greybeard Looking for Grandboy

Characters: 孙"grandson"; 逊"modest"; 荪"an aromatic plant"; 猢 "macaque".

Grandpa takes 孙 to an amusement park to have some fun, but he loses sight of the young boy out of carelessness.

Sweating with anxiety, the old man is searching here and there for his grandson.

"Hey, 孙. You are enjoying yourself in a sling chair!" says Grandpa delightedly upon seeing 逊. "I've been looking everywhere for you."

"You are 孙!" replies the other, clearly annoyed.

"I'm sorry," Grandpa says with a sense of guilt. "It was a mistake."

Then the old chap sees 荪, whom he believes to be his grandson.

"Kid, grass on top, you are playing hide and seek with me!" says the old man, breathing heavily.

"Sorry, monsieur, but I'm not your grandson," replies 荪, a courteous gentleman. "I'm afraid you've got the wrong person."

Grandpa continues his search until he comes upon 狲.

"Finally I've got you, boy!" he gasps, grabbing hold of the other. "You are playing with a dog!"

"Sorry, sir, but I'm not your grandson," grins 狲, blinking his eyes. "I'm a monkey, man's ancestor. Let me help you find your boy, and call me forefather after we dig him out."

With an angry cry, Grandpa rolls down his bed.

It turns out to be a dream.

Note: 逊 is composed of 孙 enclosed by the radical 辶 resembling a sling chair; 荪 is composed of 孙 with the radical 艹 "grass" on top; 狲 is composed of 孙 with the radical 犭 "dog" on the left.

两男之间

出场角色：天（tiān）；无（wú）。

天和无都爱上了美女沉鱼。

沉鱼犹豫再三，也拿不定主意该嫁给谁。

"不错，无是个穷光蛋，一无所有。"沉鱼暗自思忖，"可是他向我求婚的时候是一条腿跪着。而天是两条腿岔着……"

沉鱼把两个人的照片带回家，征求父母的意见。

"无是个穷小子，跟了他你不会幸福的。"沉鱼的母亲说。

"他是真心爱我的。您看他向我求婚时的样子，我真的好感动！"

"你仔细看看，他那条腿本来就是弯的。"母亲的一句话点醒了沉鱼。

"我知道了，我应该选天！"沉鱼激动地说。

"选天？"一直沉默的父亲突然插话了，"天要是成了你的老公，可就是个无头之夫啊！"

A Difficult Choice

Characters: 天"heaven"; 兂"nothing".

天 and 兂 both fall for a fair lady, Chen Yu, who struggles to choose who of the two to marry.

"True, 兂 is dirt-poor, without a penny to his name, but he proposes to me on one knee, " the girl thinks to herself. "天 pops the question with his legs apart ..."

Then she brings home the photos of the two guys to ask her parents for advice.

"You wouldn't be happy living with a man as poor as a church mouse," says her mother.

"But she really loves me. Look at the way he gets down on one knee. I'm so touched."

"Take a closer look. His leg is born bent."

"I see! Then I shall choose 天 as my man," awakened, the daughter says excitedly.

"Him?" the father, who has been silent, suddenly chimes in. "If you were married to 天, you'd have a headless husband!"

Note: 兂 is shaped like someone on one knee and 天 someone standing with the legs apart; the left-falling stroke in 天 simply touches the top horizontal line while the one in 夫"husband" runs across the top with the extended part representing the head.

头足倒置黑老大

出场角色：甲（jiǎ）；由（yóu）。

黑社会老大甲被官府正法，尸体倒悬在城门楼上。

甲的妻子见丈夫几天没有回家，很不放心。她让儿子出去找找。

儿子回家告诉母亲，他没有找到父亲，只看见城门悬挂了一个叫由的家伙。

A Gangster Boss Hung Upside Down

Characters: 甲"first"; 由"cause".

甲, a gangster boss, has been executed by the local government, his body hung by the feet at the town gate.

Ill at ease, the boss's wife sends her son to look for his dad who is not back home for days.

The boy returns home, telling his mom that he has not found his father but seen 由 hung at the gate of the town.

Note: 由 resembles 甲 upside down.

喜从天降

出场角色：丁（dīng）；衣（yī）。

丁先生一直爱着衣小姐，只是苦于不知道如何表白。

突然有一天，衣小姐微笑着对丁说："小丁，我好喜欢你。"

"是吗？"丁先生激动得有些语无伦次了，"能得到衣小姐的青睐，是我一生的荣幸。我一定会给你幸福的。"

衣扑哧一声笑了："小丁，你误会了。我喜欢你是因为你长得有趣，特别像一个衣架。"

"是有点像，"丁懊恼地说，"可惜我的挂钩没长在上边。"

"人无完人，丁无完丁嘛！"衣笑嘻嘻地说。

A Stroke of Good Luck

Characters: 丁"fourth"; 衣"dress".

Mr. 丁 has a crush on Miss 衣, but he is at a loss as to how to declare to her.

One day, 衣 suddenly says to 丁 with a smile, "I really like you."

"Are you sure?" 丁 is incoherent with excitement. "It's my lifelong honor to be favored by Miss 衣. I will definitely give you happiness."

"You've got me wrong, 丁," chuckles 衣. "I like you because you look funny, just like a hanger."

"Sort of, " says 丁, annoyed. "It's a shame my hook is not at the top."

"Nobody is perfect," says 衣 with a grin.

Note: 丁 resembles a coat hanger with a hook at the bottom.

第二章　形态可疑

Chapter 2　Something Fishy

匾（biǎn）

出场角色：匾。

匾是台湾的一个大法官。

据媒体报道，匾极有可能出任台湾陈水扁贪腐案的主审法官。

匾的亲朋好友都劝他推掉这个案子。匾执意不从。于是他们都疏远了他。

匾百思不得其解。

匾一个人郁闷地到日月潭边散步。他愣了好一阵子，突然大叫道："我明白了，大伙儿之所以劝我放弃这个案子，是担心我对阿扁网开一面呀！"

A Way Out

Character: 匾 "plaque".

According to the media, 匾, one of the trial judges of Taiwan Supreme Court, is most likely to preside over the case of 扁, who is accused of corruption.

Highly confused, 匾 finds his family and friends estranged from him since he does not take up their suggestion that he should shrink from the case.

In a gloomy mood, 匾 goes for a walk around Sun-Moon Lake all alone. He gazes into space for a while and then lets out a sudden cry, "Now I see! They try to talk me out of the case for fear that I might give 扁 a way out."

Note: 匾 is structured with 扁 enclosed by a radical from top, left and bottom sides, with the right side open representing "a way out".

说 "不" 的代价

出场角色：本（běn）；不（bù）。

本与不是兄弟俩。他俩虽然是一个娘胎里出来的，可性情很不一样。

本为人处事谨小慎微，从不得罪任何人。

本的弟弟不可就不一样了。不心直口快，只要他认为不对的，就直言不讳地对当事人讲出来。他甚至公然在大庭广众之下批评经理的决策。

不幸的是，经理是一个心胸狭窄的人。他非常忌恨不，明里暗里地给不使绊子、穿小鞋。有一段时间，不被整得狼狈不堪。

不去找哥哥本诉苦。

本痛心地对不说："兄弟，你快照照镜子吧！你不但腰带被扯掉了，连头也丢了。"

不恨恨地说："我知道了，哥。这就是说'不'的代价啊！可我不会屈服的！"

A Heavy Price for Saying No

Characters: 本"self"; 不"no".

Although born to the same mother, 本 and 不 differ greatly in personality. 本 is timid and cautious, never giving offence to anyone, while the younger brother 不 is frank and outspoken, pointing out whatever he believes is wrong to the person concerned, even complaining in public about the decisions made by the manager, who, unfortunately, is so narrow-minded as to harbour some resentment and deliberately make things awkward for 不.

Being given a hard time, 不 gets into a sorry state, so he comes to his brother to seek comfort.

"Take a look at yourself in the mirror, bro," says 本. "You've lost your head as well as your belt."

"I know," 不 says in a bitter tone. "This is the heavy price to pay for saying NO. But I'll never give in!"

Note: 不 is graphically similar to 本 without the extended part of the vertical stroke across the top horizontal line representing the head, and without the lower horizontal stroke resembling a belt.

黑猩猩

出场角色：颜（yán）。幕后角色：言（yán）。

森林宾馆的服务员黑猩猩总是对客人皱眉头。

"这家伙怎么天天凶神恶煞的？我看他不是个善良之辈。"喜鹊悄声对啄木鸟说。

"也许他心地不错，只是不善于表露而已。"啄木鸟猜测道。

"我看未必。俗话说，颜为心声。他的尊荣已经让我看透他了。"喜鹊给出了他的结论。

注释：本文中的"颜为心声"是成语"言为心声"的戏仿。

A Black Chimpanzee

Onstage Character: 颜"look". Offstage Character: 言"speech".

A black chimpanzee, attendant of the forest inn, constantly scowled at the guests.

"Why is he always looking so fierce?" a magpie whispered in a woodpecker's ear. "I don't think he is a nice guy."

"Maybe he has a kind heart, but is not good at expressing himself on his face," speculated the woodpecker.

"That's not how I see it. 'Look is the echo of the heart,' as the proverb says. His face has betrayed his true nature," concluded the magpie.

Note: "Look is the echo of the heart" is a parody of the Chinese idiom "Speech is the echo of the heart" meaning spoken words usually reflects one's thoughts and feelings. The send-up and its original sound exactly the same in Mandarin.

刀把子不能丢

出场角色：分（fēn）；八（bā）。
分对八说："兄弟，刀把子可不能丢啊。"

Hold On To Your Knife

Characters: 分"separate"; 八"eight".
"Oh, buddy," 分 sighs at 八. "You really shouldn't have given away your knife."

Note: 分 is structured top to bottom with 八 and 刀 "knife".

谁大谁小

出场角色：官（guān）；宫（gōng）。
官对宫说："少了一道，当不成官儿了吧？"
宫抚掌笑道："再大的官儿，到了我这儿还不是个小人物吗！"

Nobody or Somebody

Characters: 官"official"; 宫"palace".
"You can never be an official with the line missing," says 官 to 宫.
"Officials of whatever high rank would be dwarfed by me," smiles the other, clapping his hands.

Note: 官 is composed similar to 宫, with the component ß in 官 shaped like the component 吕 in 宫 linked by a vertical line on the left side.

一语道破

出场角色：干（gàn）；王（wáng）。

干问王："朋友啊，你我只差了一道。可为啥我干了一辈子，却混得这么惨，你却有享不尽的荣华富贵呢？"

王看了看干，不紧不慢地说："你活了一辈子也没明白。我比你多的这一道，可是决定命运的一道啊！"

The Plain Truth

Characters: 干"do"; 王"king".

"Oh, my friend," 干 asks 王. "What tells you from me is a mere line, but how come you live off the fat of the land while I live hand to mouth in spite of my best efforts?"

"You've been pig ignorant all your life," replies 王 calmly as he casts an eye over 干. "It is the line that decides our fates."

Note: 王 has one more horizontal stroke at the bottom than 干.

谁会发动政变？

出场角色：钩（gōu）；猪（zhū）；猴（hóu）。幕后角色：诛（zhū）；侯（hóu）。

老虎得到密报，国中有人试图发动政变。但苦于情报过于简单，只知道猪和猴子的嫌疑最大。

老虎问狐狸，猪和猴子谁更可能是叛徒。

狐狸歪着脑袋想了想，肯定地说："是猴子。古语说，窃钩者猪，窃国者猴。意思是猪至多偷大王的钩子，而猴子却要偷大王的国家呀。"

老虎听了狐狸的分析，觉得很有道理，于是将猴子就地正法了。

注释：本文中的"窃钩者猪，窃国者猴"是成语"窃钩者诛，窃国者侯"的戏仿。

Who Would Mount a Coup?

Onstage Characters: 钩"hook"; 猪"pig"; 猴"monkey". Offstage Characters: 诛"execute"; 侯"lord".

A secret message came to King Tiger that someone in the kingdom was trying to launch a coup, but the intelligence was too simple, only suspecting a pig and a monkey most, one of whom was plotting a revolt. Then the tiger asked Minister Fox who was more likely to be the traitor. "It's the monkey," replied the fox confidently after thinking a while with his head tilted. "As the old saying goes, 'He who steals a hook is a pig, while he who steals a state is a monkey.' That is to say, the pig is to take nothing more than a hook but the monkey is to take your kingdom." The tiger found the fox's analysis perfectly reasonable and then ordered to put the monkey to death on the spot.

Note: "He who steals a hook is a pig, while he who steals a state is a monkey" is a parody of the Chinese idiom "He who steals a hook is executed, while he who steals a state becomes a lord" which was used in ancient times to criticise the hypocritical and irrational legislation. The spoof and the original sound alike but mean quite differently with two characters changed.

皇帝的感慨

出场角色：皇（huáng）。

已经执政四十年的皇照着镜子，无可奈何地叹道："公道世间唯白发，贵人头上不曾饶。"

An Emperor's Sigh

Character: 皇"emperor".

Looking at himself in the mirror, 皇, who has held power for forty years, sighs hopelessly, "All is unfair but white hair; noble heads are not ever spared."

Note: 皇 is composed of 王"king" with 白"white" on top representing white hair.

烂尾工程

出场角色：回（huí）；叵（pǒ）。

回端详着叵好大一会儿，指责说："偷工减料，必有蹊跷。"

注释：叵，不可。

Good Start and Poor Finish

Characters: 回"chapter"; 叵"impossible".

Sizing up 叵 for quite a while, 回 remarks reproachfully, "Cutting corners on the project, you must have some dark secret."

Note: 叵 is composed similar to 回, without the vertical stroke on the right.

身陷囹圄

出场角色：卷（juǎn）；圈（juān）。
卷对圈说："兄弟，你犯啥事啦，让人给圈起来啦？"

Behind Bars

Characters: 卷"embroil"; 圈"confine".
"You are cooped up, man," says 卷 to 圈. "What have you done wrong to end up in here?"

Note: 圈 is composed of 卷 fully enclosed by a semantic radical 囗 "enclosure".

钻营高手

出场角色：尖（jiān）。
尖照着镜子，自鸣得意道："瞧我这长相，上头小，下头大，走遍天下都不怕。"

Fearing Nothing High and Low

Character: 尖"tip".

Looking in the mirror, 尖 grows complacent about his image. "Small above, big below, I fear nothing high and low," he hums proudly.

Note: 尖 is composed of a semantic radical 小"small" at the top and 大 "big" at the bottom.

真假难辨

出场角色：酒（jiǔ）；洒（sǎ）。

在一次聚会上，酒遇见了洒。

酒愤怒地对洒说："我一看见你就来气。"

洒惊问："兄台此话怎讲？"

酒道："很多人把你看作了我。可你完全没有我的醇厚和甘美啊！你让我名誉扫地呀！"

Real or Fake

Characters: 酒"wine"; 洒"spill".

Coming across 洒 at a party, 酒 says to him angrily, "I can't bear the sight of you."

"What do you mean, bro?" asks the other in surprise.

"Many people mistake you for me, but you are not as mellow or fragrant in the least, " replies 酒. "So you ruin my reputation!"

Note: Graphically similar to 洒, 酒 has one more horizontal stroke enclosed on the lower right.

歪有歪理

出场角色：开（kāi）；升（shēng）。

开对升说："兄弟，你的顶棚歪了。"

升笑道："不歪能升上去吗？"

The Benefit of a Slope

Characters: 开"open"; 升"rise".

"Mate, your roof is slanted," says 开 to 升.

"How else could I go up without that slope?" responds the other with a smile.

Note: The top vertical line in 开 resembles a roof while the top left-falling stroke in 升 resembles a slanting roof.

缺一不可

出场角色：冒（mào）；昌（chāng）。

冒对昌说："少划一道，绝对假冒。"

昌对冒说："我不是冒，何来假冒？"

Every Single One Helps

Characters: 冒"false"; 昌"prosperous".

"A line missing, you must be a fake," says 冐 to 昌.

"Just being myself, how can I be counterfeit?" comes the reply.

Note: 昌 is composed of two 日 one on top of the other (with the top narrower); 冐 is composed of 曰 at the top and 目 at the bottom (with the top wider).

路有不平，勿忘带刀

出场角色：矛（máo）；予（yǔ）。

矛对予说："兄弟，你的腰刀呢？"

Always Be Prepared

Characters: 矛"spear"; 予"bestow".

"Hey, pal," says 矛 to 予. "Do you have your side sword with you?"

Note: Without the left-falling stroke resembling a sword, 予 differs from 矛 in composition.

牢狱之灾

出场角色：目（mù）；囚（qiú）。

目对囚说："看见老兄你的模样，我瞬间明白了一个道理。"

囚问："什么道理呀？"

"宁可目中无人，不可口中有人。"

Captured and Imprisoned

Characters: 目"eye"; 囚"prisoner".

"The instant I see you, something profound dawns on me," says 目 to 囚.

"What is it?" asks the other.

"Better have nobody in the eye than have someone in the mouth," comes the reply.

Note: 囚 is composed of 人 "person" fully enclosed by 口 "mouth".

总是有事

出场角色: 木 (mù) ; 困 (kùn) 。

木对困说: "兄弟, 身陷囹圄了? 犯啥事儿了?"

Things Happen

Characters: 木"tree"; 困"stuck".

"Bro, you are penned up?" says 木 to 困. "What has been going on?"

Note: 困 is composed of 木 fully enclosed by 口.

宁死不戴乌纱帽

出场角色: 牛 (niú) ; 牢 (láo) 。

牛对牢说: "都说宝盖儿是个宝, 我看其实未必好。"

The Higher the Climb the Deeper the Fall

Characters: 牛"ox"; 牢"jail".

"They all see the cover as a treasure," remarks 牛 to 牢. "But in my eyes, it's actually nothing desirable."

Note: 牢 is composed of 牛 with a semantic radical 宀 "cover" on top.

挤掉水分

出场角色：泼（pō）；发（fā）。

泼与发是儿时好友，长大以后分别在两个不同的城市发展。

某一年春节，泼与发不约而同地回到家乡看望长辈。他俩走进一家酒馆小酌。

泼问发："老兄，听说你这些年在生意场上风生水起，可没少挣。为啥我不能发呢？"

发听邻里说泼这些年颇为不顺。因为他常常言过其实，轻诺寡信，把生意场上的朋友得罪光了。经营多年的小店也倒闭了。

"去掉你身上的水分就可以发了。"发意味深长地说。

Droplets in the Way

Characters: 泼"splash"; 发"prosper".

泼 and 发 are childhood friends who now work in different cities.

On their visits home one Spring Festival, the two guys bump into each other and come to a tavern for a drink.

"Bro," says 泼 to 发, "I hear you have a successful business and make loads of money these years. Why is it so hard for me to make a fortune?"

From some folks 发 learns that things has not gone smoothly for 泼 over the years. All his business partners have left him because he talks big and makes hollow promises, and worse still, his small shop run for years is closed.

"Wipe the moisture droplets off your body, and you'll prosper," responds 发 meaningfully.

Note: 泼 is composed of a semantic radical 氵"water" (representing moisture beads) on the left and 发 on the right; "moisture" in Chinese figuratively means "exaggeration".

音同字不同

出场角色：囚（qiú）；求（qiú）。
囚问求：“先生贵姓？”
求答道：“姓Qiú，上下求索的求。你贵姓？”
囚道：“我也姓Qiú，不过是囚徒的囚。人比人，气死人。囚比求，泪长流。”

Homonyms

Characters: 囚"prisoner"; 求"seek".
"May I have your name, sir?" 囚 asks 求.
"My name is Qiu, which means 'to seek,'" replies the other. "And yours?"
"Also Qiu, meaning 'prisoner,'" sighs 囚. "A comparison fills one with anger; a namesake reduces me to tears."

Note: 求 and 囚 are phonetically identical.

混淆黑白

出场角色：七（qī）；皂（zào）。

七对皂说："兄弟，你咋学会挂白幡，卖黑货了？"

注释：皂，黑色。

Calling Black White

Characters: 七"seven"; 皂"black".

"Hey, guy," says 七 to 皂. "Why do you hang a white banner when selling black stuff?"

Note: 皂 is composed of 七 with 白"white" on top.

人脉的重要

出场角色：企（qǐ）；止（zhǐ）。

企对止说："兄弟，你我之间最大的区别是什么？"

止答道："不知道。"

企笑道："我上面有人，你上面没人。"

止愣了一下，恍然大悟道："怪不得我一直都是止步不前啊！"

It's Not What You Know but Who You Know

Characters: 企"expect"; 止"stop".

企 asks 止, "Buddy, what is the biggest difference between you and me?"

"No idea," comes the reply.

"I have someone up there but you don't," grins 企.

Dumbfounded for a second, 止 sees the light suddenly. "No wonder I get bogged down all the time!" he exclaims.

Note: 企 is composed of 止 with 人 "person" on top; the Chinese expression "someone up there" refers to "a friend at court".

太缺德了

出场角色：且（qiě）；县（xiàn）。
且问县："兄弟，你咋坐别人的坟头上了？"

A Wicked Act

Characters: 且"and"; 县"county".

"Hi pal, why are you sitting on a grave mound?" 且 asks 县.

Note: 县 is composed of 且 with a radical 厶 at the bottom resembling a burial mound.

太不公平

出场角色：日（rì）；月（yuè）。
日对月说："月小妹，你的光全是我给的，为什么我俩聚在一起才能叫'明'呢？"
月笑道："可能造字的仓颉没有天文学知识吧！大哥就别计较这

事啦！"

"那就将错就错吧！"日心有不甘地说。

A Bit Thick

Characters: 日"sun"; 月"moon".

"Hey, little sister. You only mirror my light," says 日 to 月. "But why do we two pairing up make the character brightness?"

"Probably because Cangjie was ignorant of astronomy," grins 月. "Don't make a fuss about it, brother."

"Then let's just leave it at that," says 日 reluctantly.

Note: 日 joined by 月 on the right forms 明"brightness"; legend has it that Cangjie was the inventor of Chinese characters.

一嘴定终身

出场角色：士（shì）；吉（jí）。

士问吉："先生，为啥我读了一辈子的书，日子却过得十分清苦。而你总是鸿运当头呢？"

吉从头到脚打量了士一番，笑道："和我相比，你缺的是一张能说会道的嘴巴呀。"

A Mouth Determining Fate

Characters: 士"scholar"; 吉"lucky".

"Sir, you were born under a lucky star while I live hand to mouth in spite of years of schooling, " 士 says 吉. "Why is that?"

"Compared with me, you lack a mouth with a silver tongue," grins 吉 as he sizes the other up.

Note: 吉 is composed of 士 at the top and 口 "mouth" at the bottom.

凡事莫出头

出场角色：矢（shǐ）；失（shī）。

矢对失说："凡事莫出头，现在你知道吃亏了吧？"

失懊恼地说："是啊，怪不得我事事不顺！"

The Importance of Keeping a Low Profile

Characters: 矢"arrow"; 失"lose".

"In no case can you poke out the head," says 矢 to 失. "Now you're aware of your losses, right?"

"You said it," replies the other with regret. "No wonder everything goes wrong with me."

Note: The left-falling stroke in 矢 touches the top horizontal line while the one in 失 runs across the top with the extended part resembling the head; the Chinese expression "extend the head" figuratively means "show off".

多嘴惹是非

出场角色：少（shǎo）；吵（chǎo）。

少对吵说："姐，言多语失。凡事多一嘴不如少一嘴。"

Out of the Mouth Comes Evil

Characters: 少"few"; 吵"quarrel".

"Out of the mouth comes evil, sis," says 少 to 吵. "More is not always better."

Note: 吵 is composed of a semantic radical 口"mouth" on the left and 少 on the right.

岂有此理

出场角色：失（shī）；矢（shǐ）。

失对矢说："这年头没处讲理去——你这无头的成了箭，我这有头的反倒没了身份。"

注释：矢，箭。

Totally Unreasonable

Characters: 失"lose"; 矢"arrow".

"This is senseless," says 失 to 矢. "Without a head, you become an arrow, while with a head, I lose my identity."

Note: The top extended part of the left-falling stroke in 失 resembles the head.

66

赵家天下

出场角色：宋（sòng）。

宋对着镜子自语道："木头带帽，皇帝姓赵。"

注释：木字上面加一个"帽子"即宝盖就是"宋"字，宋朝的开国皇帝是赵匡胤，该朝代后面的皇帝都是赵氏后裔，所以说"皇帝姓赵"。

The Surname of an Emperor

Character: 宋"the Song Dynasty（960-1279）".

"A cap on wood makes Zhao emperor," 宋 thinks aloud, admiring his refection in the mirror.

Note: 宋 is composed of 木"wood" with a radical 宀 on top resembling a cap; "Zhao" was the imperial surname of the Song Dynasty.

罪有应得

出场角色：四（sì）；罪（zuì）。

四对罪说："兄弟，你哪儿不能站，非要站这么个是非之地。这下麻烦了吧！"

Asking for Trouble

Characters: 四"four"; 罪"crime".

"Hey, pal. You can stand anywhere but here in the wrong place," 四 say to 罪. "Now you are in trouble!"

Note: 罪 is composed of a radical 罒 (resembling 四) at the top and 非 "wrong" at the bottom.

凶手在哪儿?

出场角色: 市 (shì) ; 币 (bì) 。

市对币说: "兄弟, 谁把你脑袋剁了? 把肩膀也弄斜了。"

Where Is the Butcher?

Characters: 市"market"; 币"currency".

"Pal, who has chopped off your head and slanted your shoulders?" 市 asks 币.

Note: 市 has a radical 亠 at the top resembling the head and shoulders.

有用的乌纱帽

出场角色: 申 (shēn) ; 审 (shěn) 。

申问审: "兄弟, 咱俩的出身、智商、个头都差不多, 可为啥进了衙门, 我总是堂下申诉的, 你总是堂上审案的呢? "

审笑着答道: "因为我比你多一顶乌纱帽啊! "

A Cap Tipping the Balance

Characters: 申"appeal"; 审"try".

"Look, pal. We two are quite similar in background, intelligence and height," says 申 to 审, "but how is it that whenever in court I am the claimant while you are the judge?"

"Because I've got a black gauze cap that tips the balance," replies the other with a laugh.

Note: 审 is composed of 申 with a radical 宀 on top resembling a cap; "black gauze cap" figuratively means "official post".

点化僵尸

出场角色：尸 （shī）；户 （hù）。

尸问户："呵，兄弟，又长出脑袋啦！"

"废话，没脑袋能给上户口吗？"户恼怒道。

A Conversation with a Zombie

Characters: 尸"corpse"; 户"household".

"Wow, mate. Look at you with a new head!" says 尸 to 户.

"Nonsense," responds the other crossly. "How could I even register my citizenship without a head?"

Note: 户 is composed of 尸 with a dot stroke on top resembling the head.

一定要跟对了人

出场角色：土（tǔ）；鳖（biē）。

土对鳖说："朋友，我发现一个好玩儿的地方。跟我走吧！"

鳖没好气地说："跟在你后面走，我连身价都跌了。"

注释：鳖，爬行动物，形状像龟，可食，市场价格较贵。土鳖，地鳖的通称，身体扁，卵圆形，可入药。

Follow the Right Person

Characters: 土"clod"; 鳖"turtle".

"Hi there. I've found an interesting place," 土 calls out to 鳖. "Follow me."

"Going after you, I will come down in price," replies the other crossly.

Note: 鳖 is more expensive than 土鳖"ground beetle".

到哪儿说理去？

出场角色：田（tián）；由（yóu）。

田对由说："兄弟，你长出苗来啦？"

由没好气地说："是啊，没苗的是田，我这有苗的却不是田了。"

A Bit Much

Characters: 田"field"; 由"reason".

"Mate, you've sprouted a seedling?" says 田 to 由.

"Right. But even so, I'm not a piece of cropland," replies the other in anger. "Someone without a plantlet turns out to be a field."

Note: The middle vertical line in 由 runs across the top horizontal stroke with the extended part representing a seedling.

君临天下

出场角色：王（wáng）；全（quán）。

王对全说："你上面有人顶啥用，还不是得听我的？"

The Supreme Power

Characters: 王"king"; 全"all".

"What's the point of having someone up there?" says 王 to 全. "After all, you are subordinate to me."

Note: 全 is composed of 王 with 人"person" on top.

帽子惹祸

出场角色：元（yuán）；完（wán）。

忽必烈做了一个梦。在梦中前来求和的南宋使节向他献上一顶精

71

美的帽子，上面镶嵌了很多珠宝。使节说这是南宋皇帝献给忽必烈皇帝的。

忽必烈把帽子拿在手里，越看越欢喜。他想往头上试戴一下。

"陛下莫戴此帽！"辅佐忽必烈的汉人姚枢大叫一声。

忽必烈惊问何故。姚枢解释道："陛下乃大元王朝的象征，'元'上加帽，就是'完'啊！南宋使节欺我大元朝中无人，故意献上帽子，诅咒我大元早日玩儿完。陛下不可不识啊！"

忽必烈闻言大怒，把帽子扔到地上，喝令把南宋使节推出斩首。

南宋使节的头尚未落地，忽必烈从梦中惊醒了。

Trouble Out of Hat

Characters: 元"Yuan Dynasty"; 完"over".

Kublai Khan has a dream. In his dream, a Southern Song envoy who comes to seek peace presents him a delicate hat trimmed with gems. The diplomat claims that it is a tribute from the Southern Song Emperor to Kublai.

Holding the hat in his hands, Kublai grows fond of it and feels like trying it on.

"Please don't, Your Majesty!" shouts Yao Shu, a Han person who is one of Kublai's advisors.

Surprised, the sovereign asks Yao for the reason.

"Your Majesty is the symbol of the Great Yuan Dynasty," explains the Han person. "With a hat on top, 'Yuan' would turn into 'over'. So the envoy is fooling us and attempting to cast an evil spell on the Great Yuan. Your Majesty must beware of his trick!"

Hearing this, the emperor flings the hat to the ground in a rage, and orders to behead the agent immediately.

Before the envoy's head hits the ground, Kublai wakes up from his dream.

Note: 完 is composed of 元"Yuan Dynasty" with a radical 宀 on top resembling a hat.

社稷为重

出场角色：王（wáng）；弄（nòng）。

王对弄说："朋友，像你我这样身系社稷安危的人，就不要只图个人痛快，玩什么踩高跷这样的游戏了。"

Business before Pleasure

Characters: 王"king"; 弄"play".

"Hi, there. Men like you and me shouldn't take pleasure in such things as walking on the stilts," says 王 to 弄, "as we are responsible for the destiny of the kingdom."

Note: 弄 is composed 王 at the top and a radical 廾 at the bottom resembling a pair of stilts.

无奈之举

出场角色：夕（xī）；多（duō）。

夕对多说："兄弟如手足，岂可相欺呀！"

多无可奈何地说："两个'夕'字手拉手就不是字了。"

A Reluctant Act

Characters: 夕"evening"; 多"many".

"A brother is your own flesh and blood," says 夕 to 多. "You cannot bully each other."

"If hand in hand, we would not form a complete character," responds the other regretfully.

Note: 多 is composed of two 夕 one on top of the other.

歹徒的下场

出场角色：歹（dǎi）；夕（xī）。

歹："兄弟救命，快把我放下来！"

夕："我看你不像是好人。你干什么坏事了，快点从实招来！"

歹："入室抢劫，被人吊起来了。"

夕："哼。真是罪有应得！"

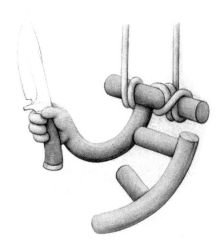

A Criminal's Fate

Characters: 夕"evening"; 歹"bad".

歹: "Brother, please save me! Get me down from here!"

夕: "You don't look like an honest guy. What did you do? Come clean right away!"

歹: "I broke into a house. They hung me up like this."

夕: "Hmph. It serves you right!"

Note: 歹 is composed of 夕 with a horizontal line on top.

羡慕不已

出场角色：层（céng）；尸（shī）。

层和尸是多年好友。自从尸下葬以后，两个人就没有机会见面了。有一天，层在梦中与尸相会了。

层激动地问尸："尸兄：你我一别数年。你在墓地里还好吧？"

"还好，冬暖夏凉，是个养老的好地方。"尸流着口水说，"可我还是羡慕你的层次高啊！"

A Twinge of Envy

Characters: 层"class"; 尸"dead body".

In a dream 层 meets his late good friend 尸 who has gone for long.

"Hey buddy. It's been years," he asks in excitement. "Are you doing okay in the burial chamber?"

"Not bad. Warm in winter and cool in summer, it's a nice place to retire," replies the other, drooling. "Still, I envy you being in a higher class."

Note: 层 is composed of 云"cloud" enclosed from upper and left sides by 尸.

"真贱！"

出场角色：贝（bèi）；见（jiàn）。

贝问见："老弟，你为啥单腿下跪呀？你可真是贱啊！"

见闻言惊喜道："大哥，你咋知道我的名字啊？我就是见啊！"

"我说你是贱骨头的贱！"贝不屑地说。

Cheap in Character

Characters: 贝"currency"; 见"meet".

贝 asks 见, "Brother, why are you kneeling on one leg? You're really cheap!"

见 replies with surprise, "How do you know my name? I AM 见!"

"I mean you're cheap in character!" resorts 贝 with disdain.

Note: 见 and 贱"cheap" are homophones.

人靠衣装

出场角色：保（bǎo）；褒（bāo）。

囚犯保越狱逃走了。

保知道狱警肯定会追捕他。

他风驰电掣般地跑进一家服装店，买了一件时尚衣服穿在身上。

两个狱警走进时装店里，见到了保。没有认出他来。

"请问先生贵姓？"狱警彬彬有礼地问。

"我叫褒，褒奖的褒。"保镇定地答道。

"你看见一个从监狱跑出来的逃犯没有？"一个狱警问。

保摇摇头。

狱警急匆匆地向前追赶了。保深情地抚摸着身上的时装，感激涕零地说："我终于知道啥叫'人靠衣装'了。"

Clothes Make the Man

Characters: 保 "protect"; 褒 "honor".

保, a prisoner who has successfully escaped from jail, knows that the prison guards will be on the hunt for him.

He rushes into a clothing store and purchases a stylish outfit to dress himself in.

Two guards enter the store and spot 保, but fail to recognize him.

"Excuse me, sir. What's your name?" one of the guards politely inquires.

"My name is 褒, meaning 'honor'," he responds calmly.

"Have you seen an escaped prisoner?" the guard asks.

保 shakes his head.

The guards quickly leaves the store in pursuit of the fugitive.

保 fondly touches his new clothes and says with tears in his eyes, "Now I finally understand the saying, 'Clothes make the man'."

Note: 褒 is structured like 保 in the middle of 衣 "clothe".

"谁有我馅儿大？"

出场角色：包（bāo）；旬（xún）；句（jù）；勺（sháo）。

有一天，包和旬、句、勺聚在一起。

包对旬、句和勺道："瞧瞧你们仨，一个比一个馅儿少。这不是坑害顾客嘛！"

"你自个儿是个包子，就以为别人也是包子啊！"旬、句和勺冷冷地答道。

A Debate over Fillings

Characters: 包"dumpling"; 旬"ten"; 句"sentence"; 勺"spoon".

One day, 旬, 句, and 勺 gather together.

包 says to them, "Look at you three, each with fewer fillings than the other. You are deceiving customers!"

"Just because you're a bun with fillings, you think everyone else has to follow your footsteps?" 旬, 句, and 勺 respond coldly.

Note: 旬, 句, and 勺 have similar shapes, with each successive one having fewer strokes.

宁要乌纱不要头

出场角色：晨（chén）；宸（chén）。

晨问宸："兄弟，你比我少颗头，却多了一顶帽子。你这不是丢了西瓜捡了芝麻吗？"

宸笑道："我反复做过比较，要想在社会上混，有一顶官帽比有一个脑壳更方便。"

Better Hat Than Head

Characters: 晨"morning"; 宸"house".

晨 says to 宸, "Brother, compared to me, you lack a head but boast a hat. Isn't this like losing a watermelon and picking up a sesame seed?"

晨 replies with a smile, "Having compared the two, I've found that in order to navigate through society, it's more convenient to have an official hat than a functioning head."

Note: 晨 is composed of 辰 with 日 on top representing a head, and 宸 is composed of 辰 with the radical 宀 on top representing a hat; the Chinese expression "official hat" refers to an official post with power and influence.

吃相不同

出场角色：乞（qǐ）；吃（chī）。

乞走进一家餐馆，看见正在大快朵颐的吃。

乞对吃说："你长着一张大嘴，一看就是个吃货。"

吃瞟了一眼乞，笑道："我虽是吃货，却自食其力。有人倒是没有嘴，可是靠要饭过日子。"

A Foodie and a Beggar

Characters: 乞"beg"; 吃"eat".

乞 walks into a restaurant and sees 吃, who is eating heartily. The former says to the latter, "You have a big mouth, so you must be a foodie."

吃 glances at 乞 and laughs, "Foodie though I am, I earn my own living. There is someone who has no mouth but relies on begging to survive."

Note: 吃 is composed of the radical 口 "mouth" on the left and 乞 "beg" on the right.

"你受屈了！"

出场角色：屈（qū）；出（chū）。

屈问出："兄弟，为啥我这一辈子活得这么憋屈呢？"

出同情地说："因为你一直被死人压着呀！"

A Suffocating Life

Characters: 屈 "bend"; 出 "rise".

"Hey, bro. Why has my life been so suffocating?" 屈 asks 出.

"Perhaps because you're living under the weight of a dead body," replies the other sympathetically.

Note: 屈 is composed of 出 with 尸 "corpse" on top.

"我不是空心树！"

出场角色：树（shù）；村（cūn）。

树对村道："兄弟，你咋空心啦？是不是让蛀虫咬的？"

村不悦地说："看清楚了，我不是一棵空心树。我是村呐。我肚子里装几百棵树没啥问题。"

Not a Hollow Tree

Characters: 树"tree"; 村"village".

树 says to 村, "Brother, why are you hollow? Did the worms eat you?"

"Take a closer look," 村 replies crossly. "I am a village, not a hollow tree. It's no problem to have hundreds of trees growing within my boundaries."

Note: 树 is structured like 村 with 又 enclosed.

要有信心

出场角色：豕（shǐ）；家（jiā）。

豕每日吃的是残渣剩饭，住的是又脏又臭的窝棚，而且不能自己主宰命运。他觉得自己真是太不幸了。

"家兄，和你一比，我真是猫狗不如啊！"豕眼圈红红地问家，"难道我只能这样过一辈子吗？"

"不要对生活失去信心。"志得意满的家开导着豕，"据我观察，哪怕是一头愚不可及的猪，戴上乌纱帽也会有一个温馨的归宿。"

注释：豕，猪。

Never Lose Faith in Life

Characters: 豕"pig"; 家"home".

豕 eats leftovers every day, and lives in a filthy and smelly shack. He believes he was born under an unlucky star with no control over his own destiny.

"Bro, compared to you, I am worse off than a cat or dog," 豕 says to 家 with red eyes. "Do I have to live like this for the rest of my life?"

"Don't lose faith in life," 家 comforts 豕 with pride. "From what I have observed, even an ignorant pig can have a favorable outcome if wearing a black hat."

Note: 家 is composed of 豕 with the radical 宀 "cover" on top representing a hat; "wearing a black hat" in Chinese culture means being an government official with power and influence.

命运不同三兄弟

出场角色：杏（xìng）；困（kùn）；呆（dāi）

杏对困和呆说："我们仁都是木傍口。只是因为位置不同，命运大不同。口下木呆傻一生；口含木穷困潦倒；口上木酸甜适中。"

Three Brothers, Three Fates

Characters: 杏"apricot"; 困"poor"; 呆"silly".

"Each of us has a tree connected to the mouth, but we differ greatly in fate simply because of the position of the tree," says 杏 to 呆 and 困. "The one with the tree under the mouth is as silly as a goose; the one with the tree in the mouth is as poor as a church mouse; the one with the tree on top of the mouth is perfectly balanced, neither too sweet nor too sour."

Note: 杏 is composed of 木"tree" at the top and 口"mouth" at the bottom;

困 is composed 木 fully enclosed by 口; 呆 has 口 above and 木 below.

畜生多嘴要不得

出场角色: 羊 (yáng) ; 王 (wáng) 。

羊对王说: "兄弟, 为了当个头, 你付出的代价太大了——头上的犄角和尾巴全掉了。"

王大怒道: "多嘴的畜生, 再敢对本王说三道四, 我叫人把你的犄角和尾巴全砍下来!"

羊哈哈大笑道: "那我不也变成'王'了吗? 你愿意这儿再添一个'王'跟你争地盘吗?"

Shut Your Mouth

Characters: 羊"sheep"; 王"king".

"Pal, you've lost all your horns and tail," says 羊 to 王. "It's a heavy price to pay for being the head."

"Shut up, or I'll have yours cut off!" yells the other.

"In that case I would be a king, too," responds 羊 with a loud laugh.

"Would you like someone to split your territory?"

Note: 王 is shaped like 羊 without the top radical ㅛ (resembling a pair of horns) or the bottom extended part of the vertical line (resembling a tail).

形态可疑

出场角色: 鱼 (yú) ; 了 (liǎo) 。

鱼看见了了, 盯了它老半天, 怯生生地问: "朋友, 为啥我一看见你就害怕呢？"

　了哈哈大笑道："因为我长得像只鱼钩啊！"

Something Fishy

Characters: 鱼"fish"; 了"end.

Fixing his eyes on 了 for quite a while, 鱼 asks timidly, "Why do I feel frightened at the sight of you?"

"Because I look like a hook," replies the other with a loud laugh.

Note: 了 is shaped like a fishing hook.

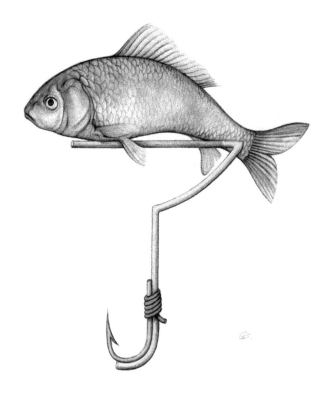

未遂政变

出场角色：羊（yáng）；王（wáng）。

羊想成为群羊之王——头羊，欲串联几个好友发动政变，推翻现任统治者——王。不幸消息走漏了，羊被王捉住了。残暴的王命令刀斧手割掉图谋不轨的羊的尾巴，凿掉犄角。

"你现在也是'王'了。"王看着奄奄一息的受难者，冷冷地说。

An Abortive Coup Attempt

Characters: 羊"sheep"; 王"king".

Desiring to be head of the flock, 羊 is planning a coup to bring down the current ruler with some friends joining hands. Unfortunately, the plot is uncovered and 羊 gets caught by 王, the bellwether, who is so ruthless that he orders to cut off the plotter's horns and tail.

"Now you are 王 too," says the head sheep in an icy tone, glaring at the dying victim.

Note: 王 is shaped like 羊 without the top radical ⼨ (resembling a pair of horns) or the bottom extended part of the vertical line (resembling a tail).

跟错了人

出场角色：正（zhèng）；不（bù）。

正没好气地对不说："当你的下属，只有走邪路了。"

注释："不"字下面加"正"字，即为"歪"。此处的"下属"暗指在下面。

Following the Wrong Person

Characters: 正"straight"; 不"no".

"Under you, I could do nothing but go astray," says 正 to 不 crossly.

Note: 正 joined by 不 on top forms 歪 "astray".

尚有一条看家狗

出场角色：仄（zè）；厂（chǎng）； 厌（yàn）。

仄对厂说："你厂子的人都跑光了。你瞧瞧厌老弟，它至少还有一条狗。"

The Owner of a Watchdog

Characters: 仄"narrow"; 厂"factory"; 厌"detest".

"There isn't a soul left in your factory," says 仄 to 厂 . "Look at brother 厌. At least he has a dog."

Note: 仄 is composed of 人 "person" enclosed (from upper and left sides) by 厂 "factory"; 厌 is composed of 犬 "dog" enclosed by 厂.

莫让邻里不安宁

出场角色：歹（dǎi）；夕（xī）。

歹对夕说："兄弟，学学我，安块天花板吧。晴天遮阳，雨天挡雨。"

夕打量了歹一眼，笑道："不行啊！我不能只图自己舒服，而让邻里和朋友忐忑不安啊！"

A Good Neighbour

Characters: 歹"bad"; 夕"eve".

"Hey, buddy," says 歹 to 夕. "Fix a ceiling as I have done, to protect yourself against sun and rain."

"No way!" laughs 夕, casting an eye over the other. "I cannot seek ease and comfort for myself while putting my friends and neighbours in fear."

Note: With a horizontal stroke at the top, 歹 differs from 夕 in composition.

大有大的烦恼

出场角色：蜂（fēng）。幕后角色：风（fēng）。

"老兄今日为何叹气呀？"小草问身旁的马尾松。

"今天早上来了一群讨厌的马蜂，在我身上做了个窝。"马尾松叹道，"他们这会儿出去散心了，不过马上就该回来了。"

"老兄真是树大招蜂啊！"小草笑道。

注释：本文中的"树大招蜂"是成语"树大招风"的戏仿。

Big Trees Have Big Worries

Onstage Character: 蜂"wasp". Offstage Character: 风"wind".

"Hey, buddy. Why are you moaning and groaning today?" a little grass asked his neighbour, a pine tree.

"This morning a swarm of wasps came to build a nest in me," sighed the pine. "Now they are out for pleasure and will be back soon."

"A tall tree invites wasps," teased the little grass.

Note: "A tall tree invites wasps" is a parody of the Chinese idiom "A tall tree invites wind" meaning a person who has made a name or a fortune is liable to attract attention and get into trouble. "Wasp" has the same speech sound as "wind" in Mandarin.

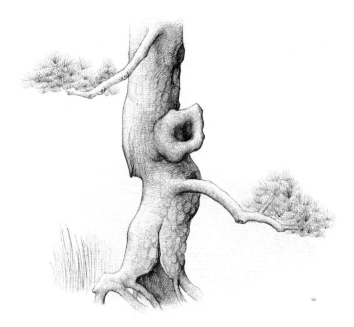

韬光养晦

出场角色：不（bù）；木（mù）。

不和木是一起长大的伙伴。从上学到工作一直在一起。

不发现木在公司里经常直言不讳地发表自己的看法，甚至为了同事的利益与老板针锋相对地争论。

不担心木这样做会影响他自己的前程。

不把木邀到一个酒馆。三杯下肚之后，不谈了他对好友的看法。他对木道："记住，轻易不要出头。"

木琢磨了不的意见，觉得他说的很有道理。木惭愧道："是啊，我这个人咋这么木呢！"

A Word of Advice

Characters: 不"no"; 木"dump".

不 and 木 are co-workers, and they go back a long way, growing up together and going to school together.

Unlike 不, 木 often voices his opinions bluntly and even stands up to the boss in the interest of his teammates.

Concerned about his friend's future in the job, 不 invites 木 out to a drink at a pub. After three glasses 木 speaks his mind, "Bear in mind, old pal, never stick out your head rashly."

Turning the advice over for a while, 木 finds it fairly sensible, and says ashamedly, "How dumb I am!"

Note: The extended part of the vertical stroke across the top horizontal line in 木 represents the head, while the vertical stroke in 不 starts at the left-falling stroke, not crossing the top horizontal line; the Chinese "to stick out one's head" figuratively means pushing oneself forward.

穷人的困惑

出场角色：代（dài）；贷（dài）。

代问贷："兄弟，为啥大伙都找你借钱，却没人找我借呢？"

贷看了看代，大笑道："因为你没钱啊！"

A Bum at a Loss

Characters: 代"replace"; 贷"loan".

"Hey, buddy. Why does everybody come to you for a loan but not me?" 代 asks 贷.

"Because you're penniless," laughs the other.

Note: 贷 is structured with 代 at the top and 贝 "money" at the bottom.

各显神通

出场角色：闪（shǎn）；介（jiè）；众（zhòng）；页（yè）；黎（lí）；队（duì）；肉（ròu）；会（huì）；囚（qiú）；内（nèi）；怂（sǒng）；人（rén）。

一帮老同学聚会。

一个同学提议道："现在没人啥事也办不成。各位说说自己哪里有关系，今后谁有了麻烦也能互相照应一下。

闪迫不及待道："我里边有人。"

介："我上边有人。"

页："我下面有人。"

黎："我中间有人。"

队："我侧面有人。"

肉："我内部有人。"

会："我高层有人。"

众："我上下都有人。"

囚："我嘴上有人。"

内："我里外有人。"

怂："我心上有人。"

从："我左右有人。"

参加聚会的同学里，只有人默不作声。

"看来只有你是孤家寡人了！"大伙朝人开起了玩笑。

人涨红了脸，羞愧得无地自容。突然，他茅塞顿开，抓起一面镜子，对众人大喊道："我镜子里有人。"

站在人旁边的众瞟了一眼镜子，大笑道："你骗我们，镜子里明明是个'入'嘛！"

人看了看镜子，还真是个"入"。

人气得拂袖而去。

A Friend at Court

Characters: 闪"flash"; 介"between"; 众"crowd"; 页"page"; 黎"multitude"; 队 "team"; 肉"meat"; 会"meet"; 囚"prisoner"; 内"inside"; 怂"terrified"; 人"man".

At a class reunion, one says, "Nowadays you can do nothing without a friend at court. Let's speak out where we have connections, whom anyone of us can turn to in times of trouble."

"I've got someone indoors," responds 闪, too impatient to wait.

介: I've got a man on top.

页: I've got a man below.

黎: I've got a man in the middle.

队: I've got a man at the side.

肉: I've got a man inside.

会: I've got a man above.

众: I've got men above and below.

囚: I've got a man in the mouth.

内: I've got a man inside and outside.

怂: I've got men on the mind.

从: I've got men on either side.

Everyone speaks up except 人.

"So you are the only one who is all alone," laugh the others.

Blushed with shame, 人 hits upon an idea. He grabs a hand glass and calls out, "I've got a man in the mirror."

"You are lying!" casting a glance into the mirror, 众, who stands right beside

人, says with a loud laugh. "Obviously it's '入' in the glass."

Taking another look into the mirror and realising the truth, 人 walks off in anger.

Note: Each of the characters 闪, 介, 众, 页, 黎, 队, 肉, 会, 囚, 内 and 怂 contains 人"man" in a different position; 人 reflects in the mirror as 入.

财大腰粗

出场角色：享（xiǎng）；亨（hēng）。

在纽约的一条大街上，享见到了亨。

享问亨："这位仁兄，你怎么连腰带也不系就出门啊！"

亨瞪了享一眼："少见多怪，大亨我就这身打扮，整个曼哈顿，还没有我进不去的地方。"

An Arrogant Tycoon

Characters: 享"enjoy"; 亨"prosperous".

享 comes across 亨 on an avenue in New York.

"Why, buddy, you're out without a belt on the waist!" says 享 to 亨.

"You are so fussy!" replies 亨, shooting a glare at the other. "In Manhattan all doors open to me, a tycoon."

Note: Without a horizontal stroke across the 了 below, 亨 differs from 享 in composition.

圈儿里圈儿外

出场角色: 卷 (juàn); 口 (kǒu)。

卷与口是儿时的好朋友。但是长大以后，卷开始看不起口了。

"你为啥不愿意搭理我了呢？"口直言不讳地问。

卷答道："我是圈儿里的，你是圈儿外的。我们俩的分量不一样。"

The Interior and the Exterior of the Circle

Characters: 卷"book"; 口"mouth".

卷 and 口 are childhood friends, but these days the former has grown to despise the latter.

"Why do you keep me at a distance?" 口 asks the other straightly.

"I'm the interior but you are the exterior of the circle," replies 卷. "We weigh differently."

Note: 卷 enclosed by 口 forms 圈"circle".

位置不同

出场角色: 陪 (péi); 部 (bù)。

风姿绰约的陪小姐在某公司聚会上见到了气宇轩昂的部先生。

"请问先生贵姓？"陪主动问部先生。

"在下姓'部'，部长的部。我是鄙公司的发展部部长。"部笑着答道，"敢问小姐尊姓？"

陪羡慕地说："我姓陪，陪酒的陪。陪酒就是我的工作。都是一只耳朵，一个立，一个口。可为啥咱俩的命差这么多呢？"

部看了看陪，认真地说："看来耳朵长在哪个位置还真的很重要。"

Where It Grows Counts

Characters: 陪"tend"; 部"department".

At a business party, a gorgeous lady 陪 meets a distinguished-looking gentleman 部.

"May I have your name, sir?" she asks him.

"My name is 部, which means 'department', and I'm the Development Director of the company, " responds the man. "And how should I address you?"

"I'm 陪, meaning 'tend', and my job is to serve drinks," says the woman.

"I possess a 阝, a 口 and a 立, exactly the same way as you do, but why do we two meet totally different fates?"

Taking a closer look at the other, the man says seriously, "It appears that where the ear grows counts a whole lot."

Note: 陪 is structured left to right with the radical 阝"ear" and 咅 while 部 left to right with 咅 and 阝.

什么世道

出场角色：口（kǒu）；国（guó）。

口无所事事地在街上闲逛。

口遇到了国。看到国神气十足的样子，口叹着气道："我是家徒四壁，你是怀揣美玉。这世道真是太不公平了。"

国安慰口说："你只靠着一张嘴，就长了跟我差不多大的块头。你该知足了。"

Life Is Unfair

Characters: 口 "mouth"; 国 "state".

Strolling down the street, 口 bumps into 国.

"Life is unfair," sighs 口, impressed by the dignified air of the other. "You are blessed with beautiful jade while I have nothing but bare walls."

"But even so, you match up to me in size just by the mouth," says 国 soothingly. "You should be well pleased."

Note: 国 is composed of 玉 "jade" enclosed by 口.

化险为夷

出场角色：且（qiě）。

死刑犯且试图越狱。

他收买了一个看守。这个看守给他提供了凿墙的工具。

且成功地把囚室的墙凿了一个洞。正当他准备钻洞而逃时，囚室的门突然打开了，监狱长来查房了。

且在囚室的一面墙下站立不动，屏住呼吸，听候命运的安排。

"快去追！"监狱长气急败坏地喊道，"这个家伙越狱了！"

原来监狱长把贴墙而立的且看成了一架梯子。

From Danger to Safety

Character: 且 "and".

且, a convict on death row, attempts to break out of jail.

He bribes a guard, who supplies him with tools to chisel through the cell wall.

且 finally manages to create a hole in the wall. He is just about to crawl through the hole when suddenly the cell door opens, and in strides the warden for a routine check. 且 remains still leaning against the wall, holding his breath and waiting for his fate.

"Chase him! Hurry up!" the jailer barks furiously. "This guy has escaped!"

As it turns out, the prison head has mistaken 且 for a ladder.

Note: 且 resembles a ladder.

跑进了死胡同

出场角色：巴（bā）。

巴被人诬陷抓捕入狱了。

夜黑风高，巴越狱了。

发现巴越狱后，狱警数十人分路追赶。

巴不幸跑进了一条死胡同。

无路可走的巴急中生智，他紧贴着一面墙站立不动，嘴里发出"嘶嘶"的声音。

狱警看见了巴，不但没有抓他，反而转身跑掉了。

原来，跑得气喘吁吁的狱警把巴当成了一条眼镜蛇。

A Narrow Escape

Character: 巴"wish".

Framed up, 巴 is in prison.

One dark and windy night, he manages to break out of jail.

Finding 巴 escaped, the prison guards, several dozens in number, immediately launch a manhunt for him in different directions.

Now the escaping prisoner strays into a bind alley. With no way out, he tactfully clings to a wall, standing motionless and making a hissing sound.

Some of the guards run in and spot 巴; however, instead of capturing him, they turn around and run away.

It turns out that the breathless guards have mistaken 巴 for a cobra.

Note: 巴 resembles a cobra.

靠山的重要

出场角色：人（rén）；仙（xiān）。

人对仙道："仙兄，看见你的模样，我才知道，一个人有没有靠山大不一样啊！"

A Background Mountain

Characters: 人"man"; 仙"immortal".

"Brother 仙, your appearance leads me to believe that a background mountain makes a big difference to a man," says 人 to 仙.

Note: 仙 is structured with a semantic radical 亻"man" on the left and 山 "mountain" on the right; the Chinese expression "background mountain" figuratively means "patron".

君子爱财，取之有道

出场角色：贼（zéi）；戎（róng）。

贼对戎道："兄弟，你身上咋一文不名啊？"

戎看了看贼，说："我身在行伍，哪有功夫挣钱啊！再说了，来路不正的钱我也不会粘的。"

Money Talks，but Integrity Speaks Louder

Characters: 贼"thief"; 戎"army".

"Why are you broke, man?" 贼 asks 戎.

"Serving in the ranks, how can I have the time to make bucks?" says 戎

as he throws a glance at 贼. "And I won't touch the stuff off the back of a lorry."

Note: 贼 is composed of 贝"currency" on the left and 戎 on the right.

根本区别

出场角色：颜（yán）；须（xū）。

颜问须："兄弟，知道我俩的根本区别在哪儿吗？"

"不知道啊！"须老老实实地答道。

"你是无产者，我是有产者。"颜得意地说。

Fundamental Difference

Characters: 颜"face"; 须"beard".

颜 asks 须, "Brother, do you know the core contrast between us?"

"I have no idea," 须 answers honestly.

"You are a proletarian and I am a bourgeois," says 颜 with pride.

Note: 须 lacks 产"property" in composition compared to 颜.

公鸡与公鸭

出场角色：冠（guān）。幕后角色：官（guān）。

公鸡很羡慕公鸭能够下河戏水和捕捉小鱼小虾。

"为什么我一下水就沉底呢？"公鸡无可奈何地问公鸭。

公鸭朝公鸡晃了晃脑袋，嘎嘎地说："因为我无冠一身轻啊。"

注释：本文中的"无冠一身轻"是谚语"无官一身轻"的戏仿。

A Rooster and a Drake

Onstage Character: 冠"crown". Offstage Character: 官"official".

A rooster felt envious of a drake able to paddle in the river catching tiddlers and shrimps.

"How come I sink to the bottom every time I enter the water?" asked the rooster hopelessly.

"No crown, no weight," quacked the drake to the rooster, swaying his head.

Note: "No crown, no weight" is a parody of the Chinese proverb "Out of office, out of care" meaning one feels carefree when relieved of his official duties. The proverb was generally used by a feudal bureaucrat to comfort himself after leaving office, and now normally means that a person feels at ease without any obligations. The send-up and its original are phonetically identical.

逃过一劫

出场角色：凶（xiōng）；区（qū）。

凶杀了人后夺路而逃。警察在后面紧追不舍。

眼看就要被警察追到了，凶立即躺倒在地。

"你是谁呀？"赶到的警察问凶。

"我是区呀！"凶狡猾地说。

"可是你很像我们追捕的凶啊？"

"不可能，凶是上面开口，我是右边开口啊！"

粗心大意的警察放过了凶，继续往前追了。

A Close Call

Characters: 凶"murderer"; 区"district".

凶, a murderer, is heading for the hills, with a policeman in hot pursuit.

Just about to be run down, the criminal throws himself on the ground.

"Who are you?" asks the cop.

"I'm 区," replies 凶 foxily.

"But you look a lot like the guy we are hunting," says the police officer.

"How ridiculous!" argues the murderer. "凶 gaps on top but I open on the right."

Then, the mindless cop picks up his chase, leaving 凶 at large.

Note: 区 resembles 凶 lying on the side.

第三章　不想成为一条狗
Chapter 3　No Desire to Be a Dog

犄角与腿

出场角色：并（bìng）；兵（bīng）。

在一次朋友聚会上，并第一次见到兵。并打量了兵好一阵，惊异地问："为什么我的犄角长在上边，你的犄角却长在下边呢？"

兵微笑着说："看好了，先生，那是我的两条腿。"

Horns and Legs

Characters: 并"union"; 兵"soldier".

并 meets 兵 for the first time at a party. Sizing the other up for quite a while, 并 asks in surprise, "How come your horns are at the bottom while mine at the top?"

"Take a good look, sir," smiles 兵. "These are my legs."

Note: 并 has a radical ⿱ above resembling the horns and 兵 has a radical 八 below resembling the legs.

"你的右腿呢？"

出场角色：兵（bīng）；乒（pīng）。

在一次退伍老兵聚会上，兵见到乒，惊问："你的右腿呢，兄弟？"

乒苦笑着答道："我从一生下来就没有右腿呀！"

Born with Only One Leg

Characters: 兵"soldier"; 乒"first character in ping-pong".

At a gathering of veterans, 兵 sees 乒. "Where's your right leg, buddy?" asks the former in surprise.

"I was born with only one leg," replies the latter with a bitter smile.

Note: 兵 has a radical 八 shaped like two legs at the bottom; 乒 has a left-falling stroke resembling a left leg at the bottom.

无头之鬼

出场角色：卞（biàn）；下（xià）。

卞对下说："无头鬼，你在我面前甘拜下风吧！"

下笑道："无所谓了，我的名字就是'下'呀！"

A Headless Monster

Characters: 卞"impetuous"; 下"lower".

"Hey, headless monster," says 卞 to 下. "Just bow to my superiority!"

"It makes no odds," smiles the other. "'Lower' is my name."

Note: 卞 is composed of 下 with a dot stroke on top representing the head.

无用武之地

出场角色：丛（cóng）；从（cóng）。

丛对从道："我们这才是双人舞。你们连地板也没有，跳什么舞啊！"

A Partner Dance

Characters: 丛"cluster"; 从"from".

"Look at us. This is a real partner dance," 丛 says to 从. "How are you supposed to dance without a floor?"

Note: 丛 is composed of 从 with a horizontal stroke at the bottom resembling a floor; 从 is structured left to right with a pair of 人"person" representing two persons doing a partner dance.

"谁拽走了你一块肉啊？"

出场角色：串（chuàn）；中（zhōng）。

串对中说："兄弟，谁拽走了你一块肉啊？"

A Chunk of Meat

Characters: 串"string"; 中"middle".

串 asks 中, "Who has torn a chunk of flesh off your body, bro?"

Note: Compared with 串, 中 lacks a 口 resembling a chunk of meat.

奢靡之风不可有

出场角色：此（cǐ）；些（xiē）。

此对些说："钱多得没处花了吧，还铺双层地毯。"

Waste Not, Want Not

Characters: 此"this"; 些"some".

"Wow, you've got a double-layer carpet," says 此 to 些. "Money burns a hole in your pocket."

Note: 些 is composed of 此 at the top and two horizontal strokes at the bottom representing two carpets laid one on top of the other.

兄有大难

出场角色：晨（chén）；辰（chén）。

晨见了辰，大惊失色道："兄弟，谁把你脑袋砍啦？"

A Stroke of Bad Luck

Characters: 晨"morning"; 辰"dragon".

晨 is taken aback upon seeing 辰 and exclaims, "Ah, buddy! Who chopped off your head?"

Note: 晨 is composed of 辰 with a radical 日 on top representing the head.

心力交瘁

出场角色：车（chē）；辇（niǎn）。
车对辇说："兄弟，你载着两个人，真够累的。"

注释：辇，古代以人拉着走的车子，后多指天子或王室乘坐的车。

Much to Bear

Characters: 车"cart"; 辇"royal carriage".
车 says to 辇, "Hey, buddy. You must be tiring yourself out carrying two men."

Note: 辇 is composed of 车 with two 夫"man" on top.

毫毛虽细，视之可察

出场角色：敞（chǎng）；氅（chǎng）。
敞对氅说："兄弟，啥时候长的毛啊？"

An Eye for Fine Hair

Characters: 敞"open"; 氅"overcoat".
敞 asks 氅, "Bro, when did you start growing the hair at the bottom?"

Note: 氅 is structured top to bottom with 敞 and 毛 "hair".

心旷才能神怡

出场角色：又（yòu）；叉（chā）。
又问叉："心里又有疙瘩了吧？"

A Light Heart, a Free Spirit

Characters: 又"again"; 叉"fork".
又 asks 叉, "You've got a knot in your heart again?"

Note: 叉 is composed of 又 with a dot stroke enclosed representing "a knot in the heart" which in Chinese refers to a petty annoyance on one's mind.

提防海龟

出场角色：龟（guī）。幕后角色：归（guī）。
章鱼问大虾："你觉得海龟怎么样，能不能与它做朋友呢？"
"俗语说，'龟心似箭'，不可不防啊。"大虾语重心长地答道。

注释：本文中的"龟心似箭"是成语"归心似箭"的戏仿。

Beware of the Sea Turtle

Onstage Character: 龟"turtle". Offstage Character: 归"return".

"How do you feel about making friends with the sea turtle?" an octopus asked a prawn.

"You must be on guard against him," replied the prawn seriously. " 'A turtle's heart is like an arrow,' as the idiom says."

Note: "A turtle's heart is like an arrow" is a parody of the Chinese idiom "A returning heart is like an arrow" which metaphorically describes the feeling of wanting to return home as fast as an arrow just shot. The send-up and its original have the same speech sound in Mandarin.

分工不同

出场角色：叼（diāo）；叨（dāo）。

叼对叨说："你我各有一张嘴，可术有专攻啊。"

Different Roles

Characters: 叼"hold in the mouth"; 叨"grumble".

叨 says to 叼, "We are both blessed with a mouth, but each has his own expertise."

Note: 叼 and 叨 are both structured with a semantic radical 口"mouth" on the left.

认错了人

出场角色：大（dà）；天（tiān）。

大问天道："兄弟呀，你头上顶块板子干啥呀？"

天皱着眉头答道："看好喽，我不是你兄弟。"

Caught in the Wrong Shoes

Characters: 大"big"; 天"sky".

"Brother, why do you carry a board on your head?" 大 asks 天.

"Take a good look," replies the other, frowning. "I'm not your brother."

Note: 天 is composed of 大 with a horizontal stroke on top resembling a flat board.

顶棚不见了

出场角色：等（děng）；寺（sì）。

等对寺说："兄弟，你啥时候把竹顶棚拆啦？"

寺笑道："我从打地基到完工，一根竹子也没用过呀！"

The Roof Gone

Characters: 等"wait"; 寺"temple".

"Hey, buddy," 等 says to 寺. "When did you tear down your bamboo roof?"

"Not a single bamboo stick has ever been used from top to bottom," smiles the other.

Note: 等 is composed of 寺 with the semantic radical ⺮ "bamboo" on top.

又认错了人

出场角色：弟（dì）；克（kè）。

弟望着克，呆呆地说："兄啊，你啥时候信的基督啊？"

克对弟微笑道："老弟，我不信基督。另外，我也不是你的兄。"

Neither Christian nor Brother

Characters: 弟"younger brother"; 克"gram".

弟 seems at a loss as he looks at 克. "When did you start to believe in Christ, brother?" he asks.

"Dude, I'm not a Christian," smiles the other, "nor am I your brother."

Note: 克 is composed of 兄"elder brother" with a radical 十 on top resembling a Christian cross.

放在哪里？

出场角色：大（dà）；犬（quǎn）。

大对犬说："你最近有点得意呀。带着一个肩章就趾高气扬啦？"

犬苦笑道："那我怎么办，像'太'那样把这玩意儿藏裤裆里？"

Where to Put It

Characters: 大"big"; 犬"dog".

"You look kind of cocky lately," 大 says to 犬. "Do you get a swelled head from the badge on your shoulder?"

"What am I supposed to do then?" smiles the other bitterly. "Do I have to hide the stuff under my thighs as 太 does?"

Note: 犬 is composed of 大 with a dot stroke representing a badge on the upper right while 太 has a dot stroke below starting at the left-falling stroke.

防身之器不可丢

出场角色：兑（duì）；况（kuàng）。

在一次聚会上，兑见到了新朋友况。

兑仔细打量了况好一阵，惊问："兄弟，犄角是我们的防身武器呀！你怎么把它们弄断了？"

Horns for Self-Defense

Characters: 兑"convert"; 况"condition".

兑 gets to know 况 at a party.

Looking the other up and down for a long while, 兑 asks in surprise, "Buddy, our horns are for self-defense, but how come you've got yours broken?"

Note: 兑 has a radical ⌄ at the top resembling a pair of horns while 况 has a radical 冫 on the left representing a pair of broken horns.

只差一点

出场角色：刁（diāo）；习（xí）。

刁和同事习到餐馆喝酒。

席间，刁对习笑着说："人家都说咱俩长相相近。确实，我比你只差了一点儿。"

习笑了笑，没有说话，只是在心里道："就这一点儿，你一辈子也追不上啊。"

A Little Dot Difference

Characters: 彐"a surname"; 习"a surname".

彐 treats his workmate 习 to a drink at a restaurant.

"They all say we two look alike," smiles 彐 at the table. "In fact, what distinguishes between you and me is just a little dot."

Cracking a grin, 习 thinks to himself, "That little dot is beyond your reach all the life."

Note: With an extra dot stroke, 习 differs from 彐 in composition.

何为人样?

出场角色：大（dà）；人（rén）。

大不满地对人说："你连胳膊也没有，还有点人样吗？"

"可我确实是人啊！"人笑道。

Barely Looking Human

Characters: 大"big"; 人"person".

大 seems displeased upon seeing 人. "Without upper limbs, do you look anything like a human?" he says.

"But I am a human indeed," smiles the other.

Note: 大 is shaped like 人 "person" with a horizontal line running through the upper middle representing the arms.

116

羡慕

出场角色：儿（ér）；兀（wù）；元（yuán）。

儿对兀和元羡慕地说："两位老哥都有顶棚！元兄还是双层的。"

A Sincere Admiration

Characters: 儿"son"; 兀"erect"; 元"first".

"How I envy you guys having roofs!" 儿 says to 兀 and 元 with admiration. "And brother 元 is even under two ones."

Note: 兀 is composed of 儿 with a horizontal stroke on top resembling a roof and 元 with a radical 二 on top representing two roofs.

记性太差

出场角色：而（ér）；斋（zhāi）。

而对斋说："兄弟，你啥时候又起了一层楼？"

斋笑道："而老弟，你的记性太差了。我这屋舍一直就是上下两层啊！"

A Poor Memory

Characters: 而"but"; 斋"room".

"When did you add another floor, pal?" 而 asks 斋.

"Buddy, you have a memory like a sieve," replies the other. "I have been a two-storey house all along."

Note: 斋 is composed of 而 with a radical 文 above representing a top storey.

赞美朋友

出场角色：儿（ér）；兆（zhào）。

儿对兆说："兄弟，你身上这四面小旗真不赖。"

A Compliment

Characters: 儿"son"; 兆"sign".

"Hey, bro," 儿 says to 兆. "The four little flags suit you well."

Note: 兆 is composed of 儿 with a dot and a raising stroke on the left, a left falling and a dot stroke on the right, representing four small flags.

误解

出场角色：夫（fū）；天（tiān）。

夫看天的头一直缩着，以为天有点自卑，于是鼓励他说："兄弟，别着急。大丈夫只要奋发图强，终有出头之日。"

天知道夫误解了自己，笑道："我已经高高在上了。再出头就跑到银河系外边了。"

A Misjudgement

Characters: 夫"man"; 天"sky".

Seeing 天 keep his head retracted all the time, 夫 believes he must feel somewhat inferior.

"Take it easy, buddy," says 夫, trying to buck the other up. "Everybody has his day to poke out the head as long as he goes all out."

"In that case, I would stretch myself out of the Galaxy," laughs 天, aware of being misjudged, "as I'm already sky-high."

Note: 夫 differs from 天 by the top extended part of the left-falling stroke representing the head; the Chinese expression "poke out the head" figuratively means becoming outstanding.

天外有夫

出场角色：夫（fū）；天（tiān）。

夫看不惯天经常夸耀自己高大无比。

一日，夫对天说："兄弟，别总夸你高了，我比你还高一头。"

天仔细看了看夫，惭愧地说："是啊，没想到真是天外有天啊！"

夫笑道："应该是天外有夫！"

A Man beyond Heaven

Characters: 夫"man"; 天"heaven".

夫 is not pleased with 天, who often boasts of his height.

"Stop bragging, dude," says 夫. "In fact I am taller than you by a head."

"Indeed," taking a close look at the other, 天 replies, ashamed. "Now I see there is a heaven beyond Heaven."

"Not exactly," smiles 夫. "Actually, there is a MAN beyond Heaven."

Note: 夫 differs from 天 by the top extended part of the left-falling stroke representing the head.

谁比谁强

出场角色: 夫 (fū) ; 失 (shī) 。
夫对失说: "你咋只有一个肩章呢? 另一个丢了? "
失看了看夫, 微笑着说: "有一个也比一个没有强吧。"
夫红着脸走了。

One Is Better Than None

Characters: 夫"man"; 失"lose".

"How come you have only one badge on your shoulder?" 夫 asks 失. "The other is lost?"

"One is better than none," smiles 失 as he glances at 夫.

Blushed, 夫 walks away.

Note: 失 is composed of 夫 with a left-falling stroke on the upper left resembling a badge.

以量取胜

出场角色：丰（fēng）；羊（yáng）。

丰对羊道："我俩若是比试起来，你肯定比我厉害。"

羊诧异道："何以见得？"

丰笑着说："你有俩犄角，我有一个犄角。一个斗不过俩。"

One Is No Match for Two

Characters: 丰"plentiful"; 羊"goat".

"You must be stronger than me if we lock horns with each other," 丰 says to 羊.

"Why do you think so?" asks the other in surprise.

"I have one horn while you have a pair," smiles 丰. "One is no match for two."

Note: The top extended par of the vertical line in 丰 represents a horn and the radical ⌄ at the top of 羊 resembles a pair of horns.

谁比谁苦

出场角色：抚（fǔ）；跌（diē）。

抚对跌说："咱俩的命是半斤八两啊。我没了手，你丢了脚。"

Birds of a Feather

Characters: 抚"comfort"; 跌"fall".

"We two share more or less the same fate," 抚 says to 跌. "I failed to keep my hands and you lost your feet."

Note: 抚 is structured left to right with a semantic radical 扌"hand" and 无 "no", and 跌 with a semantic radical 𧾷"foot" and 失"lose".

"别小看这一截"

出场角色：竿（gān）；竽（yú）。

竿看着竽，认真地说："你脚底下有一截没修理干净。"

竽自豪地对竿说："老兄，你可别小看这一截，我就凭它比你的身价高啊！"

注释：竽是一种古簧管乐器。

The Value of a Knot

Characters: 竿"pole"; 竽"a musical instrument".

Staring at 竽, 竿 says seriously, "A bump is still not trimmed off on the bottom of your foot."

"Don't underrate the knot, old chap," replies the other proudly. "It makes me superior to you in value."

Note: With an additional hook stroke at the bottom, 竽 differs from 竿 in composition.

命悬一线

出场角色：告（gào）；靠（kào）。

告目不转睛地盯着靠，自言自语道："我这兄弟跑天线上站着，万一掉下来咋办呐？"

Hanging by a Thread

Characters: 告"tell"; 靠"lean".

Gazing at 靠, 告 says to himself, "It's really silly of the fellow to stand on the antenna array. What if he falls?"

Note: 靠 is structured top to bottom with 告 and 非 resembling an antenna array.

威风顿失

出场角色：宫（gōng）；吕（lǚ）。

宫对吕说："兄弟，我比你多了个盖子，怎么样，富丽堂皇吧！"

吕笑道："你虽然富丽堂皇，可毕竟是供别人住的。我祖上可是汉朝大名鼎鼎的吕后，后半辈子一直在宫里住着。"

Loss of Prestige

Characters: 宫"palace"; 吕"a surname".

"Buddy, I'm blessed with a roof while you are not," says 宫 to 吕. "Don't

123

you find me magnificent?"

"Splendid as you look, you are a mere dwelling for others," smiles the other. "One of my ancestors, the renowned Empress Lu of the Han Dynasty, spent most of her later life in the palace."

Note: 宫 is composed of 吕 with a radical 宀 on top representing a roof.

天无二日

出场角色：亘 (gèn)；二 (èr)。

亘对二说："你天地俱备，可惜独缺一日啊！"

二苦笑道："是啊，宇宙中仅有一日，被你夺走了。"

注释：亘，表示空间和时间上延续不断。

One and Only

Characters: 亘"eternal"; 二"two".

"You possess both heaven and earth," says 亘 to 二. "It's a shame there is not a sun in between."

"Indeed," replies the other with a bitter smile. "But you've grabbed away the only one in the cosmos."

Note: 亘 is composed of 日"sun" in the middle of 二 representing heaven and earth.

评头品足

出场角色：光（guāng）；兴（xīng）。

光对兴说："你头顶中间那根头发是歪的。"

兴笑道："我还没嫌你的一条腿不直呢！"

Splitting Hairs

Characters: 光"light"; 兴"delighted".

"The central hair on your top is leaning to the side," says 光 to 兴.

"Do I have to remind you that one of your legs is bent?" replies the other with a sneer.

Note: 兴 has a component (composed of 2 dots and a left-falling stroke) at the top resembling three hairs with the one in the middle tilting to the left; 光 has a radical 儿 at the bottom resembling the legs with the right one bent.

骨之不存，肉将焉附？

出场角色：共（gōng）；其（qí）。

共对其道："我俩长得真是有点像啊！"

其笑道："但是我有肋骨，你没肋骨啊！"

Similar but Different

Characters: 共"common"; 其"its".

"We look like two peas in a pod," says 共 to 其.

"You have no ribs," smiles the other. "But I do."

Note: 其 has two more horizontal strokes than 共 resembling the ribs.

自知之明

出场角色：个（gè）；人（rén）。

个对人说："人啊，最要紧的是不能没有脊梁骨。"

人笑道："你倒是有一根，可是你却不是人啊！"

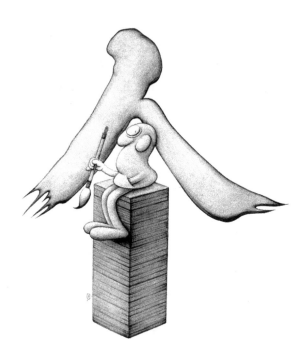

The Wise Man Knows Himself

Characters: 个"individual"; 人"man".

"A spine is indispensable to a man," says 个 to 人.

"You've got one, but you are not a human," smiles the other.

Note: 个 is structured top to bottom with 人 and a vertical stroke resembling a backbone.

只有半桶水

出场角色：甘（gān）；廿（niàn）。

甘和几个朋友在三亚的海滩上晒太阳。

今天的太阳可真辣。

甘看见大伙带的水都喝完了，于是对几个朋友道："我肚子里的水味道不错，各位如果不嫌弃，就尝几口吧。"

几个朋友笑着摆摆手："算了，你一共就半桶水，我们一人一口，你就变成廿了。"

注释：廿，二十。

A Half-Full Bucket

Characters: 甘"sweet"; 廿"twenty".

One day, 甘 and some of his friends are sunbathing on the beach in Sanya.

Exposed to the scorching sun, the bathers soon drink their bottled water to the last drop.

"Hey, guys, I've got some sweet water here inside me," 甘 says to his mates. "Have a taste if you'd like."

"Forget it," smile the others, making hand gestures to decline. "As a half-full bucket, you'd turn into the empty vessel 廿 if we each took a sip of the water."

Note: 廿 resembles an empty bucket while 甘 is shaped like a bucket half filled with water (with one more horizontal line enclosed).

"哈哈！"

出场角色：合（hé）；哈（hā）。

合对哈说："你比我多了一张嘴就是为了笑吗？哈哈！"

Ha-Ha

Characters: 合"gather"; 哈"ha".

"You added an extra mouth just for laughing aloud?" says 合 to 哈. "Ha-ha!"

Note: 哈 is composed of a semantic radical 口"mouth" on the left and 合 on the right.

嘴不干净

出场角色：猴（hóu）；丫（yā）。

猴想吃桃子了，于是他来到一片树林里。

猴子见到丫，围着丫转了一圈，没有看见一个果子。猴子失望地问：“你丫为啥不长果子呢？”

丫狠狠瞪了猴子一眼，怒道：“你这畜生嘴里不干不净，没你好果子吃。”

You Eat with That Mouth?

Characters: 猴"monkey"; 丫"branch".

猴 comes to an orchard, with the desire to devour some peaches.

Circling around 丫, 猴 cannot find an edible yield. "How come you bastard don't bear any fruit?" asks the monkey, disappointed.

"You eat with that mouth?" replies 丫 as he darts an angry look at 猴. "Nothing good is meant for you beast."

Note: 丫 dialectally means "bastard".

另找出口

出场角色：甲（jiǎ）；由（yóu）。

甲指着由的头说：“兄弟，听我一句劝——出头的椽子先烂。”

由抿着嘴笑道：“怪不得阁下的头从屁股底下出呢！”

From under the Butt

Characters: 甲"nail"; 由"reason".

"Listen, pal," 甲 says to 由, pointing at his head. "The rafters that jut out rot first."

"No wonder your head pokes out from under the butt," sneers the other, pursing his lips.

Note: The extended part of the middle vertical stroke in 由 resembles the head.

又见山顶洞中人

出场角色：巾（jīn）；帘（lián）。
巾对帘说："姐姐，你躲在洞里干什么？"

A Cave Woman

Characters: 巾"towel"; 帘"curtain".
"Sis, why do you hide in the cave?" 巾 asks 帘 curiously.

Note: 帘 is structured top to bottom with 穴 "cave" and 巾.

大惑不解

出场角色：家（jiā）；冢（zhǒng）。
家仔细端详着冢，不解地问："你为啥把脑袋卸下来挂裙子上呢？"

注释：冢，坟墓。

All at Sea

Characters: 家"home"; 冢"tomb".
Looking at 冢 up and down, 家 asks in puzzlement, "Why have you removed your head and hung it on the skirt?"

Note: Compared with 家, the character 冢 is composed without a dot stroke on top resembling the head, but with an extra dot on the middle one of the three left-falling strokes which as a whole resembles a skirt.

重质不重量

出场角色：介（jiè）；个（gè）。

介问个："兄弟，正常人都有两条腿，你咋一条腿呢？"

个看了看介，笑道："与其一条直，一条弯，还不如我这一条腿好看呢。"

Quality above Quantity

Characters: 介"interpose"; 个"individual".
"Mate, different from others, how come you have only one leg?" 介 asks 个.
Throwing the other a glance, 个 chuckles, "With one leg straight and the other crooked, you look no better than me."

Note: 个 has a vertical stroke below resembling a leg; 介 has a left-falling stroke and a vertical line below resembling two legs with the left one bent.

宁缺毋滥

出场角色：君（jūn）；尹（yǐn）。

君问尹："兄弟，你的嘴巴呢？"

尹笑道："压屁股底下的嘴巴，不要也罢。"

Better Nothing Than Something Wrong

Characters: 君"monarch"; 尹"magistrate".

"Hey, dude," says 君 to 尹. "Where's your mouth?"

"I'd rather part with that stuff than keep it under the butt," laughs the other.

Note: 君 is structured with 尹 at the top and 口"mouth" at the bottom.

以少胜多

出场角色：几（jī）；秃（tū）。

几对秃说："别看你头上长了根苗苗，其实还不如我这一无所有的好看呢！"

Less Is More

Characters: 几"small table"; 秃"bald".

"You've got a seedling on your top while I have nothing on mine," says 几 to 秃. "But honestly, you don't look as good as I."

Note: 秃 is composed of 禾 "seedling" at the top and 几 at the bottom.

一点儿没用

出场角色：九 （jiǔ）；丸 （wán）。
九对丸说： "你明白吗，比 '九' 多一点未必是十啊！ "

No Effect

Characters: 九 "nine"; 丸 "pill".

"Nine plus one dot doesn't necessarily make ten," says 九 to 丸. "Are you clear about that?"

Note: 丸 is composed of 九 with a dot on the left-falling stroke.

就高不就低

出场角色：就 （jiù）；鹫 （jiù）。
就对鹫说： "兄弟到鸟头上高就啦。"

A High Position

Characters: 就 "move"; 鹫 "vulture".

"Wow, buddy," says 就 to 鹫. "You hold a high position on top of a bird."

Note: 鹫 is composed of 就 at the top and 鸟 "bird" at the bottom.

马上威风

出场角色：加（jiā）；驾（jià）。

加对驾说："兄弟真有你的，骑上神驹啦！"

Mounted on a Steed

Characters: 加"add"; 驾"ride".

加 says to 驾, "Buddy, you are really something mounted on a steed!"

Note: 驾 is composed of 加 at the top and 马"horse" at the bottom.

前呼后应

出场角色：空（kōng） 罕（hǎn）。

空对罕说："我多一头，君多一尾。"

罕接道："联袂出演，有头有尾。"

A Perfect Match

Characters: 空"air"; 罕"rare".

"You have a tail and I have a head," says 空 to 罕.

"Pairing up on stage, we make a perfect match," adds the other.

Note: The dot stoke at the top of 空 resembles the head, and the bottom extended part of the vertical line in 罕 resembles the tail.

名副其实

出场角色：口（kǒu）；二（èr）。

口对二说："你咋把两边的墙拆啦？你可真二啊！"

二对口说："你说对了，我本来就是二。"

注释："二"有多义，在某些汉语方言中有"缺心眼儿"的意思。

True to His Name

Characters: 口"mouth"; 二"two".

"Why have you pulled down both of your sidewalls?" says 口 to 二. "You are such a number two."

"You said it," replies the other. "I AM number two."

Note: The two vertical lines in 口 resembling the sidewalls; the Chinese "two" dialectally means "stupid" or "lacking mental agility".

难分高下

出场角色：吕（lǚ）；品（pǐn）。

吕对品说："咱俩真是难分高下。你嘴多，我嘴大。"

Neck and Neck

Characters: 吕"a surname"; 品"class".

"As for our mouths, we are neck and neck," says 吕 to 品. "You are superior in number and I am superior in size."

Note: Graphically 品 consists of three 口"mouth" and 吕 two bigger ones.

靠嘴吃饭

出场角色：吏（lì）；丈（zhàng）。

吏对丈说："兄弟，你的嘴呢？"

"你以为别人也像你一样靠嘴活着啊！"丈笑着答道。

Living by Mouth

Characters: 吏"official"; 丈"old man".

"Where's your mouth, old chap?" 吏 asks 丈.

"Do you believe everybody else should live by the mouth as you do?" replies the other with a grin.

Note: 丈 is shaped like 吏 without 口"mouth" in the middle.

尾大不掉

出场角色：立（lì）；产（chǎn）。

立在大街上遇见了产，奇怪地问："兄弟，你啥时候长了一条大尾巴呀？"

A Big Tail

Characters: 立"establish"; 产"produce".

立 comes across 产 on the street. "Buddy, since when have you grown that big tail?" asks the former curiously.

Note: 产 is composed of 立 with a left-falling stroke starting at the left end of the bottom horizontal line resembling a tail.

两个鬼东西

出场角色：磷（lín）；槐（huái）。

磷对槐说："你是鬼木。"

槐对磷道："你是鬼火。"

Two Ghost Brothers

Characters: 磷"phosphorus"; 槐"Chinese scholar tree".

"You are a ghost tree," says 磷 to 槐.

"You are a ghost fire," says 槐 to 磷.

Note: 槐 is composed of a semantic radical 木"tree" on the left and 鬼 "ghost" on the right; 磷 is seen as a ball of fire floating in the middle of night, commonly known as "ghost fire".

顶上功夫

出场角色：离（lí）；禽（qín）。

离对禽说："兄弟，你的顶棚修的不错呀！"

Impressed by the Roof

Characters: 离"leave"; 禽"birds".

"Wow, mate," says 离 to 禽. "What a nice roof you've built!"

Note: 禽 is composed of 离 with a radical 人 on top resembling a roof.

猴子的礼物

出场角色：酱（jiàng）。幕后角色：将（jiàng）。

猴子送给狗熊一瓶自制的苹果酱作为礼物。

"谢谢你。猴子兄弟。你送的礼物太珍贵了。俗话说，'千军易得，一酱难求'啊。"狗熊高兴地说。

注释：本文的"千军易得，一酱难求"是谚语"千军易得，一将难求"的戏仿。

A Jar of Apple Jam

Onstage Character: 酱"jam". Offstage Character: 将"general".

A monkey presented a bear with a jar of homemade apple jam as a gift.

"Thank you, buddy," said the bear joyfully. "This is really precious. As the saying goes, 'It is easy to get a thousand soldiers, but hard to find a single jam.' "

Note: "It is easy to get a thousand soldiers, but hard to find a single jam" is a parody of the proverb "It is easy to get a thousand soldiers, but hard to find a single general" which means it is easy to recruit a large number of soldiers but difficult to find a talented commander. In Chinese, the proverb and the parody sound exactly the same.

站没站相

出场角色：六（liù）；立（lì）。

六对立说："买了块地毯就忘乎所以啦，两条腿都站不利索了。"

Not Standing in Style

Characters: 六"six"; 立"stand".

"With a new carpet under your feet, you are too carried away to stand steady," says 六 to 立.

Note: The bottom line in 立 resembles a carpet and the radical ⸜ resembles the legs.

点卯之后

出场角色：卵（luǎn）；卯（mǎo）。

卵对卯说："兄弟，你看我：双目炯炯有神，多带劲啊。"

卯笑道："你不就比我多两个卵子么？神气啥呀！"

Don't Give Yourself Airs!

Characters: 卵"egg"; 卯"mortise".

"Look at me, pal," says 卵 to 卯. "With two bright eyes, how radiant I am!"

"Don't give yourself airs!" chuckles the other. "You've got nothing more than me but two eggs."

Note: With two extra dot strokes, 夘 differs from 卯 in composition.

闹中如何能取静？

出场角色：门（mén）；闹（nào）。

门不解地对闹说："你咋把市场引进家里来了？你不嫌吵的慌啊！"

Peace and Quiet Not Found

Characters: 门"door"; 闹"noisy".

门 seems confused to see 闹. "Why are you holding a market at home?" 门 asks. "Don't you find it noisy?"

Note: 闹 is composed of 市 "market" enclosed by 门 (from left, top and right sides).

一匹瞎马

出场角色：马（mǎ）；车（chē）；连（lián）。

主人让马套上车，到地里把刚刚挖出来的土豆拉回来。

可是，马找不到自己的老搭档——车了。马急得四下里搜寻。

突然，马在一个庭院里看见了连。

"车老弟，你居然赖在躺椅上悠哉悠哉！快跟我干活去！"马对着连嘶叫道。

连看了看马，困惑地说："干什么活呀？我不是你的车老弟呀。"

A Blind Horse

Characters: 马"horse"; 车"cart"; 连"connect".

马 is ordered by his master to hitch up and pull a load of freshly dug potatoes back home, but his partner 车 is nowhere to be found.

Anxious, 马 is searching around for 车 when suddenly he spots 连 in a courtyard.

"Hurry to work with me, old chap," yells the horse. "You cannot just stay idle in the sling chair."

"What?" replies 连 as he casts a puzzled look at the animal. "I'm not your partner!"

Note: 连 is composed of 车 enclosed from lower and left sides by a radical 辶 resembling a sling chair.

宅男

出场角色：木（mù）；闲（xián）。

木对闲说："你可真够木的，整天宅在家里，也不出去走走。"

闲看了看木，笑道："咱俩到底谁木啊？"

A Homebody

Characters: 木"numb"; 闲"idle".

"You are so numb staying cooped up at home all day and never going out for a walk," 木 says to 闲.

"Who is really numb here, you or me? " sneers 闲 as he throws the other a glance.

Note: 闲 is composed of 木 enclosed by 门 "door" (from left, top and right sides).

高攀死鬼

　　出场角色：毛（máo）；尾（wěi）。
　　毛对尾说："兄弟，你啥时候粘到死人身上啦？"

A Question about Attachment

Characters: 毛"hair"; 尾"tail".
毛 asks 尾, "Pal, since when have you glued yourself on a dead body?"

Note: 尾 is composed of 毛 enclosed by 尸"corpse" from upper and left sides.

"为啥我俩不一样？"

　　出场角色：马（mǎ）；犬（quǎn）。
　　马盯着犬看了半天，不解地问："朋友，为啥你添两张嘴就哭，我添两张嘴就骂呢？"

A Horse of Another Colour

Characters: 马"horse"; 犬"dog".
Staring at 犬 for a long while, 马 asks in confusion, "Buddy, how is it that

if we had two mouths on top, you would shed tears while I would use bad language?

Note: 马 joined by two 口 "mouth" on top forms 骂 "curse"; 犬 joined by two 口 on top forms 哭 "weep".

各就各位

出场角色：某（mǒu）；柑（gān）。

某对柑说："兄弟，你的部件安错位置了吧？"

Everything Has Its Place

Characters: 某 "some"; 柑 "orange".

"Hey, mate," says 某 to 柑. "Your parts are fitted wrong, aren't they?"

Note: 某 is composed of 甘 at the top and 木 at the bottom while 柑 is structured with 木 on the left and 甘 on the right.

灰头土脸

出场角色：皿（mǐn）；盔（kuī）。

皿盯着盔看了半天，不解地问："兄弟，你身上咋落那么多土啊？"

盔笑道："我就是因为有这一身土，才比你禁得住磕碰啊！"

注释：皿，器皿，某些盛东西的日常用具的统称。

Covered with Dust

Characters: 皿"utensil"; 盔"helmet".

皿 asks 盔 with a curious stare, "Why are you covered in a thick layer of dust, chum?"

"Thanks to the fine powder, I'm not as fragile as you are," replies the other with a mile.

Note: 盔 is composed of 皿 with 灰"dust" on top.

稳居高位

出场角色：目（mù）；鼎（dǐng）。
目对鼎说："兄弟，你的架子真不赖！"

In a High Rack

Characters: 目"eye"; 鼎"tripod".

"Wow, dude," says 目 to 鼎. "What a superb rack stand you are in!"

Note: 鼎 is graphically shaped like 目 held by a rack stand.

嘴上功夫

出场角色：名（míng）；夕（xī）。
名问夕："知道为什么我比你更有知名度吗？"
夕答道："不知道，请多指教。"

名笑着说：“因为我比你多一张能说会道的嘴呀！”

Mouth with a Silver Tongue

Characters: 名"name"; 夕"evening".

"Do you know why I'm more popular than you?" 名 asks 夕.

"No idea." replies the other. "Tell me why, please. I'm all ears."

"It's because I have a mouth with a silver tongue while you don't," grins 名.

Note: 名 is composed of 夕 at the top and 口 "mouth" at the bottom.

正该如此

出场角色：皿（mǐn）；血（xuè）。

皿见到了血，大惊说：“大兄弟，你头上咋插了一把刀啊！都流出红水了。”

血笑道：“那就对了。”

Born That Way

Characters: 皿"utensil"; 血"blood".

皿 is shocked to see 血. "You have a knife stabbed in the skull, old chap," he exclaims. "And it's bleeding!"

"That's just the way I am," grins the other.

Note: 血 is composed of 皿 with a left-falling stroke on top representing a knife.

天有不测风云

出场角色：宁（níng）；丁（dīng）。

宁对丁说："朋友，还是有个屋顶踏实啊！"

Storms May Strike Anytime

Characters: 宁"peace"; 丁"man".

"Hey, pal," says 宁 to 丁. "You'd feel more at ease if under a roof."

Note: 宁 is composed of 丁 with 宀 on top resembling a roof.

熊到家了

出场角色：能（néng）；熊（xióng）。

能对熊说："你可真是能人啊，连拉了四坨粑粑。"

熊不好意思地答道："快别叫我能人了。如今我可是熊到家了。"

A Bear at Home

Characters: 能"capable"; 熊"bear".

"Having done four piles of poo in a row, you are really something!" 能 says to 熊.

"Stop calling me something," replies the other, embarrassed. "Now I'm nothing but a bear at home."

Note: 熊 is composed of 能 with four dots at the bottom resembling four piles of poo; the Chinese expression "a bear at home" refers to a good-for-nothing.

一分为二

出场角色：牛（niú）；失（shī）。

牛见了失，好奇地围着他转了一圈儿。

失问："牛兄，找什么哪？"

牛不解地对失说："老弟，你的尾巴咋长成两岔啦？"

Splitting in Two

Characters: 牛"ox"; 失"loss".

牛 runs across 失 and starts to walk round him curiously.

"Bro, what are you searching for?" 失 asks.

"How come your tail splits in two, old chap?" replies 牛, puzzled.

Note: The vertical line in 牛 runs across the lower horizontal stroke with the extended part resembling a tail, while the bottom part in 失 resembles a tail splitting in two.

彼此彼此

出场角色：你（nǐ）；尔（ěr）。

你得意地对尔说："我和你不一样，我有人，你没有人。"

尔对你道："没人也是你，有人还是你。身份一点没变！"

Pride and Prejudice

Characters: 你"you"; 尔"you".

"Different from you, I have a man," says 你 to 尔 with pride.

"With or without the man, you are of the same identity," comes the reply.

Note: 你 is composed of a semantic radical 亻"person" on the left and 尔 on the right.

"我的头上没长角"

出场角色：前（qián）；俞（yú）。

前问俞："兄弟，你的犄角咋长成这样啦？"

俞笑道："你长了俩犄角，就以为别人也要长犄角啊！我那是屋顶。"

No Horns on Top

Characters: 前"front"; 俞"a surname".

"Hey, mate," says 前 to 俞. "How is it that your horns look so funny?"

"You believe everyone should have horns as you do?" laughs the other.

"That's my roof, not a pair of horns."

Note: 前 has 䒑 on top resembling a pair of horns while 俞 has 人 on top resembling a roof.

音符立在茶几上

出场角色：曲（qǔ）；典（diǎn）。

曲望着典，担忧地说："兄弟，你咋站茶几上了，不怕摔下来吗？"

On a Tea Table

Characters: 曲"tune"; 典"law".

Gazing at 典 with concern, 曲 says, "Buddy, aren't you afraid of falling off the tea table?"

Note: 典 is shaped like 曲 standing a tea table.

"为何将头藏起来？"

出场角色：庆（qìng）；厌（yàn）。

庆见到了厌，惊问："阁下把脑袋藏起来啦？"

Curiosity and Mystery

Characters: 庆"celebrate"; 厌"detest".

庆 is surprised to see 厌. "Sir, why are you keeping your head out of sight?" he asks.

Note: The dot stroke resembling the head in 庆 lies at the top while the dot in 厌 is enclosed (from upper and left sides).

两个忠告

出场角色：人（rén）；入（rù）。

人对入说："我给你一个忠告——好好照照镜子，你哪有个人样啊！"

入对人说："我也给你一个忠告——千万别把我当人。"

Two Pieces of Advice

Characters: 人"person"; 入"enter".

"Allow me to offer you some advice," says 人 to 入. "Just check yourself out in the mirror. You look nothing like a human!"

"Well, my advice to you would be: never see me as a human," responds the other.

Note: 人 and 入 are graphically similar but entirely different in meaning.

"我还真有个人样！"

出场角色：入（rù）；人（rén）。

入不修边幅，每日吊儿郎当。

人怒斥道："照照镜子，你哪还有个人样！"

入看着镜子里的自己；"噫，你不说我还不知道，我还真有个人样啊！"

Looking Human

Characters: 入"enter"; 人"person".

入 cares little about his appearance and fiddles around day after day.

"Examine yourself in the mirror," 人 says to him reproachfully. "Do you even look human?"

"Aha! You've pointed out something that I didn't realize," 入 exclaims, staring at his own mirror image. "I do have a human look!"

Note: 入 reflects in the mirror as 人.

"我还是我呀！"

出场角色：人（rén）；干（gān）。

人对干道："我发现一个秘密——镜子里的自己是反的。我在镜子里就不是人了。"

"是吗？"干将信将疑地来到镜子前一照。"什么反的呀！我还是干，不是士。哈哈！"

Not Reversed

Characters: 人"human"; 干"dry".

"I've discovered a secret: one's mirror image is reversed," says 人 to 干. "I am not 人 in the looking glass."

"Really?" half in doubt, 干 comes up looking into the mirror. "What are you talking about? I see 干 myself in it, not 士!" exclaims he with a hearty laugh.

Note: A mirror reverses left and right but not up and down.

一人撑起一个厂

出场角色：人（rén）；仄（zè）。

人在大街上见到了仄，吃惊地说："兄弟，你一个人就把厂子撑起来了？"

Under a Heavy Load

Characters: 人"man"; 仄"narrow".

人 appears taken back to see 仄 on the street. "Bro, you keep up the factory all on your own?" he exclaims.

Note: 仄 is composed of 人 with 厂"factory" on upper and left sides.

没有人样

出场角色：人（rén）；大（dà）。

人端详着大说："朋友，你整天端着一付肩膀，哪还有个人样啊。"

大微笑着答道："我本来就不是人啊！"

Not Looking Human

Characters: 人"man"; 大"big".

Examining 大 from head to toe, 人 remarks, "Holding your shoulders high all day, you don't look anything like a human."

"I was born a nonhuman," smiles the other.

Note: 大 is composed of 人 with a horizontal stroke across resembling the shoulders.

真是高人

出场角色：人（rén）；会（huì）。

人对会说："兄弟，真有你的，会腾云驾雾啊！"

Walking on Clouds

Characters: 人"man"; 会"can".

"Wow, buddy," says 人 to 会. "Able to walk on the cloud, you are truly one of a kind!"

Note: 会 is composed of 云"cloud" with 人 on top.

不言自明

出场角色：日（rì）；昊（hào）；杲（gǎo）。

昊和杲辩论谁高谁低，互不服气。

于是他俩请日裁决。

日对昊和杲说："两位朋友一个是天上日，一个是树上日。结论不用我说了吧。"

As Clear as Day

Characters: 日"sun"; 昊"vast"; 杲"bright".

Not convinced who is taller than the other, 昊 and 杲 come to 日 for a judgement.

"One is a sun high up in the sky and the other on top of a tree, so the conclusion is self-evident," declares 日 firmly.

Note: 昊 is composed of 天 "sky" with 日 on top; 杲 is composed of 木 "tree" with 日 on top.

口吐脏字

出场角色：人（rén）；丫（yā）。

人闲来无事，在北京南城溜达。

人看见丫在街头站着，心想："这家伙怎么在大街上拿大顶啊？"

人走进一家商厦，买了点东西后出来，看见丫还站在那里，不禁好奇地说："整天拿大顶，你丫还算个人吗？"

无缘无故挨了骂的丫怒道："说话文明点，我本来就不是人。"

注释：本文中的"丫"被人误以为是头足倒置的"人"字。丫，音yā，基本含义为分枝的和女孩子。在北京话中"丫"是带有贬义的词。在旧社会，北京话有"丫头养的"一词，指"没过门生的"，是侮辱性词汇。

Watch Your Language

Characters: 人"human"; 丫"fork of a tree".

Strolling leisurely around southern Beijing, 人 chances on 丫. "Why is the guy standing on his head in the middle of the street?" 人 wonders to himself.

Walking out of a shopping mall with some purchases, 人 notices 丫 still standing there. "On head all day long, are you bastard a human?" curious, 人 comes up asking him.

"Mind your tongue, " given a bad name for no reason, 丫 replies in anger. "I was born a nonhuman."

Note: 丫 resembles 人 upside down; 丫 dialectally means "bastard".

比上不足，比下有余

出场角色：申（shēn）； 电（diàn）。

申："兄弟，尾巴长歪了吧？"

电笑道："我好歹还有条尾巴。你看看'由'，屁股下面是秃的。"

Better Than the Worst

Characters: 申"state"; 电"power".

"Pal, your tail is crooked," says 申 to 电.

"Well, at least I have one," grins the other. "Look at 由, who has nothing at the rear end."

Note: The vertical with turn and with hook stroke in 电 runs across the bottom horizontal line with the extended part resembling a tail, and so does the central vertical stroke in 申.

左右为难

出场角色：手（shǒu）；毛（máo）。

手对毛说："向左还是向右，这是个问题。"

In a Tight Corner

Characters: 手"hand"; 毛"hair".

"To turn left or right, that is a question," says 手 to 毛.

Note: The vertical line in 手 hooks leftward at the bottom while the vertical line in 毛 turns and hooks rightward at the bottom.

旧铁壶的悲哀

出场角色：锈（xiù）；秽（huì）。幕后角色：秀（xiù）；慧（huì）。

有一只旧铁壶总是怀念自己年轻时候的时光，并且非常在意别人对它的印象。

"你觉得我还漂亮吧？"旧铁壶问它的伙伴炉子。

"锈外秽中。"炉子老老实实地答道。

注释：本文中的"锈外秽中"是成语"秀外慧中"的戏仿。

The Sorrow of an Old Iron Kettle

Onstage Characters: 锈"rust"; 秽"filth". Offstage Characters: 秀"beauty"; 慧"wisdom".

There was an old iron kettle who always missed his youthful days and cared much about what others thought of him.

"How do I look?" he once asked his companion, a stove.

"Rust on the outside, filth on the inside," replied the stove honestly.

Note: "Rust on the outside, filth on the inside" is a parody of the Chinese idiom "Beauty on the outside, wisdom on the inside" which in ancient China was used as a compliment to women who were beautiful, sensible, and cultivated. The send-up and its original have the same speech sound in Mandarin.

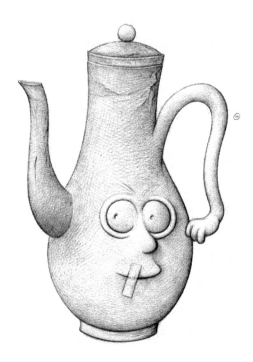

"你是无脊椎动物？"

出场角色：申（shēn）；曰（yuē）。

申问曰："兄弟，你的脊椎骨呢？"

曰笑道："我一生下来就没有那玩意儿。"

Are You an Invertebrate?

Characters: 申"state"; 曰"say".

"Where's your backbone, man?" 申 asks 曰.

"I was born without that stuff," grins the other.

Note: 申 is composed of 曰 with a vertical stroke running through resembling a backbone.

避之不及

出场角色：尸（shī）；户（hù）。

尸问户："朋友，你我相貌近似，只是头上差了一点，可为啥我走到哪里都不如你受欢迎啊！"

户用手掩着鼻子，笑道："谁挨上你谁倒霉。大伙自然对你敬而远之啦！"

"谁挨上我谁倒霉？"尸有点摸不着头脑了。

"你看，水挨上你就变潲；米挨上你就变臭；肖一挨上你就成了碎末子；比一挨上你就成了臭气。你说大伙怎么会欢迎你呢？"

What a Nuisance!

Characters: 尸"corpse"; 户"household".

"Pal, we two look quite similar, except for the dot on your head," says 尸 to 户. "But how come I am not as warmly received as you are wherever I go?"

Covering his nose with one hand, 户 replies with a chuckle, "Whoever moves close to you will get bad luck, so everyone tries to keep you at a distance."

"Whoever moves close to me will get bad luck?" 尸 repeats, feeling perplexed.

"Look. Coming close to you, 水 gets musty, 米 goes smelly, 肖 turns into crumbs, and 比 becomes fart. How could you expect others to welcome you?"

Note: With a dot stroke at the top, 户 differs from 尸 in composition; joined by 尸, 水 forms 尿"urine", 米 forms 屎"shit", 肖 forms 屑"crumb" and 比 forms 屁"fart".

一颗屎招来一身毛

出场角色：兔（tù）；免（miǎn）。

免对兔说："你真占了大便宜，拉一颗屎就长了一身长毛。"

One Pellet Resulting in a Coat of Fur

Characters: 兔"rabbit"; 免"free".

免 says 免 to 兔. "You hit the jackpot, growing a full coat of fur just by taking a pellet of poop."

Note: With an extra dot stroke (representing a pellet of poop) on the lower right, 兔 differs from 免 in composition.

牛气冲天

出场角色：天（tiān）；关（guān）。

天对关说："兄弟，你属牛的？"

关诧异道："何以见得？"

天笑着指了指关的头："你的俩犄角告诉我的。"

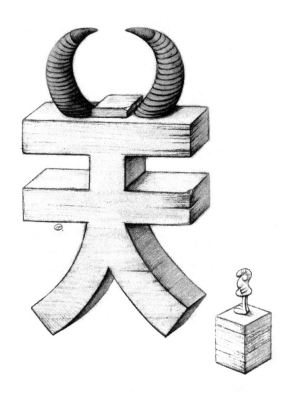

Bullish Vibe

Characters: 天"day"; 关"close".

"Hey, mate. You were born in the Year of the Ox?" 天 asks 关.

"How did you figure that out?" responds the other in surprise.

"Your horns let the cat out of the bag," grins 天, pointing at the other's head.

Note: 关 is composed of 天 with with a radical ⱽ on top resembling a pair of horns.

不动声色

出场角色：吞（tūn）；吴（wú）。

吞对吴自夸道："别看你把嘴巴伸得老高，可没我能吃。"

吴对吞说："是啊，没想到你的嘴巴不显山不露水，吃起东西来可是真不含糊。"

Lying Low

Characters: 吞"devour"; 吴"a surname".

"Even with a mouth jutted high up, you don't eat so much as I do," brags 吞 to 吴.

"Indeed. It is hard to imagine that you eat like a horse with such a modest mouth," comes the reply.

Note: 吞 has 口"mouth"at the bottom while 吴 at the top.

高度不够

出场角色：土（tǔ）；圭（guī）。

土对圭说："兄弟，你这罗汉叠得高度不够。"

Near to the Ground

Characters: 土"clod"; 圭"jade tablet".

"Pal, you are not a pile high enough," says 土 to 圭.

Note: 圭 consists of two 土 one on top of the other.

气象不同

出场角色：土（tǔ）；士（shì）。

土闷闷不乐地问士："先生，我俩相貌大体相当，个头不分伯仲，可为啥人家都高看你一头，而对我不屑一顾呢？"

士看了看土，大笑道："因为我有士气，你有土气呀！"

The Aura Makes a Difference

Characters: 土"clod"; 士"scholar".

"Sir, we look alike and are of similar height, yet how come they all have a high regard for you and hardly spare me a glance?" 土 asks 士 crossly.

"Because I am vigorous and you are cloddish," laughs the other as he throws a glance at 土.

Note: 土 has a longer bottom vertical line than the top one, as opposed to 士.

只差了一点

出场角色：王（wáng）；主（zhǔ）。

王对主道："主啊，你高高在上，不食人间烟火，受尽了顶礼膜拜。可你哪如我这个尘世的国王过得自在呢？"

主看了一眼王，笑道："一只没头苍蝇，嗡嗡啥呢？"

A Dot Difference

Characters: 王"king"; 主"lord".

"Oh, lord! You are high above, not partaking in the earthly world, and constantly receiving reverence and worship," says 王 to 主. "However, the ease I enjoy as a worldly monarch is not something you can match." Throwing the other a brief glance, 主 sneers, "Stop buzzing, you headless fly."

Note: 主 is composed of 王 with a dot stroke on top resembling the head.

身材过大

出场角色：午（wǔ）；缶（fǒu）。

午问缶："舒服吗？浴缸有点小吧？"

A Figure Too Large

Characters: 午"noon"; 缶"pottery".

"How do you feel in the bathtub? Isn't it a bit small for you?" 午 asks 缶.

Note: 缶 is composed of 午 with a component below resembling a bathtub.

赢了两毛

出场角色：兴（xīng）；六（liù）。

兴在大街上见到了六。他围着六转了一圈儿，兴奋地对六说："大伙儿都笑话我只有三根毛，没想到还有比我头发更少的。"

Two More Hairs

Characters: 兴"rise"; 六"six".

兴 bumps into 六 on the street. "Everyone laughs at me for having only three hairs, but I never expected to meet someone with even fewer," exclaims 兴 excitedly as he walks around 六 in a circle.

Note: 兴 has two dots and a left-falling stroke at the top resembling three hairs while 六 has one dot stroke above resembling one hair.

没有过不去的坎

出场角色：县（xiàn）；悬（xuán）。

县见到了忧心忡忡的老朋友悬。他诚恳地对悬说："听我一句劝，兄弟，别总是提心吊胆的。世上没有过不去的坎。"

No Hurdles Too High to Jump

Characters: 悬"suspence"; 县"county".

Coming across his old friend 悬 who appears troubled, 县 earnestly advises him, "Listen to me, bro. Don't always be so anxious and fainthearted. In this world, there is no hurdle that is too high to jump over."

Note: 悬 is composed of 县 above and 心"heart" below.

\

搭个竹顶好开心

出场角色：笑（xiào）；夭（yāo）。
笑对夭："兄弟，搭个竹顶子吧。"

Delight of Shelter

Characters: 笑"smile"; 夭"die young".

"Hey, guy. Why not build yourself a bamboo roof?" says 笑 to 夭.

Note: 笑 is composed of 夭 with a semantic radical ⺮"bamboo" on top representing a bamboo roof.

少一嘴不如多一嘴

出场角色：兄（xiōng）；儿（ér）。

兄对儿说："兄弟，你掉了嘴巴，可就比我小一辈儿了。"

A Junior in Hierarchy

Characters: 兄"elder brother"; 儿"son".

"Man, with your mouth lost," says 兄 to 儿, "you rank as my junior in the family hierarchy."

Note: 兄 has 口 "mouth" at the top and 儿 at the bottom.

我可不傻

出场角色：杏（xìng）；木（mù）。

杏问木："兄弟，你的嘴巴呢?"

木笑道："我可不想跟你一样，把嘴巴压身子底下。"

杏道："那你可以顶在头上啊。"

木生气地说："你让我像'呆'一样? 我是傻瓜呀!"

Not an Idiot

Characters: 杏"apricot"; 木"tree".

"Where's your mouth, pal?" 杏 asks 木.

"I hate to put it under the body as you do," grins the other.

"Put it on top then," adds 杏.

"You'd like me to be 呆? But I don't want to be a fool," says the other, annoyed.

Note: 杏 is composed of 木 with 口 "mouth" at the bottom; joined by 口 on top, 木 forms 呆 "fool".

胖子和瘦子

出场角色：曰（yuē）；日（rì）。

曰羡慕地对日说："为啥你的身材那么好呢？你瞧我都胖成啥样了。"

日笑道："你在家里耍嘴皮子，我在天上巡逻值班。日积月累，当然是我苗条啦！"

The Chubby and the Slender

Characters; 曰 "say"; 日 "sun".

"Why do you have such a good figure?" says 曰 to 日 admiringly. "Look at me. I'm so out of shape."

"You stay at home paying lip service while I travel across the sky carrying out my duty," grins the other. "Day after day, naturally I stay slim while you become heavier."

Note: With longer horizontal strokes, 曰 looks "fatter" than 日.

上天原来不神秘

出场角色：乙（yǐ）；飞（fēi）。

乙对飞说："兄弟，看见你的模样我才知道，原来插两根毛就能上天啊！"

No Mystery

Characters: 乙"second"; 飞"fly".

"Man, seeing you, I come to know that one can take to the air with two feathers fixed on the back," says 乙 to 飞.

Note: The left-falling stroke and the dot in 飞 resemble two feathers.

核桃说花生

出场角色：仁（rén）。幕后角色：人（rén）。

生物学家达尔文来到乡间考察。

"你觉得花生的秉性如何？"达尔文问核桃。

"他呀，仁小心不小。"核桃笑着告诉达尔文。

注释：本文中的"仁小心不小"是谚语"人小心不小"的戏仿。

A Walnut's View on a Peanut

Onstage Character: 仁"kernel". Offstage Character: 人"man".

Biologist Darwin came to the countryside on a research journey.

"What do you think of the nature of the peanut?" he asked a walnut.

"A small kernel has a big heart," grinned the walnut.

Note: "A small kernel has a big heart" is a parody of the Chinese proverb "A little man has a great mind" which means a young child may have a deep insight or good judgement. The parody and the proverb have the same speech sound in Mandarin.

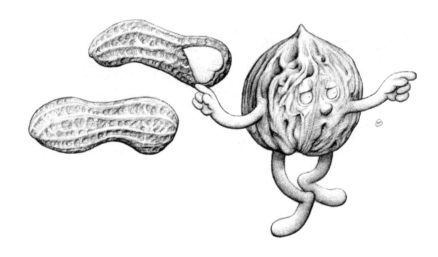

脊梁不可弯

出场角色：用（yòng）；甩（shuǎi）。

用对甩说："你脊椎骨下边怎么弯了？快去医院看医生吧。"

Spine Must Not Bend

Characters: 用"use"; 甩"toss".

"How is it the lower part of your spine is bent?" says 用 to 甩. "Go to see a doctor."

Note: 甩 has a vertical with turn and hook stroke (different from the vertical stroke in 用) resembling a bent spine.

使命感

出场角色：由（yóu）；笛（dí）。
由对笛说："你不就比我多个竹顶子嘛，用得着整天吹吗？"
笛尖声答道："我来到世上，唯一的使命就是'吹'呀！"

Sense of Mission

Characters: 由"reason"; 笛"flute".
"You have the edge over me simply by the bamboo top," says 由 to 笛.
"But do you have to blow your own trumpet all day long?"
"I come to the world only to blow," replies the other in a piercing voice.

Note: 笛 is composed of 由 with a semantic radical ⺮"bamboo" on top representing a bamboo cap.

人多分量重

出场角色：又（yòu）；桑（sāng）。
又看着桑，忧心忡忡地说："你们三兄弟站在一棵树上，不怕把树压断了吗？"

桑看了看又，不解地说："我本人就是一棵树，哪有你说的什么'三兄弟'呀！"

The More, the Heavier

Characters: 又"again"; 桑"mulberry".

"The tree may break under the weight of you three brothers,"

says 又, worried as he stares at 桑. "Aren't you afraid of that?"

桑 takes a glances at the other and says in confusion, "As a tree myself, I don't have anything as the three brothers you're talking about."

Note: 桑 is composed of 叒 (three 又) at the top and 木"tree" at the bottom.

事出有因

出场角色：又（yòu）；戏（xì）。

又看见戏总是带着兵器，好奇地询问缘由。

戏对又说："我是个唱戏的。唱戏能不舞刀弄枪吗？"

Every Why Has a Wherefore

Characters: 又"again"; 戏"play".

又 notices that 戏 always carries a weapon and asks curiously for the reason.

"As an opera actor, how could I perform the martial play without a spear or sword?" replies 戏.

Note: 戏 is composed of 又 on the left and 戈"spear" on the right.

为何今日月不明

出场角色：月（yuè）；育（yù）。
月对育说："兄弟，你这出戏叫《云遮月》吧？"

Faint Moonlight

Characters: 月"moon"; 育"rear".
"You are acting the scene A Cloud Covering the Moon, aren't you?" 月 asks 育.

Note: Graphically 育 has 云"cloud" at the top and 月 at the bottom.

帽上何须再扣帽

出场角色：宜（yí）；且（qiě）。
宜问且："兄弟，你为啥不学我，也戴一顶帽子呢？"
且笑道："人家说我本人就像一顶帽子啊！"

Hat on Hat Not Needed

Characters: 宜"proper"; 且"and".
"Pal, why not wear a cap as I do?" 宜 asks 且.
"They say I already look like a hat," grins the other.

Note: 宜 is composed of 且 with a radical 宀 on top resembling a cap; 且 is shaped like a tall hat.

莫把上衣当裤子

出场角色：裔（yì）； 装（zhuāng）。

裔问装："兄弟，你咋把上衣当裤子穿啊？"

A Coat Taken for Trousers

Characters: 裔"descendant"; 装"clothing".

"Hey, man. Why do you wear your jacket as pants?"

Note: 裔 has 衣"coat" at the top while 装 has 衣 at the bottom.

后顾之忧

出场角色：座（zuò）； 痤（cuó）。

座对痤说："兄弟，你后背上长了两个瘤子。"

Worries about the Back

Characters: 座"seat"; 痤"acne".

"Regrettably, I must inform you that you have two tumours on your back," announces 座 to 痤.

Note: Compared with 座, 痤 has an extra 冫 on the left resembling two tumours.

为何工厂无人影？

出场角色：仄（zè）；厂（chǎng）。

仄对厂说："整个厂子连个人影都没有了，你这企业咋办的？"

厂笑道："我这是机器人控制的全自动化工厂。"

Not a Soul in Sight

Characters: 仄"narrow"; 厂"factory".

"There isn't a soul in sight in the entire factory," says 仄 to 厂. "What's wrong with your business?"

"In front of you is a fully automated plant run by robots," grins the other.

Note: 仄 is composed of 人"person" enclosed (from upper and left sides) by 厂.

四坨粑粑热乎乎

出场角色：执（zhí）；热（rè）。

执对热说："你拉了四坨粑粑，还是热乎的。"

Four Piles of Poo

Characters: 执"execute"; 热"hot".

"You've just done four piles of poo," says 执 to 热, "and they are still steaming."

Note: 热 is composed of 执 with a radical 灬 at the bottom resembling four piles of poo.

抬头不见低头见

出场角色：庄（zhuāng）；压（yā）。

庄见到了压，仔细端详了对方好大一会儿，发出一阵惊叹："你把头藏得真妙，我差点儿没发现。"

Out of Sight and in Sight

Characters: 庄"village"; 压"press".
Staring at 压 for quite a while, 庄 exclaims, "You hide your head so tactfully that I can barely see it."

Note: 庄 has dot stroke at the top resembling the head.

"你做手术啦？"

出场角色：占（zhàn）；卤（lǔ）。
占问卤："兄弟，你肚子上的纱布是咋回事啊？做手术啦？"

The Bandaged Belly

Characters: 占"occupy"; 卤"stew in soy sauce".
"Mate, why is your belly bound with gauze?" 占 asks 卤. "You just came

out of surgery?"

Note: The left-falling stroke together with the dot enclosed in 卤
resembles two strips of gauze.

自上而下

　　出场角色：止（zhǐ）； 正（zhèng）。
　　止问正："兄弟，你啥时候封的顶啊？"
　　正笑道："我是先盖的顶。从上往下盖。"

Top to Bottom

Characters: 止"stop"; 正"straight".
"Pal, when were you roofed?" 止 asks 正.
"I was built from top to bottom, with the roof completed first," grins the
other in response.

Note: 正 is composed of 止 with a horizontal stroke on top resembling a
roof; 正 is written from top to bottom, the top horizontal line being the
first stroke.

滑板之乐

　　出场角色：旦（dàn）； 日（yuē）。
　　旦对日说："兄弟，你也弄个滑板玩玩吧！没准儿还能减肥呢！"

Fun and Fitness

Characters: 旦"dawn"; 曰"say".

"Hey, dude. Get yourself a skateboard to have some fun!" suggests 旦 to 曰. "And it may even help you shed some weight."

Note: 旦 consists of 日 above and a horizontal stroke below resembling a skateboard; 曰 looks "fatter" than 日.

动物之家

出场角色：穴（xué）；八（bā）。

穴对八说："兄弟，加个顶子吧。没个顶子不是家呀！"

八看了看穴，笑道："你倒是家——动物之家。"

A Home for Animals

Characters: 穴"cave"; 八"eight".

"Build yourself a rooftop, dude." says 穴 to 八. "No home should be without a roof."

Taking a look at the other, 八 smiles, "You are a home indeed, home for animals."

Note: 穴 is composed of 八 with 宀 on top representing a roof.

奴才有罪

出场角色：奴（nú）；皇（huáng）；凰（huáng）。

奴跟随皇出去狩猎。因为皇的马太快了，把奴甩了十几里地。

皇丢了，这可是千刀万剐的罪呀！奴找了一夜也没有找到皇。

黎明时分，又困又乏的奴突然发现了凰。他大喜过望，马上在凰面前跪下："皇上，您原来在帐篷里休息呐。奴才罪该万死，没跟上您的龙驹！"

A Guilty Slave

Characters: 奴"slave"; 皇"emperor"; 凰"female phoenix".

A slave, escorting 皇 out on a hunting trip, lags some ten miles behind His Majesty mounted on a faster horse.

Having lost the emperor, the servant deserves a death by a thousand cuts! The poor man searches throughout the night but to no avail.

At the crack of dawn, the slave, weary and drowsy, stumbles upon 凰, and he is so delighted that he immediately falls to his knees before the fellow.

"Your Majesty! You turn out to be resting in the tent," exclaims the servant. "Punish me for failing to keep up with your steed."

Note: 凰 is composed of 皇 enclosed by 几 resembling a tent.

心里发毛

出场角色：手（shǒu）；毛（máo）。

手问毛："兄弟，你咋长成这模样啦？看得我心里发毛。"

毛笑道："你心里发毛就对了。我就是毛啊！"

Hair Standing on End

Characters: 手"hand"; 毛"hair".

"How do you grow into such a shape, buddy?" 手 asks 毛. "You make my hair stand on end."

"You said it," laughs the other. "I AM a hair."

Note: The vertical line in 毛 turns and hooks right, different from the one in 手 hooking left.

出了岔子

出场角色：大（dà）；丈（zhàng）。
儿去找大。没有找到。看见了丈。
"大，你出岔子啦？"儿惊慌地问。
"这孩子，真不会说话。"丈皱着眉头道，"谁出岔子啦！"

Something Wrong

Characters: 儿"son"; 大"father"; 丈"senior".

儿 goes out in search of 大 and comes across 丈.

"Something has gone wrong with you, da?"

"Mind your tongue, kid," says 丈 with a frown. "There's nothing wrong with me!"

Note: 大 and 丈 are composed of the same strokes; 丈 differs from 大 in the right-falling stroke, which runs across the left-falling one representing "go wrong".

"原来是个老前辈"

出场角色：老（lǎo）；考（kǎo）。

老对考说："别人的尾巴都往上翘，你怎么往下垂呀！真难看。"

考叹着气回答道："我已经上西天了，哪还有力气翘尾巴呀！"

"失敬了，阁下原来是比我还老的前辈了！"

注释：考是父亲的尊称，特指已经逝世的父亲。

A Senior Figure

Characters: 老"old"; 考"deceased father".

"Everyone else has an upraised tail," 老 says 考. "How come yours hangs down? It's ugly as sin."

"I have gone the way of all flesh," 考 replies with a heavy sigh. "How can I have the muscle to lift my tail?"

"Your Honour turns out to be a senior! Forgive me for being disrespectful. " says 老.

Note: The last stroke (vertical curved hook) in 老 represents an tail curled up, and the last stroke (vertical folding hook) in 考 represents a hanging tail.

骂人与杀人

出场角色：匕（bǐ）；叱（chì）。

匕在大街上散步时，听见叱正在无缘无故地责骂一个路人，不禁厉声说："你小子长一张嘴就是为了骂人吗？"

叱看了看匕，冷冷地回敬道："我不过是嘴上凶一点。阁下可是刺刀见红的主儿啊。"

A Confrontation on the Street

Characters: 匕"dagger"; 叱"scold".

Strolling down the street, 匕 overhears 叱 dressing down a passerby without rhyme or reason. He cannot help but step forward and snap, "You have a mouth only for foul language?"

Casting the other a look, 叱 retorts harshly, "Maybe my tongue is sharp, but you are bloodthirsty by nature."

Note: 叱 is structured with a radical 口"mouth" on the left and 匕 on the right.

礼帽的作用

出场角色：兵（bīng）；宾（bīn）。

在大街上，兵看见宾特别受人尊重。无论男女老少，谁见了宾都会朝他微笑点头。

而兵就没这个福气了。很多人看见他就远远地躲开了。实在躲不过去的也是低着头与兵擦肩而过。

兵不知道宾为什么这么得到别人尊重。他就此诚恳地向宾请教。

宾看了看兵，微笑着说："和阁下不同的是，我总是戴着一顶礼帽啊。"

The Advantage of a Hat

Characters: 兵"warrior"; 宾"guest".

On the street, 宾 is so much respected that whoever sees him will give him a smile and nod, while 兵 is not as favoured, shunned by many or ignored by those who have to walk past him.

Curious about what helps him earn the esteem of everyone in town, 兵 asks 宾 sincerely for advice.

Looking at 兵 for a while, 宾 smiles, "What makes a distinction between you and me is the hat I wear all the time."

Note: 宾 is structured with a radical 宀 at the top resembling a hat and 兵 at the bottom.

抬杠

出场角色：包（bāo）；抱（bào）。

包和抱是一个胡同里长大的。他们一见面就要抬杠。

一天，包嘲弄抱说："你就一只手也敢叫抱？"

抱反唇相讥道："你连一只手也没有，不是也号称能包东西吗？"

Arguing for the Sake of Arguing

Characters: 包"wrap"; 抱"embrace".

Despite growing up in the same alley, 包 and 抱 cannot help but bicker and argue every time they come face to face.

One day, 包 sneers at 抱, "With only one hand, how dare you boast you can hug?"

"Aren't you the one who has no hand at all but claims to be able to wrap things up?" 抱 retorts bitterly.

Note: 抱 is structured with a semantic radical 扌"hand" on the left and 包 on the right.

爱挑剔的家伙

出场角色：贝（bèi）；见（jiàn）。

贝总是用挑剔的眼光看待别人。

一天，贝对见说："兄弟，你右腿咋打弯了？"

见一直对贝没好印象，见他找上门来挑衅，于是没好气地答道："别总是盯着别人的缺点。你低头看看，你两条腿可是一长一短啊！"

An Avid Nitpicker

Characters: 贝"treasure"; 见"sight".

贝 is always finding fault with others.

One day, he says to 见, "Buddy, how is it that your right leg is bent?"

"Stop fixing your eyes on the flaw in others," disgusted with 贝, 见 responds to his provocation in an angry tone. "Just look down at your own legs, one shorter than the other."

Note: 见 is structured with a component at the bottom resembling two legs with the right one bent while 贝 with the right one shorter than the left.

冒犯兄弟

出场角色：布（bù）；希（xī）。

布见到了希，惊问道："兄弟，你犯啥错误啦，头上咋顶个大叉叉？"

A Big Cross

Characters: 布"cloth"; 希"hope".

布 sees 希 and exclaims in surprise, "What have you done wrong, buddy? Why is there a big cross on top of your head?"

Note: 希 is composed of 布 with a left-falling stroke plus a dot on top resembling a cross.

酒后责友

出场角色：办（bàn）；为（wéi）。

办和为本是好朋友，但是办最近对为有点不满意。

一次，办和为一起喝酒。办借着酒劲儿，指责为说："我为朋友两肋插刀，你倒好，举着一把藏着一把。"

Dutch Courage

Characters: 办"manage"; 为"become".

Lately, 办 feels a little annoyed with 为, though they have been good friends.

Then at a party, fueled by alcohol, 办 says to 为 in a reproachful tone, "In the interest of a friend, I'd rather have each side of my chest pierced by a knife, but you simply put up one knife and lock up the other."

Note: 办 is composed of a radical 力 with two dot strokes resembling two knives, one on the left and the other on the right, while 为 one on the top left and the other in the centre.

认错了兄弟

出场角色：叉（chā）；山（shān）。

叉在路上走着，眼前出现了山。

叉围着山转了又转，好奇地说："你这把叉子真怪，咋没有把儿了？"

山看了一眼叉，没好气地答道："你才怪呢。自己是把叉子，就把别人也看成你的同类。"

A Strange Fork

Characters: 叉"fork"; 山"mountain".

叉 comes across 山 on the road.

"What a strange fork you are!" says 叉 curiously as he walks around 山

over and over. "How come you have no handle?"

"YOU are a strange fork," casting a glance at 叉, 山 replies in annoyance, "so strange that you see others as your own kind."

Note: 山 graphically resembles a fork without a handle.

平平淡淡才是真

出场角色：茶（chá）；泉（quán）。

泉从山上流下来，正好驻足在茶的脚下。

茶看了看泉，讥讽道："看见阁下的尊容，让我想起了'白开水'，淡而无味。"

泉笑着答道："阁下若是离开了'白开水'，恐怕没人知道你是什么味儿吧！"

The Simplest Is the Best

Characters: 茶"tea"; 泉"spring".

泉 runs down a mountain, coming across 茶.

"Hey, buddy," sneers 茶. "Your appearance reminds me of 'plain boiled water', light and tasteless."

"Without 'plain boiled water', I'm afraid no one would know what you taste like," replies 泉 with a smile.

Note: 泉 is structured top to bottom with 白"white" and 水"water"; the Chinese "white water" means plain boiled water.

"离我远点！"

出场角色：臣（chén）；卜（bǔ）。

臣刚刚从王宫出来，远远看见卜迎面而来。

"离我远点，一挨上你，我就得趴下。"臣厌恶地对卜说。

注释："臣"字与"卜"字合成为"卧"字。

Get Out of My Way

Characters: 臣"minister"; 卜"foretell".

Stepping out of the palace, 臣 sees 卜 coming straight to him from a distance.

"Get out of my way," 臣 calls out to 卜 in resentment. "Every time you get close to me, I'll fall over."

Note: 臣 joined by 卜 on the right forms the character 卧 meaning "lie".

主心骨

出场角色：串（chuàn）；吕（lǚ）。

串望着吕的模样，语重心长地说："兄弟，有个主心骨儿太重要了。"

吕不屑地答道："一个胡同串子，还想跟我谈人生哲理？"

串毫不在意吕的顶撞，又重复了一遍刚才的话："兄弟，有个主心骨儿太重要了！"

吕反唇相讥说："啥主心骨啊，插一根搅屎棍子就不得了啦？"

串叹了一口气，语重心长地说："朋友，我最后再说一遍，做人没有主心骨儿可不行啊！"

　　吕怒道："糖葫芦儿也有主心骨，还不是让人啃的命！"

A Backbone

Characters: 串"chain"; 吕"a surname".

Looking at 吕, 串 says earnestly, "It means a lot to have a spine, pal."

"What?" replies 吕 with a disdainful look. "A loafer is trying to teach me the philosophy of life?"

"It means a lot to have a spine, pal." 串 repeats without taking any offence.

"What spine?" sneers 吕. "Who do you think you are with that stirring stick?"

"Buddy," with a sigh, 串 says seriously, "I'll say it one last time. One cannot do without a backbone."

"Look at the sugarcoated haws on a stick," 吕 yells. "Still, they are meant to be gnawed!"

Note: 串 dialectally means "idler", composed of 吕 with a vertical line running through resembling a backbone or a stick; 串 is shaped like a stick of sugarcoated fruit, with the vertical stroke resembling a stick and the component 吕 resembling two pieces of fruit.

反唇相讥

　　出场角色：川（chuān）；三（sān）。

　　川对三说："兄弟，躺倒不干啦？"

　　三生气地说："谁躺倒啦？我看你倒是站姿不对。"

A Sharp Retort

Characters: 川"river"; 三"three".

川 says to 三, "Buddy, you lie down and quit?"

"It is not that I lie down," replies the other crossly. "It's just that you stand in a wrong posture."

Note: 三 looks like 川 lying on the side; 川 is graphically shaped like someone standing in a wrong posture with the left-falling stroke resembling a leg slanted outward.

家有家样

出场角色: 闯 (chuǎng); 门 (mén)。

闯对门说:"兄弟, 你的马呢?"

门没好气地答道:"你以为都跟你一样, 把家变成马厩啊!"

A House or a Stable

Characters: 闯"rush"; 门"door".

"Hi there," says 闯 to 门. "I was wondering where your horse has gone."

"Never will I turn my house into a stable as you do," replies 门 in annoyance.

Note: 闯 is composed of 马"horse" enclosed by 门"door" from left, top and right sides.

以己度人

出场角色：查（chá）；旦（dàn）；杳（yǎo）。

查对旦和杳说："你们俩去照照镜子——一个头上没树，一个脚下没土，发育不全吧？"

旦对杳说："这家伙总是以己度人。恨不得天下人都长得跟他一模一样才好。"

注释：杳，无影无声；幽暗。

Every Shoe Fits Not Every Foot

Characters: 查"check"; 旦"dawn"; 杳"dark".

"Check yourselves out in the mirror," 查 says to 旦 and 杳. "One has no tree above and the other no earth below, so are you both under-grown?"

"That fellow is always measuring others against himself," 旦 says to 杳. "He'd rather everyone on earth looked exactly like him."

Note: Compared with 查, the character 旦 is structured without the component 木"wood" on top, 杳 without the horizontal stroke below representing soil.

请君自重

出场角色：人（rén）；介（jiè）。

人对介说："兄弟，你长腿啦？可俩腿咋不一般直呢？"

介对人说："你又不是大人物，我没必要对你保持立正姿势吧？"

Mind Your Manners

Characters: 人"person"; 介"upright".

"Hey, guy. You have legs?" says 人 to 介. "But why aren't they equally straight?"

"You are not a big shot, so I don't have to stand at attention showing respect for you, do I?" comes the reply.

Note: 介 is composed of 人 at the top and a left-falling stroke plus a vertical line at the bottom resembling the legs.

语重心长

出场角色：叉（chā）；又（yòu）。

叉对又说：“兄弟，千丢万丢，心不可丢啊！”

又大笑道：“你不过是个大叉子而已，装什么有心人啊！”

From the Bottom of Heart

Characters: 叉"fork"; 又"again".

"Hey, buddy," 叉 says to 又. "Remember, you can lose everything but your heart."

"Don't pretend to be someone with a heart," chuckles 又. "You are nothing but a mere fork."

Note: 叉 is composed of 又 with a dot stroke enclosed representing a heart.

"去你的！"

出场角色：去（qù）；丢（diū）。

在一次同学聚会上，去见到了丢。

去鄙夷地说："兄弟，你真丢人啊，随便找块抹布就往头上顶啊！"

丢怒道："去你的！"

Go to Hell!

Characters: 去"go"; 丢"lose".

去 meets 丢 at a class reunion.

"With a dishcloth on your head, you are making a fool of yourself!" says 去 in disdain.

"Go to hell!" responds the other with anger.

Note: 丢 is composed of 去 with a left-falling stroke on top representing a wash-up cloth.

自以为是

出场角色：呆（dāi）；杏（xìng）。

呆看着杏，大惊小怪道："你这是咋长的，把嘴长到身子下面了。你的样子好傻呀！"

杏撇着嘴回敬说："咱俩到底谁傻，大众自有公论。"

Self-Arrogance

Characters: 呆"stupid"; 杏"apricot".

As 呆 looks at 杏, he seems surprised and exclaims, "Why is your mouth at the bottom? What a blockhead you look like!"

"As for who of us is a blockhead, the public will have their own opinion," retorts the other, curling his lips.

Note: 呆 is composed of 口"mouth" on top of 木 while 杏 reverses order.

手下无情

出场角色：丁（dīng）；打（dǎ）。

丁在大街上看见打正在对一个老者挥舞拳头，马上制止了他。

丁对打说："兄弟，你长手的目的就是对人施暴吗？"

A Cruel Hand

Characters: 丁"a surname"; 打"hit".

Seeing 打 swinging his fist at an old man on the street, 丁 intervenes to stop him. "Hey, man," he says. "You have a hand only for doing violence to others?"

Note: 打 is composed of a semantic radical 扌"hand" on the left and 丁 on the right.

头足倒置为哪般？

出场角色：士（shì）；干（gān）。

士对干说："老弟，你为啥要拿大顶啊？头足倒置的事我可不干。"

干看了一眼士，冷冷地说："你自己坐在屋里卖卖嘴皮子也就算了，居然还指责踏踏实实做事的人！"

Standing on the Head

Characters: 士"scholar"; 干"do".

"Hey, man. Why are you standing on your head? " 士 asks 干. "I would never do anything like that."

Casting the other a glance, 干 responds coldly, "It's all right for you to stay indoors paying lip service, but too much to point finger at someone who works like a horse."

Note: 干 is shaped like inverted 士.

一百个不愿意

出场角色：大（dà）；力（lì）。

工地正在招打夯工。

大兴冲冲地对力说："你我联袂出场，保证力敌万夫。"

力酸溜溜地说："你出头，我出力，是吧？"

注释："大"上"力"下，合成"夯"字。

A Show of Reluctance

Characters: 大"big"; 力"force".

A construction site is seeking a worker with ramming skills.

"United as one, we two will be strong as an ox," 大 says to 力 with excitement."

"Then you stick out and I toil away, right?" sneers the other.

Note: 大 and 力 put together top to bottom compose the character 夯 "ram".

两根高跷不一般

出场角色：二（èr）；亓（qí）。
二对亓说："兄弟，瞧你踩的高跷，一根直一根弯。"

注释：亓，姓氏。

Stilts off Balance

Characters: 二"two"; 亓"a surname".

"Pal, look at the stilts you are walking on," 二 says to 亓. "One is straight and the other bent."

Note: 亓 is structured with 二 at the top, a left-falling stroke and vertical line at the bottom resembling a pair of stilts with the left one bent.

"你肚子上的痦子呢？"

出场角色：凡（fán）；几（jǐ）。

凡在游泳池边见到了几，好奇地问："兄弟，你肚子上的痦子呢？"

几皱着眉头对凡说："你以为是人都像你一样，肚子上非长个疙瘩不可？"

Where Is the Mole on Your Belly?

Characters: 凡"all"; 几"some".

凡 meets 几 at the edge of a swimming pool. "Buddy, where is the mole on your belly?" the former asks curiously.

"Do you believe everyone should have a blemish on the stomach as you do?" replies the latter with a frown.

Note: 凡 is composed of 几 with a dot stroke enclosed (from three sides) representing a mole on the stomach.

好为人师

出场角色：凡（fán）；几（jǐ）。

凡见到了久违的老朋友几，教训他说："几年不见了，没想到你还是老样子。一个人胸无点墨，如何在社会上立足啊！"

几对凡冷笑道："别好为人师了，你不就比我多个痦子吗？"

Talking like a Master

Characters: 凡"all"; 几"some".

凡 bumps into his old friend 几 and begins to lecture him.

"It's surprising that you haven't changed at all over the years," says 凡.

"How can one establish himself in the society without a bit of ink in the chest?"

"Don't talk down to me like a master," responds the other with a sneer.

"You have nothing more than me but a mole, right?"

Note: 凡 is composed of 几 with a dot stroke enclosed representing a mole or a drop of ink; the Chinese idiom "not having a bit of ink in the chest" means being unlearned or ignorant.

不知天高地厚

出场角色：夫（fū）；天（tiān）。

夫对天说："天啊，你不能总是把头藏到脖子里。大丈夫要做顶天立地之人，绝不能遇到点事儿就当缩头乌龟。"

天鄙夷地答道："你以为长个小脑袋就顶天立地啦。比你高的人有的是。"

High and Mighty

Characters: 夫"man"; 天"sky".

"Oh my! You should not keep your head retracted all the time," 夫 says to 天. "A great man stands like a giant and never shrinks from danger like a turtle."

"Do you see yourself as a giant with that small head?" replies the other in disdain. "There are many men taller than you are."

Note: 夫 differs from 天 by the top extended part of the left-falling stroke representing the head.

争老大

出场角色：方（fāng）；万（wàn）。

方和万准备联袂登场，但是为出场顺序争执起来。

万说："我财大气粗，有气场。应该我先出场。"

方理直气壮地说："你连脑袋都没有，腰缠万贯又有什么用。应该我先出场。"

万反驳道："应该我排前面，词典说'仪态万方'嘛。"

两个家伙因为谈不拢，最后不欢而散。

Who Is to Be the First

Characters: 方"aspect"; 万"ten thousand".

As partners going on stage, 万 and 方 engage in a heated dispute over the order of appearance.

"Wealthy and charismatic," says 万, "I should be the first to take the stage."

"What's the point of being cash rich but headless?" says 方 with complete confidence. "So I should make an appearance before you."

"I am the one who's to show up first," retorts 万, "because an idiom in the dictionary says 'have an appearance attractive in ten thousand aspects.' "

Failing to see eye to eye, the two fellows end up going separate ways.

Note: 方 is composed of 万 with a dot stroke on top representing the head; "万" appears before "方" in the Chinese idiom quoted by 万.

遭人非议

出场角色：非（fēi）；丰（fēng）。

非问丰："兄弟，你的脊椎咋那么细呀？"

丰不悦道："看来你真是名如其人，总喜欢挑别人的毛病。"

Snide Remarks

Characters: 非"fault"; 丰"abundance".

非 asks 丰, "Why is your spine so slim, dude?"

"You're always finding fault with others," replies the other, annoyed. "How the name fits you!"

Note: The vertical stroke in 丰 represents a backbone, and the two vertical lines in 非 combined represents a thicker spine.

肋骨弯了

出场角色：丰（fēng）；韦（wéi）。

丰问韦："兄弟，你一根肋骨咋打弯儿啦？"

A Bent Rib

Characters: 丰"abundance"; 韦"leather".

"Hey, pal," 丰 asks 韦. "Why has one of your ribs become bent?"

Note: 韦 differs from 丰 by the extra turning with a hook stroke on the lower right resembling the bent part of a rib.

多管闲事

出场角色：古（gǔ）；右（yòu）。

在一次酒会上，古见到了老朋友右。

好开玩笑的古指着右说："老弟，你脖子歪啦！"

右喝了一口五粮液，回敬道："你自己都作古了，就别多管闲事啦！"

None of Your Business

Characters: 古"ancient"; 右"right".

古, who loves playing practical jokes, bumps into his old friend 右 at a wine party.

"Buddy, you have a crooked neck!" says 古, pointing at 右.

"As you have become ancient, just keep your nose out of it," retorts the other as he takes a sip of grain alcohol.

Note: 古 has a vertical stroke at the top representing a neck while 右 has a left-falling stroke on the upper left resembling a crooked neck; the

201

Chinese expression "become ancient" is a euphemism for "die".

凶相毕露

出场角色：瓜（guā）；爪（zhuǎ）。

瓜对爪说："兄弟，你这模样长得有问题呀！"

爪对瓜说："谁是你兄弟呀。滚开，不然我给你一爪子，让你的瓢子流出来！"

A Fierce Look

Characters: 瓜"melon"; 爪"claw".

瓜: Something is wrong with your look, bro.

爪: Don't bro me. Get lost, or I'll claw the pulp out of you.

Note: With an extra raising stroke together with a dot at the bottom, 瓜 differs from 爪 in composition.

爱抬杠的家伙

出场角色：工（gōng）；三（sān）。

工与三是两个有名的爱抬杠的家伙。

这不，今天他俩又"杠"上了。

"兄弟，你的脊梁骨咋横着长呢？"工问三。

"我还想问你呢，你的肋骨咋是竖着长呢？"三反唇相讥道。

Two Argumentative Fellows

Characters: 工"work"; 三"three".

Known for their argumentative personalities, 工 and 三 find themselves once again at odds with each other.

"Buddy, how come you've got a horizontal spine?" asks 工.

"I was just wondering why one of your ribs is vertical," the other resorts sarcastically.

Note: The middle horizontal stroke in 三 resembles a rib but maliciously regarded by 工 as a horizontal spine, while the vertical line in 工 resembles a spine but maliciously seen by 三 as a vertical rib.

算卦

出场角色：冈 （gāng）；凶 （xiōng）。

冈好给别人算命。一天，凶找到冈，请他给自己算一卦。

冈打量了一下凶，语调沉重地说："阁下头足倒置，不是吉相啊。"

A Visit to a Fortune Teller

Characters: 冈 "hill"; 凶"disaster".

One day, 凶 comes to 冈, who is fond of fortune-telling, to inquire about his future.

After taking a close look at the other, 冈 states in a deep tone, "Sir, your top and bottom are reversed, which bodes ill for your days to come."

Note: 凶 is shaped like 冈 upside down.

对面是个小人物

出场角色：公（gōng）；翁（wēng）。

公望着翁，口中念念有词地嘟囔道："能立在羽毛上的家伙，不是什么有分量的人物。"

Face to Face with a Lightweight

Characters: 公"a noble man"; 翁"an old man".

Looking up at 翁, 公 mumbles to himself, "A man standing on a feather doesn't carry much weight."

Note: 翁 is structured top to bottom with 公 and 羽"feather".

莫与寡人称兄道弟

出场角色：关（guān）；朕（zhèn）。

关对朕说："兄弟，跟月亮傍肩儿啦，你的位置可不低呀！"

朕冷冷地答道："谁跟你是兄弟呀。朕懒得搭理你！"

注释：朕，该字有多义，此处指皇帝的自称。

Not on Equal Terms

Characters: 关"close"; 朕"I or me (used by an emperor)".

"Bro, you stand shoulder to shoulder with the moon," says 关 to 朕.

"What a high position you hold!"

"Who do you think you are to bro me?" replies the other coldly. "Leave ME alone."

Note: 朕 is composed of a semantic radical 月"moon" on the left and 关 on the right.

各有所长

出场角色：个（gè）；丫（yā）。

个："兄弟，你的顶棚咋反着修啊？你这个顶子容易存水呀！"

丫："凡是长相跟你不一样的都是反的？我防水是不如你，可遮阳不比你差呀。"

Each Has His Own Strengths

Characters: 个"individual"; 丫"crotch".

个: "Hey buddy, how come your roof is built reversed? It's prone to getting waterlogged."

丫: "What's different from you is simply reversed? I am as shady as you are, though not as water-proof."

Note: 个 is structured with a radical 人 at the top resembling a roof, while 丫 structured with a radical ⩊ at the top representing a roof upside down.

差距很大

出场角色：甘（gān）；廿（niàn）。

甘在一次聚会上第一次见到廿。他好奇地打量了对方很久，终于忍不住对廿说："原来你是个空桶啊！"

廿听到如此无理的话，看了甘一眼，冷冷地回应道："是啊，比起你这个'半桶水'，我还是差距很大呀！"

A Big Difference

Characters: 甘 "sweet"; 廿 "twenty".

Meeting 廿 for the first time at a party, 甘 sizes him up curiously for quite a while, blurting finally, "Actually you are an empty vessel!"

Offended by the insulting remark, 廿 casts the other a look and replies coldly, "Sure I am, and I have a long way to go before matching up to you, a half-full bucket."

Note: 廿 resembles an empty bucket while 甘 is shaped like a bucket half filled with water (with one more horizontal line enclosed).

想立传的老虎

出场角色：文（wén）。幕后角色：闻（wén）。

老虎大王让狐狸给他写个传记，将他开疆拓土的伟绩传扬出去。

"虎大王一生穷兵黩武，残害了无数生灵。他的生平臭不可闻。这个传记没法写呀！"领了任务的狐狸对妻子叹道。

注释：本文中的"臭不可文"是成语"臭不可闻"的戏仿。

King Tiger's Biography

Onstage Character: 文"write". Offstage Character: 闻"sniff".

King Tiger ordered Minister Fox to write a biography of him, to spread his great feats in expanding the territory.

"All his life King Tiger has been waging war after war, claiming countless lives. His life story is too nasty to write. How can I complete such a sticky task?" sighed the fox to his wife.

Note: "Too nasty to write" is a parody of the Chinese idiom "too stinky to sniff" used to describe someone notorious. The parody and the idiom are phonetically identical in Mandarin.

四肢有缺

出场角色：几（jī）； 厂（chǎng）。

几盯着厂看个不停。

"看什么呀？" 厂奇怪地问。

"兄弟你发育不全啊。" 几惋惜地叹道。

Not Fully-Developed

Characters: 几"small table"; 厂"factory".

几 stares fixedly at 厂.

"What's wrong?" asks 厂 curiously.

"You are not fully developed yet, pal," sighs 几 with regret.

Note: Compared with 几, 厂 is composed without the stroke 乚 (vertical with turn and hook) on the right.

不知自重

出场角色：今（jīn）； 令（lìng）。

今对令说："会拉个羊屎块儿就指手画脚啊！"

Lack of Self-Restraint

Characters: 今"present"; 令"order".

"Stop ordering others around," 今 says to 令. "Who do you think you are with the piece of sheep dung?"

Note: 令 has an extra dot stroke at the bottom compared with 今.

人不可貌相

出场角色：巾（jīn）；币（bì）。

巾对币说："瞧你这点本事，安个顶棚还是歪的。"

币笑道："我的本事大不大，你到市场上走一圈儿就知道了。"

Never Judge by Appearances

Characters: 巾"towel"; 币"money".

"It's so clumsy of you to have built the roof crooked," 币 says to 巾.

"Just go around the market," laughs the other, "and I'll show you what I am made of."

Note: 币 is composed of 巾 with a left-falling stroke on top resembling a slanting roof.

大哥的风范

出场角色：甲（jiǎ）；由（yóu）。

甲对由说："老大就要有老大的样子，不能由着性子拿大顶。"

The Style of a Boss

Characters: 甲"first"; 由"follow".

"A boss should act like a boss," says 甲 to 由. "You can't stand on your head at pleasure."

Note: 甲 is shaped like a reversed 由.

不过是个架子工

出场角色：加（jiā）；架（jià）。

加望着架好大一会儿，不屑地说："兄弟，你以为站在树上就能高人一等吗？别摆臭架子了！"

The Arrogant Perch

Characters: 加"addition"; 架"frame".

"Dude, do you see yourself as superior standing on top of a tree?" looking up at 架 for quite a while, 加 says in disdain. "Don't put on that disgusting airs!"

Note: 架 is composed of 加 at the top and 木"tree" at the bottom.

谁是老大？

出场角色：甲（jiǎ）；申（shēn）。

甲对申说："越是强出头越当不了老大。这就是生活给你的教训。"

申朝甲笑了笑，说："找本字典，看看'申'是不是全中国的老大！"

注释：申有多义，其中之一是中国最大的城市上海的别称。

Who Is Number One

Characters: 甲 "first"; 申 "a nickname of Shanghai".

"The harder you try to stick out your head, the less likely you are to become a boss ," says 甲 to 申. "This is a lesson that life teaches you."

"Consult the dictionary, and you'll know who is the number one in the country," smiles the other.

Note: The middle vertical stroke in 甲 touches the top stroke, while the middle vertical stroke in 申 sticks out of the top stroke with the extended part representing the head; the Chinese "stick out one's head" figuratively means "become prominent"; 申 "Shanghai" is the largest city in China.

求全责备

出场角色：卡（kǎ）；上（shàng）；下（xià）。

卡见到了上和下。

卡对上说："兄弟，下半身截肢了？"又对下说："兄弟，你的上半身呢？"

上和下齐声道："恭喜阁下到火葬场时有个全须全尾。"

Demanding Perfection

Characters: 卡 "card"; 上 "up"; 下 "down".

卡 runs into 上 and 下.

"Hey, guy," says 卡 to 上. "You had your lower body amputated?"

Then he turns to 下, asking, "And where's your upper half, dude?"

"Congratulations, sir!" say 上 and 下 in unison. "You're going to be buried intact in the memorial park."

Note: 卡 is graphically structured with 上 at the top and 下 at the bottom.

谁晕了？

出场角色：晕（yūn）；晖（huī）。

晕问晖："朋友，你晕头转向了吧？脑袋都耷拉一边了！"

晖看了看晕，不禁笑道："你自己晕了，就以为别人也跟你一样吗？"

Who Is Dizzy

Characters: 晕"dizzy"; 晖"sunshine".

"Mate, your head droops to one side," 晕 says to 晖. "Are you feeling dizzy or something?"

Glancing at the other, 晖 cannot help but laugh, "Being lightheaded, you find others the same as you?"

Note: 晖 has 日 on the left and 晕 has 曰 at the top representing the head.

空空如也

出场角色：空（kōng）；穴（xué）；工（gōng）。

空、穴和工在一起小聚。

借着酒力，空对穴和工说："你们俩咋长的？一个有头无尾，一个有尾无头。"

穴和工耳语道："他自以为自己十全十美，其实他是空洞无物啊。"

As Empty as a Drum

Characters: 空"empty"; 穴"cave"; 工"work".

空, 穴 and 工 meet up for a drink.

Fueled by liquid courage, 空 says to the other two, "Guys, what makes you grow like that? One has a head but no tail and the other has a tail but no head."

"He sees himself as perfect," whispers 穴 to 工. "But in fact, he's as empty as a drum."

Note: 空 is composed 穴 at the top representing the head and 工 at the bottom representing the tail.

以多胜少

出场角色：田（tián）；品（pǐn）。

田与品互不服气，各自摆出自己的本事。结果还是半斤八两。

突然，田发现了自己的优势，马上大叫道："我四张嘴，你三张嘴。四比三，我赢了。"

品无可奈何道："你嘴多，你有理。"

Victory by Number

Characters: 田"field"; 品"product".

田 and 品 are challenging each other to see who is superior. Having displayed all their skills, they remain neck and neck.

Suddenly 田 finds his edge over 品. "I have four mouths while you have three," he exclaims. "Four to three, I am the winner."

At his wit's end, 品 says, "You talk more sense with one more mouth."

Note: 品 is composed of three 口"mouth" while graphically 田 consists of four 口.

专注旁人下半身

出场角色：考（kǎo）；老（lǎo）。

考对老说："兄弟，你的下半身长的不对呀！"

老不悦地答道："你一有闲工夫就考证别人的下半身啊！"

The Lower Half

Characters: 考"research"; 老"old".

"Something seems off with your lower body, old chap, " 考 says to 老.

"You seem to enjoy examining the lower parts of others once you have time to spare," replies the other, annoyed.

Note: 考 and 老 are structured with the same top 耂 but each with a different bottom, the former 丂 the latter 匕.

互不对眼

出场角色：吝（lìn）；齐（qí）。

吝对齐说："兄弟，我咋瞅你长得这么别扭呢？"

齐对吝说："是吗？我还看你不顺眼呢。我下面是腿，你下面咋是嘴呢？"

Looking Down on Each Other

Characters: 吝"stingy"; 齐"neat".

"Pal, why do you look so oddly shaped?" says 吝 to 齐.

"Do I? You are out of shape in my eyes too," replies the other. "Here at the bottom are my legs, but why is your mouth at the end?"

Note: 吝 and 齐 are structured with the same top 文 but each with a different bottom, the former with 口"mouth" the latter with a left-falling stroke plus a vertical line resembling the legs.

古调莫弹

出场角色：古 (gǔ) ； 叶 (yè) 。

古望着随风摆动的叶说："阁下站没站相，坐没坐相啊！"

叶笑道："作古之辈，怎知道我翩翩起舞之乐呀！"

Swaying in the Wind

Characters: 古"ancient"; 叶"leaf".

"You never stand or sit properly," says 古 to 叶 who is swaying in the wind.

"Someone resting in peace never knows the joy of dancing," sneers the other.

Note: 叶 resembles 古 lying on the side.

不容瑕疵

出场角色：十（shí）；斗（dòu）。

十对斗说："你两个肩章咋缝一边了？"

斗对十说："就你十全十美，没事总挑别人毛病！"

A Critical Eye

Characters: 十"ten"; 斗"fight".

"Why do you sew both badges on just one shoulder?" 十 asks 斗.

"Always picking on others, you see yourself as flawless in every way?" retorts the other.

Note: The two dot strokes in 斗 represents two badges.

自恋有术

出场角色：术（shù）；木（mù）。

术对木说："我已经有一个肩章了。你什么时候有呀？"

木不屑地说："看把你美的，不就肩膀上长了个瘤子嘛！"

The Way to Parade Your Wares

Characters: 术"skill"; 木"tree".

"Look, I have a badge on my shoulder," says 术 to 木. "When will you get one?"

"Don't flatter yourself," scoffs the other. "It's nothing but a growth."

Note: With an extra dot stroke (representing a badge or tumor) on the upper right, 术 differs from 木 in composition.

个人看法不相同

出场角色：个（gè）；人（rén）。

个在大街上见到了人。他看了看人的模样，笑道："兄弟，别看你人五人六的样子，咋没个主心骨呢？"

"要是有了那根打狗棍，我还是人吗？"人反唇相讥道。

A Matter of Personal Opinion

Characters: 个"individual"; 人"man".

个 comes across 人 on the street.

Casting a glance at the other, 个 smiles, "Full of airs and graces, how come you don't have a backbone to match?"

"If I had that stick, would I still be a man?" retorts 人.

Note: 个 is composed of 人 with vertical stroke below resembling a spine or a stick.

多放了一个 "屁"

出场角色：穴（xuè）；帘（lián）。

穴在大街上见到了帘，开玩笑道："兄弟，你几岁了，还系着屁帘儿啊？"

帘大怒道："你这么没有教养。我是帘，不是屁帘儿！"

注释："屁帘儿"是中国北方小孩子在开裆裤外面加的一个棉布做的帘子，有两个带子系在腰上，防止露出的屁股受凉。

A Bottom Drape

Characters: 穴"cave"; 帘"curtain".

As 穴 walks down the street, he comes across 帘.

"You are not young enough to be wearing a bottom drape, buddy," jokes 穴.

"Watch your mouth!" replies the other, outraged. "I'm a drape, not a bottom one."

Note: 帘 is composed of 穴 with 巾 at the bottom representing a bottom drape; some children in the north of China wear bottom drapes made of cotton cloth outside their split pants to protect their buttocks from the cold.

白字

出场角色: 白 (bái) ; 臼 (jiù) 。

白在大街上看见了臼, 一把将后者抓在手里:"哈哈, 今天我终于逮住了一个白字。"

臼困惑地说:"我不是白字啊!"

白哈哈大笑道:"你不是白字, 谁是白字? 看看你的长相, 该连上的地方都没有连上。"

臼不服气地说:"咱俩谁是白字你说了不算, 要让大伙评评理。"

"莫非我还怕评理?"白扯着臼, 对着大街上的行人喊道:"大伙给评评理, 看看我俩谁是白字?"

"你是白字!"过路的行人指着白, 异口同声地说,

A White

Characters: 白"white"; 臼"joint".

白 bumps into 臼 on the street. "Finally, I've caught a White, ha-ha," exclaims the former as he grabs the latter.

"But I'm not a White," says 臼, perplexed.

"Who else is supposed to be if you are not?" laughs 白. "Look at the lines on you, which are not as they should be."

"It's not up to you to decide who is one," argues 臼. "Let the public make a judgment."

"The public?" With the other in his grip, 白 calls out to the passers-by,

"Hello, everybody, please tell me which of us is a White."

"It's you!" shout the bystanders in unison, pointing at 白.

Note: 白 graphically resembles 白 with the top two horizontal lines in error; the Chinese phrase "white character" means "wrongly written character".

自讨没趣

出场角色：面（miàn）；而（ér）。

面问而："兄弟你咋长的，发育不全？"

而反击道："我还说你发育过度呢！整天'发'不离口。不知道的以为你是个款爷，其实就是一块软面团。"

Asking for a Retort

Characters: 面"flour"; 而"but".

"You look peculiar," 面 says to 而. "Are you underdeveloped?"

"I could say you are overdeveloped!" retorts the other. "Talking of 'develop' all day, you may strike some people as a moneybag. In reality, you are nothing but a ball of dough."

Note: Graphically 面 has three more horizontal lines in composition than 而.

不知所云

出场角色：伞（sǎn）；个（gè）。

伞对个说："偷工减料，不可救药。"

个对伞说："以己度人，不知所云。"

Asking for Mockery

Characters: 伞"umbrella"; 个"individual".

"Cutting corners in composition, you are hopeless," says 伞 to 个.

"Judging others against yourself, you are ridiculous," comes the retort.

Note: With three extra strokes (a horizontal and two dots), 伞 differs from 个 in composition.

一毛不能拔

出场角色：毛（máo）；乇（tuō）。

毛问乇：“兄弟，你咋少了一根毛啊？”

乇正色道：“你自己是毛，就以为别人都跟你一样啊？”

Every Single Hair Counts

Characters: 毛"hair"; 乇"torr (a unit of pressure)".

"Buddy, how is it that you've lost a hair?" 毛 asks 乇.

"Just because you are a hair, do you think everybody else is exactly the same as you?" replies 乇 with a stern look.

Note: 毛 has one more horizontal line in composition than 乇.

敢问大名是何意？

出场角色：木（mù）；杰（jié）。

木问杰："杰兄，你的大名是啥意思啊？"

杰得意地说："出类拔萃，就是非同一般啊。"

"啥出类拔萃呀，不就比我多几个歪点子嘛！"木不屑道。

What Does Your Name Mean?

Characters: 木"tree"; 杰"hero".

"What does your name mean, bro?" 木 asks 杰.

"Outstanding," replies the other proudly. "That is to say, I'm exceptionally prominent."

"Outstanding?" says 木 in contempt. "You have nothing more than me but some slanting dots."

Note: 杰 is composed of 木 with four dot strokes below; the Chinese phrase "slanting dots" means "bad ideas".

更胜一筹

出场角色：淼（miǎo）；众（zhòng）。

淼对众说："纵然你人多势众，也敌不过我烟波浩渺。"

注释：淼，水大的样子。

One Up

Characters: 淼"(of water) vast"; 众"crowd".

"You a mob of men are no match for me an expanse of water," says 淼 to 众.

Note: 淼 consists of three 水"water" and 众 three 人"person".

林子大了

出场角色：鸟（niǎo）；乌（wū）；马（mǎ）。

鸟一向看不起乌和马。一天，鸟看见乌和马在一起谈天，于是上前说道："瞧瞧你们俩的尊容——一个头上没眼，一个既没眼又没毛。"

乌对马说："他怎么总喜欢对别人评头品足？真是林子大了什么鸟儿都有啊！"

It Takes All Sorts

Characters: 鸟"bird"; 乌"crow"; 马"horse".

鸟 holds 乌 and 马 in contempt all the time.

One day, noticing the two chatting with each other, 鸟 approaches and says, "Look at you two. One has no eye and the other has neither eyes nor feathers."

"Why is he always finding fault with others?" says 乌 to 马. "It takes all sorts to make a world!"

Note: With an extra dot stroke resembling the eye, 鸟 differs from 乌 in composition; compared with 鸟, 马 graphically lacks a dot stroke resembling the eye and a left-falling stroke representing the feather.

宁可丢钱，不可丢人

出场角色：去（qù）；丢（diū）。

去对丢说："顶个方巾四处招摇，丢人现眼。"

Never Make a Fool of Yourself

Characters: 去"go"; 丢"lose".

"Swaggering around with a kerchief on top, you are making an exhibition of yourself!" says 去 to 丢.

Note: 丢 is composed of 去 with a left-falling stroke on top resembling a kerchief.

口说无凭

出场角色：品（pǐn）；口（kǒu）。
品对口说："嘴多有理。"
口答道："嘴大有理。"

Word of Mouth Is No Proof

Characters: 品"taste"; 口"mouth".

"More mouths talk sense," says 品.

"A bigger mouth talks sense," 口 responds.

Note: 品 is composed of three 口 (one on top of the other two).

鄙人可以说"不"

出场角色：丕（pī）；不（bù）。
丕问不："兄弟，买块地毯吧？"
不答道："不！"

I Can Say No

Characters: 丕"big"; 不"no".

"Hey, guy. Why don't you considering buying a carpet?" suggests 丕 to 不.

"No way!" replies the other dismissively.

Note: 丕 is composed of 不 with a horizontal stroke at the bottom resembling a carpet.

有弃有取

出场角色：平（píng）；乎（hū）。

平见到了乎，不屑地说："你上头歪，下面拐。"

乎笑道："我宁可上歪下拐，也不学你的四平八稳。"

Two Sides to Every Story

Characters: 平"flat"; 乎"a modal particle".

"You lean over and bend under," 平 says in contempt upon running into 乎.

"I'd rather have my top slanted and bottom crooked than live a flat life as you do," sneers 乎 in response.

Note: 乎 has a left-falling stroke at the top and a vertical line with hook, different from 平 (which has a flat top and a vertical line without a hook).

不想成为一条狗

出场角色：犬（quǎn）；尤（yóu）。

犬看了看尤，说："兄弟，你的右腿弯了。"

尤冷冷地答道："没什么，这不过是不想做一条狗的代价。"

No Desire to Be a Dog

Characters: 犬"dog"; 尤"a surname".

"Hi, mate. Your right leg is crooked," says 犬 looking at 尤.

"No matter," replies the other coldly. "It's just a price to pay for not being a dog."

Note: The vertical with turn and hook stroke in 尤 resembles a bent leg.

"你的两条腿呢？"

出场角色：乔（qiáo）；夭（yāo）。

乔对夭说："虽说我两条腿不一般直，可聊胜于无啊。兄弟，你的两条腿呢？夭啦？"

Where Are Your Legs

Characters: 乔"tall"; 夭"die young".

"Though my legs are not symmetrically straight, they are better than nothing," says 乔 to 夭. "Where are yours, pal? Lost in your infancy?"

Note: 乔 is composed 夭 at the top and a left-falling stroke together with a vertical line at the bottom resembling two legs.

缺一不可

出场角色：全（quán）；仝（tóng）。

全对仝说："兄弟，你的部件不全啊！"

仝笑道："看来求全责备是你的本性啊。"

One Part Missing

Characters: 全"complete"; 仝"same".

"Pal, your parts are incomplete," says 全 to 仝.

"Now I see it's your nature to demand perfection from others," sneers 仝.

Note: 全 has one more horizontal line than 仝.

眼前尽是高帽子

出场角色：且（qiě）；目（mù）。

且好奇地盯着目看了很久，最后忍不住问目："兄弟，我走南闯北，也没见过你这样的高帽子，居然没有帽檐。"

目看了一眼且，冷笑道："你自己是一顶帽子也就罢了，怎么还以为别人也是帽子？"

An Eye for Nothing but Hats

Characters: 且"and"; 目"eye".

Staring curiously at 目 for a long while, 且 finally blurts, "Buddy, I've traveled far and wide, but never seen a top hat like you, with no brim at all."

"It's all right for you to be a topper, but why must you assume I am one too?" sneers 目 as he casts a glance at 且.

Note: With the bottom stroke longer than that of 目, 且 resembles a high hat.

校园里的孤家寡人

出场角色：齐（qí）；吝（lìn）；文（wén）。

齐、吝和文是一个班的同学。但是齐和吝不喜欢跟文玩。

229

"你们俩为什么不带我玩呢？" 文闷闷不乐地问道。

"你呀，要腿没腿，要嘴没嘴。配跟我俩玩儿吗！" 齐和吝讽刺道。

A Loner in School

Characters: 齐"neat"; 吝"stingy"; 文"culture".

As classmates, 齐 and 吝 are reluctant to hang out with 文.

"Why do you two always leave me out of your fun?" asks 文, depressed.

"Without leg or mouth, are you really fit to be our playmate?" sneer the other two.

Note: 齐 is composed of 文 at the top and a left-falling stroke plus a vertical line at the bottom resembling the legs; 吝 is composed of 文 at the top and a semantic radical 口"mouth" at the bottom.

柳眉倒竖

出场角色：兑 (duì)；只 (zhǐ)。

兑问只："姐姐，你的眉毛咋长在嘴下边了？"

只看了看兑，不悦道："有人的眉毛倒是在嘴上边，可像俩犄角。吓死人了。"

Eyebrows under the Mouth

Characters: 兑"exchange"; 只"only".

"Hey, sis. Why do your brows grow below your mouth?" 兑 asks 只.

"Someone has his eyebrows above his mouth, but they look like a pair of horns," replies 只 crossly as she casts an eye over the other. "It's quite frightening, actually."

Note: 只 has a radical 八 below and 兑 has a radical ⱱ above representing the eyebrows.

人心叵测

出场角色：人（rén）；从（cóng）。
人对从说："这俩兄弟，咱仨结伴走吧。众人拾柴火焰高。"
从对人道："想得倒美，结伴还不是你在上头。"

A Cheap Trick

Characters: 人"person"; 从"follow".
"Hi there. Shall we keep each other company on the trip?" 人says to 从.
"The more, the merrier."
"In your dreams!" replies the other. "I would be under you if we paired up."

Note: 从 joined by 人 on top forms 众"many".

出言不逊

出场角色：肉（ròu）；内（nèi）。
肉对内说："兄弟，你丢人了吧？"
内大怒道："你这块臭肉怎么如此无理？我哪里丢人了？"
肉困惑地说："你明明下面丢了一个'人'，怎么反倒骂我是'臭肉'？"

A Personal Remark

Characters: 肉"meat"; 内"inside".

肉 says to 内, "Hey mate. You've lost a man, haven't you?"

"Why are you bad meat so rude?" responds the other furiously. "How can I be disgraced?"

"Clearly a man is missing down there," says 肉, totally confused. "But how come you give me a bad name?"

Note: With an additional 人 "man" enclosed, 肉 differs from 内 in composition; the Chinese expression "lose a man" means "lose face".

说倒容易做却难

出场角色：真（zhēn）；直（zhí）。

真对直说："兄弟，两条腿都没了，还能站得直吗？"

Easier Said Than Done

Characters: 真"real"; 直"straight".

"With both legs missing, how can you stand up straight?" 真 asks 直.

Note: Compared with 直, 真 has an radical 八 at the bottom resembling the legs.

活像两个二流子

出场角色：孑（zǐ）；孓（jié）；孓（jué）。

孑对孓和孓说："你们俩的裤腰带咋系的？"

注释：孑孓，蚊子幼虫。

Coming Off as Two Loafers

Characters: 孑"son"; 孓"all alone"; 孓"wriggler".

"Your belts seem fastened out of place," 孑 remarks to 孓 and 孓.

Note: Each of 孑, 孓 and 孓 has a stroke resembling a belt across the vertical with hook stroke.

一无是处

出场角色：真（zhēn）；且（qiě）。

真对且说："你快照照镜子吧——上无头，下掉腿，胸腔里还缺根肋骨，你这模样谁待见啊！"

Nothing Right

Characters: 真"real"; 且"and".

"Just take a look at yourself in the mirror," says 真 to 且. "Who'd care for someone without a head above or legs below and with one rib missing in the chest?"

Note: Compared with 且, 真 has an extra radical 十 at the top (resembling the head), another extra radical 八 at the bottom (resembling the legs) and still another extra horizontal stroke in the middle (resembling a rib).

不过尔尔

出场角色：山（shān）；马（mǎ）。

山对马说："常言道，'望山跑死马'，看来我是阁下的克星啊！

马看了山一眼，抖了抖鬃毛，冷笑道："什么克星啊！你在我眼里就是个没把儿的粪叉子。"

No Great Shakes

Characters: 山"mountain"; 马"horse".

"'The mountain ahead tires a horse to death,' as the saying goes," says 山 to 马. "It appears that I'm the bane of your life."

Throwing the other a brief glance, the horse shakes his mane and resorts with a sneer, "In my eyes, you are nothing but a manure fork with no handle."

Note: 山 resembles a fork without a handle.

稀奇骨怪

出场角色：中（zhōng）；曰（yuē）。

中打量着曰，好奇地问："你的脊椎骨咋横着长啊？"

曰看了一眼对方，不快地说："我还正要问你那，阁下的肋骨咋竖着长啊！"

Bones Not Right

Characters: 中"middle"; 曰"say".

Staring at 曰, 中 asks curiously, "How come your spine is horizontal?"

"I'm just wondering why your rib is vertical," responds 曰 crossly, darting a brief glance at the other.

Note: 中 has vertical line through the middle resembling a spine.

一分小胜

出场角色：早（zǎo）；昃（lá）。

早对昃说："我有十日，你有九日。十比九，我赢了。"

One-Point Victory

Characters: 早"morning"; 昃"corner".

"I have ten suns and you have nine. So, I've won, ten to nine!" boasts 早 to 昃.

235

Note: 早 is composed of 日"sun" at the top and 十 "ten" at the bottom while 晃 has 九 "nine" at the bottom.

求全责备

出场角色：真（zhēn）；直（zhí）；具（jù）。

真对直和具说："你俩一个有头无尾，一个有尾无头。"

直和具笑着答道："只有你是全须全尾。"

Nobody Is Perfect

Characters: 真"real"; 直"straight"; 具"tool".

"Look at you two," says 真 to 直 and 具. "One has a head but no tail and the other has a tail but no head."

"You are an intact corpse," laugh other two.

Note: 直 has a radical 十 at the top resembling the head; 具 has a radical 八 at the bottom resembling the legs.

爱惜羽毛

出场角色：孑（zǐ）；孚（fú）。

孑对孚道："至于嘛，你总共就三根毛，还顶个头巾护着。"

Hairs Highly Valued

Characters: 子"son"; 孚"inspire confidence in".
"With only three hairs on top, do you have to cover them with a headscarf?" says 子 to 孚.

Note: 孚 is composed of 子 with a radical 爫 on top resembling three hairs covered by a kerchief.

尸道尊严

出场角色：尾（wěi）；尸（shī）。
尾问尸："兄弟，在太平间呆久了吧，身上的毛都掉光了？"
"我好歹也是一具全尸，你不过是一条可有可无的尾巴。"尸冷冷地答道。

A Tail Good for Nothing

Characters: 尾"tail"; 尸"dead body".
"You stay in the mortuary too long to keep your hair, right?" 尾 asks 尸.
"At least I am a complete body," replies the other coldly. "But you are simply a tail good for nothing."

Note: 尾 is composed of 尸 with 毛"hair" below.

不是一路货

出场角色：瓦（wǎ）；瓷（cí）。

瓦在一次聚会上见到了瓷。

瓦问瓷道:"兄弟,人家都说你的身价比我高多了。我看不见得。"

瓷看了看瓦,没有说话。

瓦见瓷不搭理他,怒火一下子冒了出来:"你撒泡尿照照自己,分明是一片次瓦,怎么能比我的身价高呢?"

瓷只是笑了笑,转身走了。

Not Two of a Kind

Characters: 瓦"tile"; 瓷"porcelain".

瓦 comes across 瓷 at a party.

"Buddy, they all say you are worth much more than me," says 瓦 to 瓷. "But that's not how I see it."

Casting the other a glance 瓦, 瓷 does not say a word.

Feeling ignored, 瓦 flares up and yells, "Who do you think you are? As a defective tile, how can you possibly be more precious than me?"

瓷 makes no reply, but simply walks away with a grin.

Note: 瓷 is composed of 瓦 with 次"defective" on top.

光彩照人

出场角色:兀(wù);光(guāng)。

兀不服气地对光说:"你不过头上比我多了三根毛,神气啥呀?"

光严肃地对兀说:"你可别小看这三根毛。我光顾的地方阁下未必能去啊。"

Chapter 3 No Desire to Be a Dog
第三章　不想成为一条狗
Chapter 3　No Desire to Be a Dog

Bright Flashes

Characters: 兀"bare"; 光"light".

"With only three hairs on top, why are you so swollen-headed?" says 兀 to 光 harshly.

"Don't look down on the three hairs," replies the other seriously. "They allow me to visit places you may not be able to reach."

Note: 光 is composed of 兀 with a radical ⺍ on top resembling three hairs.

长短不齐

出场角色：文（wén）；齐（qí）。

文对齐说：“兄弟，你这两条腿咋不一般长啊？”

齐对文说：“我在稍息。再说了，我的腿就是真不一般长，也比你这‘无腿将军’强啊！”

Off Balance

Characters: 文"article"; 齐"neat".

"Man, why are your legs not equally straight?" 文 asks 齐.

"I stand at ease," replies the other. "Besides, someone legless bears no comparison with me."

Note: 齐 is composed of 文 at the top and and a left-falling stroke plus a vertical line at the bottom resembling the legs.

无事生非

出场角色：无（wú）；元（yuán）。

无对元说："你咋没脖子呀？"

元反唇相讥道："那也比你这个一无所有的家伙强。"

Much Ado about Nothing

Characters: 无"nothing"; 元"first".

"How is it that you have no neck?" says 无 to 元.

"Having nothing to your name, you stand no comparison with me," retorts the other.

Note: The left-falling stroke in 元 starts at the lower horizontal line while the one in 无 touches the top with the extra part resembling the neck.

绝妙反击

出场角色：未（wèi）；来（lái）。

未对来说："兄弟，咱俩同台献技时，你总是排我后面出场。"

来笑着答道："是啊，导演老是让我唱大轴。谁让我比你多两下子呢。"

A Witty Retort

Characters: 未"not"; 来"come".

"Pal, every time we two give a stage performance together, you always make the appearance after me," says 未 to 来.

"You said it," grins 来. "I'm always cast in the grand finale to display my two extra skills."

Note: 未来"future" is a set phrase and 来 has two more strokes (a dot and a left-falling stroke representing "two skills") than未.

自愧不如

出场角色：行（háng）；街（jiē）。

行不屑地对街说：“当间儿摆两堆土就是街道啦？”

街惭愧地答道：“没法子，当初老祖宗就是这么设计的。”

It Runs in the Family

Characters: 行"line"; 街"street".

"Two mounds of earth piled in the middle make you a street?" scoffs 行 at 街.

"I was born this way," replies the other, ashamed. "It runs in the family."

Note: 街 is graphically composed of 行 with two 土"soil" in the middle.

有个毛用

出场角色：兴（xīng）；六（liù）。

兴对六说：你有头无臂，发育不全吧！

六对兴说：就你那三根细毛，还想冒充头与臂！

Hairs of No Use

Characters: 兴"rise"; 六"six".

兴 says to 六, "Having a head but no arm, are you underdeveloped?"

"Stop passing off those three fine hairs as your head and arms!" retorts the other.

Note: 兴 has two dots and a left-falling stroke at the top resembling three hairs while 六 has one dot stroke above resembling the head.

一个无神论者的质疑

出场角色：兄（xiōng）；克（kè）。

兄对克说："朋友，你以为头上顶个十字架就能战无不胜啊！"

A Question by a True Skeptic

Characters: 兄"brother"; 克"conquer".

"Mate, do you see yourself as all-conquering with a cross on top?" says 兄 to 克.

Note: 克 has a radical 十 at the top resembling a cross.

谁对谁错

出场角色：凶（xiōng）；区（qū）。

凶恶狠狠地对区说："站直了，别趴下！"

区看了看凶，不紧不慢地说："别那么凶巴巴的。我看你才是趴着呢！"

Who Is in the Wrong Posture?

Characters: 凶"fierce"; 区"district".

"Stand up straight," 凶 yells at 区 with a fierce look. "Don't lie down!"

"Don't bark at me," throwing a glance at 凶, 区 replies calmly. "In my eyes, you are the one lying on the side."

Note: 区 resembles 凶 lying on the side and vice versa.

眼力太差

出场角色：羊（yáng）；兰（lán）。

羊在草原上见到了兰，大为震惊："兄弟，你脊梁骨咋没啦？是不是让狼吃了？"

兰笑道："你仔细看看我，拿鼻子闻闻也成。我是你的兄弟吗？"

A Bad Eyesight

Characters: 羊"sheep"; 兰"orchid".

羊 is terribly stunned to see 兰 on the grassland. "Bro, what happened to your spine?" asks the sheep. "Chowed down by a wolf?"

"Take a closer look or even give me a sniff," smiles 兰. "Are you certain that I am your brother?"

Note: With one more vertical line resembling a spine, 羊 differs from 兰 in composition.

鸡同鸭讲

出场角色: 鸭（yā）; 鸡（jī）。

鸭对鸡说: "人人都叫你又（幼）鸟，看来你总也长不大。"

鸡对鸭说: "人人都叫你甲（假）鸟，看来你是个冒牌货。"

A Talk between Two Fowls

Characters: 鸭"duck"; 鸡"chicken".

"They all call you 'young bird', so you can never mature," says 鸭 to 鸡.

"They all call you 'phony bird', so you must be a fraud," comes the reply.

Note: 鸡 is composed of 又 (a homophone of 幼"young") on the left and 鸟 "bird" on the right; 鸭 is composed of 甲 (a homophone of 假"phony") on the left and 鸟 on the right.

眼中异类

出场角色: 羊（yáng）; 丰（fēng）。

羊对丰说: "我有两只角，你有一只角。你是何方神圣？"

An Alien in the Eye

Characters: 羊"sheep"; 丰"abundant".

"I have two horns while you have one. Who in the world are you?" says 羊 to 丰.

Note: 羊 has a radical ⱽ at the top resembling a pair of horns; the vertical stroke in 丰 runs through the three horizontal lines with the top extended part resembling a horn.

谁的分量重？

出场角色：羽（yǔ）；习（xí）。

羽对习说：“兄弟，半边身子咋丢啦？”

习笑道：“没有啊，我生下来就是这个样子。”

羽望着习，对他说：“阁下的体重只是我的一半啊！”

习瞟了一眼羽，轻声道：“先生想必是一个很有分量的人物啰！”

一阵风吹了过来，被吹得摇摇晃晃的羽红着脸告辞了。

Who Carries More Weight?

Characters: 羽"feather"; 习"study".

"Where's your other half, bro?" 羽 asks 习.

"I was born this way," smiles the other.

"So you merely have half of my weight," says 羽, gazing at 习.

"Then you must be someone who carries a lot of weight," 习 responds gently, throwing a glance at 羽.

Blushed with shame, 羽 staggers away in a gust of breeze.

Note: 羽 consists of two 习.

多余的心

出场角色：亚（yà）；恶（è）。

亚对恶说："兄弟呀，你这颗心长得多余呀！"

A Heart to No Avail

Characters: 亚"second"; 恶"evil".

"Pal, the heart is more than you need!" says 亚 to 恶.

Note: 恶 is composed 亚 at the top and 心"heart" at the bottom.

附庸风雅

出场角色：乙（yǐ）；艺（yì）。

乙对艺说："头上顶两棵草就装上高雅啦！"

An Elaborate Pretense

Characters: 乙"second"; 艺"art".

"You are acting elegant with two blades of grass on top!" says 乙 to 艺.

Note: 艺 is composed 乙 with a semantic radical 艹"grass" on top representing two straws.

攀比之心

出场角色：杳（yǎo）；查（chá）；香（xiāng）。

杳看见了查、香，先是气呼呼地问查："凭啥你有地毯我没地毯？"

查没有搭理杳。

杳又生气地问香："凭啥你有头巾我没头巾？"

香一声不吭地跟查走了。

Keeping Up with the Joneses

Characters: 杳"distant"; 查"check"; 香"fragrance".

杳 comes across 查 and 香. "How is it that you have a carpet while I don't?" 杳 asks 查 crossly.

Ignored by 查, 杳 turns to 香. "Why do you possess a scarf but I don't?" asks杳, outraged.

香 makes no reply, but simply walks away with 查.

Note: Compared with 杳, 查 has an extra horizontal stroke at the bottom resembling a carpet and 香 has an extra left-falling stroke at the top resembling a scarf.

你的主在教堂

出场角色：玉（yù）；主（zhǔ）。

一基督徒去教堂做礼拜。路上他见到了正在晒太阳的玉。

"主啊，谁把你的头拧下来啦？" 基督徒泪流满面地问。

"谁是你的主啊！" 玉没好气地说，"上教堂找你的主去吧！"

Your Lord Is in the Church

Characters: 玉"jade"; 主"lord".

On his way to church, a Christian runs across 玉 who is basking in the sun.

"Oh, my lord. Who wrenched off your head?" asks the Christian with tears running down his cheeks.

"What are you talking about?" replies the other, annoyed. "Go to find your lord in the house of worship!"

Note: 玉 is shaped like 主 with the top dot stroke (resembling the head) removed to the lower right.

各执一词

出场角色：主（zhǔ）；王（wáng）。

主对王说："有头方为主。"

王对主说："无头才是王。"

Each Has a Version

Characters: 主"lord"; 王"king".

"The lord is the lord only if he has the head," says 主 to 王.

"A king is a king only if headless," comes the reply.

Note: 主 is composed of 王 with a dot stroke on top resembling the head.

"你着急了吧？"

出场角色：刍（chú）；急（jí）。
刍对急说："兄弟，我不让你多心，你偏不听。这下该着急了吧！"

An Anxious Heart

Characters: 刍"hay"; 急"anxious".
"I told you not to have a heart, but you simply didn't listen," says 刍 to 急.
"Now you've got an anxious heart!"

Note: 急 is composed of 刍 with 心"heart" below.

无用之人

出场角色：甩（shuǎi）；用（yòng）。
甩愤愤不平地问用："为啥大伙都说我没你有用呢？"
"因为你爱翘尾巴呀。"用严肃地答道。

A Good-for-Nothing

Characters: 甩"toss"; 用"use".
"Why do they all say that I am not as helpful as you are?" 甩 asks 用
resentfully.
"Because you are always curling your tail up," replies the other seriously.

Note: Different from 用, the middle vertical stroke in 甩 turns and hooks, with the turn and hook resembling a tail being curled up; the Chinese expression "curl up the tail" figuratively means "get cocky".

人可以貌相

出场角色：夯（hāng）；劣（liè）。

夯对劣说："一看你这副样，就知道你不是个好干活的。"

注释：夯，砸地基用的工具；用夯砸。

You Can Judge a Man by His Appearance

Characters: 夯"rammer"; 劣"inferior".

"Judging by your look, I know you are a lazy bum," says 夯 to 劣.

Note: 夯 is structured top to bottom with 大"big" and 力"effort" while 劣 with 少"little" and 力.

该出头时就出头

出场角色：开（kāi）；井（jǐng）。

小酌之后，开推心置腹地对井说："兄弟，听我一句——莫出头，莫出头。凡事莫出头。"

井抿了一口酒，幽幽地答道："我不出头你有水喝吗？"

Just Do It

Characters: 开"open"; 井"water well".

"Listen, pal," 开 says to 井 earnestly over a drink. "You should never stick out, under any circumstances."

Taking a sip, 井 replies calmly, "But would you have water to drink without me sticking out?"

Note: The left-falling and vertical strokes in 开 touch the top horizontal line while the same strokes in 井 run across the top, representing "stick out"; it is commonly believed that "sticking out" is liable to invite trouble.

夸夸其谈

出场角色：亏（kuī）；夸（kuā）。

亏对夸说："亏不可怕，可怕的是大亏以后还自吹自擂。"

Blowing His Own Trumpet

Characters: 亏"deficit"; 夸"boast".

"It's not a terrible thing to slip into a deficit," says 亏 to 夸. "But it's really awful that one blows his own trumpet after running a huge deficit."

Note: 夸 is composed of 大"big" at the top and 亏 at the bottom.

心术不正

出场角色：忡（chōng）；忠（zhōng）。

"我心里为啥总是不痛快呀！" 忡愁眉苦脸地问忠，"你帮我琢磨琢磨。"

忠看了看忡，笑道："因为你的心没摆正啊！"

A Heart Out of Place

Characters: 忡"uneasy"; 忠"loyal".

"Why do I always have a heavy heart?" 忡 asks 忠 with a dejected expression. "Help me find the cause, please."

Casting the other a glance, 忠 smiles, "It's because your heart is in the wrong place."

Note: 忡 is composed of a radical忄"heart" on the left and 中 on the right, while 忠 is structured with 中 at the top and 心"heart" at the bottom.

身价太低

出场角色：十（shí）；千（qiān）。

十在一个数学学会年会上见到了千。他对千说："你以为戴个方巾我就不认识你啦！"

千看了看十，冷冷地答道："你我身价相差百倍，我没必要让你认识吧？"

Worth Far Less

Characters: 十"ten"; 千"thousand".

十 encounters 千 at the math society annual meeting. "Donning a kerchief on your head, do you assume I cannot recognise you?" quips 十.

Surveying the other with a chilly gaze, 千 replies curtly, "Why bother acquainting myself with someone whose worth is one hundred times less?"

Note: 千 is composed of 十 with a left-falling stroke on top resembling a kerchief.

虚荣之心不可有

出场角色：宋（sòng）；荣（róng）。

宋对荣说："兄弟，为了虚荣，用脑袋换顶草帽，值吗？"

Not Worth It

Characters: 宋"a surname"; 荣"glory".

"Pal, you've traded your head for a straw hat for the sake of vanity," says 宋 to 荣. "Is it truly worth it?"

Note: 宋 has a dot stroke at the top resembling the head; 荣 has a semantic radical 艹"grass" at the top representing a straw hat.

嘴大有理

出场角色：只（zhī）；口（kǒu）。

只对口说："有嘴有腿，胜过有嘴无腿。"

口对只说："我虽没腿，可我的嘴大呀！这年头是靠嘴吃饭，要腿有什么用啊"

A Large Mouth

Characters: 只"single"; 口"mouth".

"It's always advantageous to possess the ability to speak and move," remarks 只 to 口.

"Though born without legs, I'm blessed with a large mouth," replies the other. "In today's world, one can succeed with the power of words alone. What's the good of legs?"

Note: 只 has a radical 八 at the bottom resembling the legs.

"请允许我说'不'！"

出场角色：不（bù）；个（gè）。

不对个说："你没个顶子，看着多别扭啊！我看你还是跟我学学吧！"

个微笑着答道："先生，请允许我说'不'！"

Please Allow Me to Say No

Characters: 不"no"; 个"individual".

"How awkward you look without a roof!" 不 says to 个. "Just follow my example."

"Please allow me to say NO, sir," replies 个 with a smile.

Note: 不 has a horizontal line at the top resembling a roof, with the rest (composed of a left-falling, a vertical and a dot stroke) graphically similar to 个.

且听公论

出场角色：悬（xuán）；县（xiàn）。

悬看了一眼县，对他说："头可断血可流，唯独心不可丢啊！孟子说，'心之官则思'。没有思想，与行尸走肉无异呀。兄弟，我看你这辈子悬了！"

县看了看悬，大笑道："我悬还是你悬，且听公论吧！"

Let Us Heed the Public's Opinion

Characters: 悬"suspense"; 县"county".

悬 takes a glance at 县 and says to him. "The head can be cut off, blood can be shed, but one must never lose his heart! As Mencius said, 'The heart is the master of thought.' Without thoughts, one is no different from a lifeless shell. Buddy, I'm afraid you're in suspense about your life."

县 looks at 悬 and laughs heartily, "Who is truly in suspense? Let's hear what people have to say about that."

Note: 悬 is composed of 县 above and 心"heart" below.

好歹还活着

出场角色：亡（wáng]）；忘（wàng）。

亡问忘："兄弟，听说你记性极差，整天丢三落四的。"

"是啊，"忘笑道，"不过我好歹还苟活着。不像有的人，倒是从来也不丢三落四，可已经长眠于地下了。"

Living and Breathing

Characters: 亡"die"; 忘"forget".

亡 remarks to 忘, "Bro, I heard you have a memory like a sieve and are scatterbrained all day."

"You said it," chuckling, 忘 replies, "but at least I'm still able to live and breath. Someone never forgets anything, but has already been laid to rest underground."

Note: 忘 is composed of 亡 above and 心"heart" below.

"老兄多虑了！"

出场角色：网（wǎng）；冈（gāng）。

网看见了冈，皱着眉头问："看样子你是偷工减料的产品。咋样，逮不着鱼吧？"

冈笑道："老兄为我多虑了。我上接苍天，下连厚土，揽清风明月，拥草木入眠，岂不快哉？我怎肯与臭鱼烂虾为伍？"

"You Worry Too Much, Buddy"

Characters: 网"net"; 冈"ridge".

网 comes across 冈 and asks with a frown, "Looks like you're a shoddy product. Are you incapable of reeling in any fish?"

"You worry too much, buddy," 冈 laughs and resorts. "I reach towards the sky and ground in the earth, embrace fresh breeze and bright moon, and sleep with grass and trees. How can I bear to be with stinking fish and rotten shrimp?"

Note: Graphically similar to 网, 冈 has less strokes enclosed.

山中异类

出场角色：山 （shān）；当 （dāng）。
山对当："你也太没出息了。三棵小草就把你压倒啦！"

Not of the Same Clan

Characters: 山"mountain"; 当"equal".
"How feeble you are!" comments 山 to 当. "You've succumbed to the mere weight of three little blades of grasses."

Note: 当 is composed of ⼹ at the bottom resembling 山 lying on the side and ⺍ at the top resembling three grasses.

我把尾巴翘起来

出场角色：申 （shēn）；电 （diàn）。
申对电："兄弟，又翘尾巴了？"
电笑道："我要是不翘尾巴，今天夜里大街上就漆黑一团了。"

A Tail Curled Up

Characters: 申"appeal"; 电"electricity".

"Hey, pal. Are you raising your tail once again?" says 申 to 电.

"If I weren't, the entire street would be plunged into darkness tonight," grins the other.

Note: Different from 申, the middle vertical stroke in 电 turns and hooks, with the turn and hook resembling a tail being curled up; the Chinese expression "raise the tail" figuratively means "become cocky".

田亩之争

出场角色：田（tián）；亩（mǔ）。

田对亩说："你以为安个顶棚我就不认识你啦！"

亩对田说："别神气啦。你有多大由我说了算。"

注释：亩是面积计量单位。所以"亩"有"你有多大由我说了算"之言。

A Big Argument

Characters: 田"field"; 亩"a unit of area".

"Merely because a roof shelters you, do you presume I am unable to identify you?" says 田 to 亩.

"Stop putting on airs," retorts the other. "It's all up to me to tell the size of you."

Note: 亩 is composed of 田 with a radical 亠 on top resembling a roof; 亩 is a unit of measurement for 田.

主心骨丢不得

出场角色：申（shēn）；旦（dàn）。

申对旦说：你咋把主心骨抽出来压身子底下啦？”

Never Lose Your Backbone

Characters: 申"state"; 旦"dawn".

"Why have you pulled out your spine and placed it beneath your body?" 申 asks 旦.

Note: 申 is composed of 日 with a vertical stroke running through resembling a backbone, and 旦 is composed of 日 with a horizontal stroke below representing a spine pulled out.

无头不丈夫

出场角色：户（hù）；尸（shī）。

户到太平间里闲逛，看见了躺着一动不动的尸。

户叹息说：“这个兄弟真是太可怜了，不但人死了，咋连脑袋也掉了？”

Head of Household

Characters: 户 "household"; 尸 "corpse".

Strolling into a mortuary, 户 sees 尸 lying motionless.

"You poor thing," sighs 户. "Not only have you lost your life, but you have also lost your head?"

Note: 户 is composed of 尸 with a dot stroke on top representing the head.

遇事莫登三宝殿

出场角色：口 （kǒu）； 问 （wèn） 。

口对问说： "现在有电话了，问事没必要进人家门里了吧？"

The Ease of Communication

Characters: 口 "mouth"; 问 "ask".

"Everyone has a phone now," says 口 to 问. "So you don't have to step indoors when making inquiries, do you?"

Note: 问 is composed of 口 enclosed (from left, top and right sides) by 门 "door".

自以为是要不得

出场角色：不 （bù）； 个 （gè） 。

不对个说： "兄弟，你的顶棚呢？ 没有顶棚怎么防水呀？"

个看了看不，笑道："若论防水，我比你可是强多了。"

A Demeanour of Superiority

Characters: 不"no"; 个"individual".

不 says to 个, "Hey buddy, where's your roof? How can you be waterproof without roofing?"

个 takes a glance at the other and smiles, "When it comes to waterproofing, I am way stronger than you."

Note: 个 is graphically similar to 不 without top horizontal line; the top of 不 represent a flat roof and the top of 个 represents a pitched roof.

肚里没货

出场角色：凸（tū）；平（píng）。

凸对平道："阁下怎么相貌平平啊！"

平反唇相讥道："我是没有突出的地方，可是也不会像某些人那样，大腹便便，肚子里却是空空如也呀！"

No Substance Inside

Characters: 字"word"; 了"finish".

凸 says to 平, "Why do you have such a plain look!"

"Maybe I don't have any outstanding features, but at least I'm not like someone who has a big belly with nothing inside!" retorts 平 with a sneer.

Note: 凸 resembles someone who is overweight and has outstanding features but lacks substance inside.

大惊小怪

出场角色: 跳 (tiào)；兆 (zhào)。

跳在大街上遇见了兆。他看了兆一眼，惊叫道："哎呀，朋友，你失足啦？"

兆瞪了一眼跳，不屑地说："你谁呀，长着一只大脚丫子，有啥可炫耀的？"

A Fuss over Nothing

Characters: 跳"jump"; 兆"foretell".

跳 runs across 兆 on the street. Casting a brief glance at the other, 跳 exclaims, "Oh my, you lost the foot?"

"Who do you think you are?" responds 兆 disdainfully, giving 跳 a cold stare. "What's so impressive about having a big tootsie?"

Note: 跳 is composed of the radical 足"foot" on the left and 兆 on the right; the Chinese expression "lose foot" figuratively means going astray.

真不像话

出场角色: 字 (zì)；了 (liǎo)。

字对了说："你这个人真不像话，出门在外，既不戴帽子，也不系腰带。"

Out of Line

Characters: 字"word"; 了"finish".

字 says to 了, "Out and about without a hat or a belt, you're really out of line."

Note: Compared to 字, 了 lacks the radical 宀 representing a hat and the horizontal line representing a belt.

报丧之口

出场角色: 衣 (yī); 哀 (āi)。

衣每次遇见哀, 都看见他在哭哭啼啼。衣鄙夷地对哀说: "你比我多张嘴就是为了报丧啊?"

A Mouth to Tell Sorrows

Characters: 衣"clothes"; 哀"sad".

Every time 衣 comes across 哀, he sees the other crying tears. "You have that added mouth only to tell your sorrows?" says 衣 in contempt.

Note: Compared with 衣, 哀 has an extra 口"mouth".

成为英才有捷径

出场角色: 央 (yāng); 英 (yīng)。

央对英说: "看把你美的, 搭个草棚子就成英才啦? "

The Illusion of Genius

Characters: 央"centre"; 英"genius".

"You are so full of yourself!" says 央 to 英. "Just because of a shed built on top, you fancy yourself a genius?"

Note: 英 is composed 央 with a semantic radical 艹"grass" on top representing a shed.

衣冠禽兽

出场角色: 亵 (xiè) ; 执 (zhí) 。

亵在大街上见到了执。他盯着执看了一会, 突然大笑道: "兄弟, 你为什么光着身子上街呀! "

执冷冷地说: "别以为你穿件衣服就是正人君子了。"

A Savage in a Suit

Characters: 亵"obscene"; 执"persist".

亵 comes across 执, stares at him for a while and bursts into laughter.

"Why are you out on the street without a stitch on, dude?" asks 亵.

"Never regard yourself as a man of honour though in a suit," the other retorts harshly.

Note: 亵 is structured like 执 in the middle of 衣"garment".

以盲辨色

出场角色：乌（wū）；鸟（niǎo）。

乌："哇，整个世界漆黑一团啊！"

鸟："你没长眼，当然看不见世界的光亮。"

The Blind Judge No Colours

Characters: 乌"dark"; 鸟"bird".

乌: Wow, the whole world is just a dark mass.

鸟: Without eyes, you can never see the bright light on earth.

Note: Compared with 乌, 鸟 has one more dot stroke resembling the eye.

创口贴

出场角色：凡（fán）；风（fēng）。

凡在桑拿室见到了风。

凡对风说："朋友，你的痦子上贴了创口贴？"

A Sticking Plaster

Characters: 凡"all"; 风"wind".

凡 meets 风 in a Sauna room.

"Hey, buddy," says the former to the latter. "You've applied a sticking plaster on your mole?"

Note: 凡 is composed of 几 with a dot stroke enclosed (from three sides) representing a mole; 风 has an extra left-falling stroke across the dot resembling a sticking plaster.

兄弟买了一辆车

出场角色：非（fēi）；辈（bèi）。

非对辈说："兄弟，你啥时候买的车呀？"

A Car Just Bought

Characters: 非"not"; 辈"generation".

"Cool, buddy," 非 says to 辈. "When did you purchase the car?"

Note: 辈 is structured top to bottom with 丰 and 车"car".

多余的关心

出场角色：合（hé）；台（tái）。

合对台说："朋友，你顶棚没搭好，这样上不了台面啊！"

台笑道："老兄多虑了，我就是台面啊。"

The Stage

Characters: 合"close"; 台"stage".

"Your roof is left incomplete, pal," 合 says to 台. "You can't go on stage like that."

"Don't make a fuss about it, dude," grins the other. "I am a stage myself."

Note: The top of 合 resembles a roof while the radical 厶 in 台 resembles an incomplete roof.

第四章　人兽之间

Chapter 4　Man and Beast

人畜有别

出场角色：牛（niú）；生（shēng）。

牛对生说："兄弟，那地毯是给人类预备的，不适合咱们畜生踩。"

Worlds Apart

Characters : 牛"ox"; 生"life".

"Pal, that carpet is not for us animals but for men to tread on," says 牛 to 生.

Note: 生 is composed of 牛 with a horizontal line at the bottom resembling a carpet.

难得一见

出场角色：乒（pīng）；乓（pāng）。

在一次老兵聚会上，乒见到了乓。

乒对乓说："我追随诸葛亮北伐时丢了右腿。"

乓对乒说："我是在缅甸跟日本人打仗时掉了左腿。"

乒对乓说："咱俩能见上面全托本书作者马先生的福啊！"

A Chance Meeting

Characters: 乒"crack"; 乓"crash".

At a gathering of veterans, 乒 comes across 乓.

"I lost my right leg when following Chancellor Zhuge Liang on the northern expedition," says the former.

"I lost my left leg when fighting the Japanese invaders in Burma," says the latter.

"Thanks to Mr. Ma, author of this book, we get to meet each other," adds 乒.

Note: 乒 is composed of 丘 with a left-falling stroke at the left bottom resembling a left leg and 乓 with dot stroke at the right bottom resembling a right leg.

咏夜壶

出场角色：壶（hú）。幕后角色：湖（hú）。

某公对自己的夜壶珍爱无比。

一日，他喃喃自语道："晴湖不如雨湖，雨湖不如雾湖，雾湖不如雪湖，雪湖不如夜壶。"

注释：汉语中的咏湖谚语是"晴湖不如雨湖，雨湖不如雾湖，雾湖不如雪湖，雪湖不如夜湖"，最后的"夜湖"恰与本文中的"夜壶"同音。夜壶，过去中国男人在冬天夜晚接小便的器具。

Ode to the Chamber Pot

Onstage Character: 壶"pot". Offstage Character: 湖"lake".

A man saw his chamber pot as the apple of his eye. One day, he muttered to himself, "A clear lake is not as good as a rainy lake, a rainy lake is not as good as a foggy lake, a foggy lake is not as good as a snowy lake, and a snowy lake is not as good as a chamber pot."

Note: The Chinese proverb for praising lakes is "A clear lake is not as good as a rainy lake, a rainy lake is not as good as a foggy lake, a foggy lake is not as good as a snowy lake, and a snowy lake is not as good as a night lake", and the final "a night lake" has the same speech sound as "a chamber pot" which was a container used in the past by Chinese men to collect urine on winter nights.

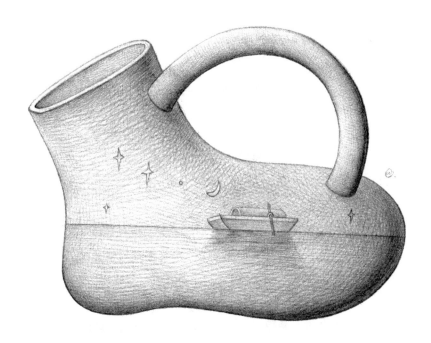

人兽有别

出场角色: 中 (zhōng) ; 衷 (zhōng) 。

中对衷说: "兄弟不参加天体运动,改穿衣裳啦?"

衷笑道: "我寻思着,人若是一丝不挂,与畜生何异呀!"

Man or Beast

Characters: 中"middle"; 衷"heart".

中 says to 衷, "You've quit the nudism movement and started wearing clothes?"

"I was just wondering how one would tell himself from a beast without a stitch on," replies 衷 with a smirk.

Note: 衷 is structured like 中 in the middle of 衣"clothes".

修蹄师与马

出场角色：蹄（tí）。幕后角色：题（tí）。

修蹄师："过来，你该钉掌了。"

马："谢谢师傅。"

修蹄师："注意……坏了……"

马："哎呀，我好疼啊！"

修蹄师："对不起，我刚才走神了，把马掌钉到你屁股上了。"

马："师傅，你可真是'离蹄万里'呀！"

注释：本文中的"离蹄万里"是成语"离题万里"的戏仿。

A Farrier and a Horse

Onstage Character: 蹄"hoof". Offstage Character: 题"topic".

Farrier: "Come over here. It's time for you to get shod."

Horse: "Thank you, sir."

Farrier: "Be careful. Oops!"

Horse: "Ouch! That hurts like hell!"

Farrier: "Sorry. I just got distracted and nailed the shoe to your buttock."

Horse: "You are a thousand miles away from the hoof!"

Note: "A thousand miles away from the hoof" is a parody of the idiom "a thousand miles away from the topic" implying an article or speech strays wildly off the subject. "Hoof"in Chinese has the same phonetic sound as "topic".

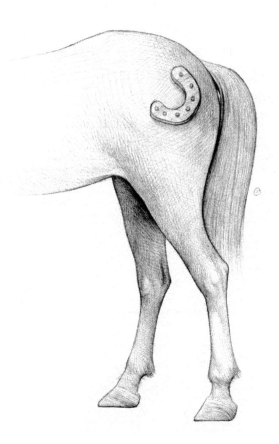

人兽之间

出场角色：闪（shǎn）；闯（chuǎng）。

闪问闯："朋友，为啥我在困难面前总是躲躲闪闪，你却能知难而上呢？"

闯看了一眼闪，笑道："因为你肚子里是瞻前顾后的人，我肚子里是不懂人情世故的马呀！"

Man and Beast

Characters: 闪"dodge"; 闯"rush".

闪 asks 闯, "Hey, buddy. Why is it that I always shrink back from difficulties, while you face them head on?"

With a glance at the other, 闯 chuckles and replies, "Because inside you is a man with cold feet but inside me is a horse ignorant of the way of the world."

Note: 闪 is composed 门 with 人"person" enclosed; 闯 is composed of 门 with 马"horse" enclosed.

跳蚤的尊严

出场角色：叉（chā）；蚤（zǎo）。

叉对蚤："兄弟，你身上长虫子了吧！"

蚤怒道："讽刺我不是？我就是虫子啊！"

The Dignity of a Flea

Characters: 叉"fork"; 蚤"flea".

"Hey, bro. I must point out there's a bug on you." says 叉 to 蚤.

"Are you attempting to mock me?" replies 蚤, irritated. "I am an insect myself."

Note: 蚤 is structured top to bottom with 叉 and 虫"bug".

猪与主人

出场角色：稀（xī）。

主人："开饭了，开饭了。"

猪："又是稀泔水。主人，你能不能往里面多加点内容呀！"

主人："你懂什么！有句谚语说得好，'物以稀为贵'。我看你是身在福中不知福！"

A Pig and His Master

Onstage Character: 稀"thin/rare".

Master: "Dinner is ready. Time for meal."

Pig: "Oh, Master! Thin swill again! Why don't you add something solid?"

Master: "How ignorant you are! As the saying goes, 'Something rare makes treasure.' You are in the midst of good fortune but not aware of it!"

Note: With "rare" and "thin" being the two different definitions of one same Chinese character, the master misinterpreted the proverb

"Something rare makes treasure" to fool the pig.

猴子取经

出场角色：笑（xiào）。幕后角色：孝（xiào）。

老虎大王见到很多到大森林踏青的人类旅游者以后，深感人类举止文雅，待人和气，完全不像森林里的野兽横冲直撞、蛮不讲理。

老虎想知道人类为什么如此善良，于是他派猴子悄悄潜到人类社会看个究竟。

猴子走了数月，终于风尘仆仆地回来了。

"快跟朕说说人类的真经。"老虎迫不可待地问。

猴子一字未说，只是哈哈大笑。

狐狸、野牛也上前向猴子打探人类的奇闻异事。无论谁问，猴子只是大笑不止。

"莫非猴爱卿疯了？"老虎和诸位大臣大惑不解。

"陛下，臣取回真经了。"猴子收住笑容，向老虎汇报他在人类社会的所见所闻。

"百善笑为先'。这就是他们亲口告诉我的真经啊！"猴子说完，又哈哈大笑起来。

注释：本文中的"百善笑为先"是汉语谚语"百善孝为先"的戏仿。

A Monkey's Mission

Onstage Character: 笑" laugh". Offstage Character: 孝"filial piety". Having witnessed many human tourists on their excursions in the woodland, King Tiger was deeply impressed with their elegant manners and courteous behaviour, entirely different from the violent and savage beats living in the forest.

Wondering what made human beings so virtuous, King Tiger sent Minister Monkey to sneak into the human society to uncover the truth. Months later, the monkey came back to the forest, dusty and exhausted. "Just tell me what their secret is," urged the tiger, too impatient to wait. Yet the monkey uttered no word. Instead, he burst out laughing. Then came Minister Fox, Minister Buffalo and others one after another, inquiring what anecdotes about humans he had to tell. Whoever asked, the monkey just responded with his chuckling.

"Is he out of his mind?" wondered King Tiger and the ministers.

"Mission accomplished, Your Majesty!" finally the monkey stopped laughing and reported what he had seen and heard in the human community.

"Laughter comes first of all virtues. That's the secret!" the monkey summed up and exploded with laughter once again.

Note: "Laughter comes first of all virtues" is a parody of the Chinese proverb "Filial piety comes first of all virtues" meaning that of all the benefactions in the human world, to support and respect one's aged parents is of utmost importance. In Chinese, "laughter" and "filial piety" are homophones.

老夫妻和他们的猪

出场角色：聋（lóng）；猪（zhū）。幕后角色：龙（lóng）；珠（zhū）。

有一对老夫妻养了一头猪。一天，猪吃完老夫妻给他的早饭以后，感觉肚子还是很空。

猪对男主人说："先生，再给我点豆渣吧！"

"什么，你要吃豆花？我们俩哪有钱买这么贵的东西给你吃啊！"有点儿耳背的老头朝猪吼道。

无奈的猪把头转向老太太："夫人，那给我点泔水总可以了吧！"

"什么，你要吃甘薯？"老太太的耳朵比老头还聋，"我们家没有甘薯啊！"

猪饿得浑身无力，叹气道："你们这是在二聋戏猪啊！"

注释：本文中的"二聋戏猪"是成语"二龙戏珠"的戏仿。二者语音相同。

An Old Couple and Their Pig

Onstage Characters: 聋"deaf"; 猪"pig". Offstage Characters: 龙"dragon"; 珠"pearl".

There was once an old couple who raised a pig. One day, having had breakfast, the pig still felt his stomach empty, so he asked his master, "Sir, give me some more bean dregs, please!"

"What? You want some bean jelly? How can we ever afford anything so extravagant for you?" yelled back the old man, somewhat hard of hearing.

At his wit's end, the pig turned to the old woman, "Madam, is it okay for me to have some slops?"

"What? You want some sweet potatoes?" responded the lady, more earless than her husband. "But we don't have any!"

Weak with hunger, the pig sighed, "You two deaf souls are playing with a pig!"

Note: "Two deaf souls are playing with a pig" is a parody of the Chinese idiom "Two dragons are playing with a pearl". The parody and the original are phonetically identical in Mandarin. Additionally, in Chinese "bean dregs" and "bean jelly" sound roughly similar, and so do "slops" and "sweet potatoes".

偷吃羊的狼

出场角色：狼（láng）。幕后角色：郎（láng）。

一条即将饿死的小狼为一个牧人所收养。牧人每天喂他肉和奶，还给他治好了身上的伤。

小狼渐渐长大了。他不但不思报答牧人的救命之恩，反而趁牧人不注意，偷吃了好几只小羊。

狼的行径终于为牧人所发现。牧人将他吊死了。

"皇天不佑负心狼啊！"临刑前，牧人对狼说道。

注释：本文中的"皇天不佑负心狼"是谚语"皇天不佑负心郎"的戏仿。

A Wolf Stealing Sheep

Onstage Character: 狼"wolf". Offstage Character: 郎"man".

A shepherd rescued a starving wolf cub, fed him meat and milk every day and healed his wounds.

As he grew up, the wolf never thought of anything to repay his benefactor, but instead ate some of the lambs behind the shepherd. Finally, the shepherd discovered the truth and hanged the wolf.

"Heaven condemns a treacherous wolf," the shepherd said to the wolf before his execution.

Note: "Heaven condemns a treacherous wolf" is a parody of the Chinese proverb "Heaven condemns a treacherous man" which means the heavens will not bless a faithless man. The proverb and its imitation have the same speech sound in Mandarin Chinese.

小斑马找朋友

出场角色：道（dào）。

小斑马想和银环蛇交朋友。斑马爸爸知道以后，告诉儿子说："你们不适合做朋友。'道不同不相为谋'，你们俩身上的道道相差太大了。"

A Young Zebra Looking for Friends

Onstage Character: 道"course/stripe".

A little zebra hoped to befriend a coral snake.

"Different courses make strangers," Father Zebra cautioned his son after hearing about his idea. "His body stripes being a far cry from yours, you two are not suitable to be friends."

Note: As "course" and "stripe" are the two definitions of one same character with a dozen meanings, the old zebra misinterpreted the maxim "Different courses make strangers" which means those who have different values and principles cannot work together to make plans for a venture.

前后有别

出场角色：巴（bā）。

巴氏兄弟上台各自介绍了自己。

巴老大："各位好，敝人姓巴，结巴的巴。"

巴老二："各位好，鄙人也姓巴，巴结的巴。"

The First and the Second

Character: 巴 "a Chinese surname".

The 巴 brothers step onto the stage and introduce themselves. The elder one says, "Greetings, everyone. My name is 巴, pronounced like 'stutter'." The younger one follows suit, saying, "Hello, all. My name is also 巴, pronounced like 'flatter'."

Note: "Flatter" and "stammer" are two-word phrases in Chinese, both of which contain the Chinese character "巴".

失望的狗

出场角色：古（gǔ）；　骨（gǔ）。

狗遇见了古。

"先生贵姓。"狗张着大嘴问。

"敝姓古。"古彬彬有礼道。

"啊，是骨头的骨吧，我就喜欢啃骨头。"狗汪汪大笑道，露出满嘴的犬牙。

"别别，我是古代的古，身上没多少肉。您就别啃了。"古连连后退，生怕狗扑上来咬自己一口。

"啊，原来是作古的古！"狗失望地叹了口气，转身走了。

A Disappointed Dog

Characters: 古"ancient"; 骨"bone".

A dog runs into 古.

"May I have your name, sir?" asks the dog with his mouth wide open.

"My name is Gu," replies 古 politely.

"Ahh, you must be the bone Gu. I love gnawing on bones," the dog laughs, revealing his sharp teeth.

"No, no, I am the ancient Gu. There isn't much flesh on me. Please don't gnaw on me," 古 keeps stepping back in fear that the dog might leap and bite him.

"Ah, it turns out that you are someone who has passed away," the dog sighs with disappointment, turns around and walks away.

Note: 古 and 骨 are homophones.

无巧不成话

出场角色：地（dì）；天（tiān）；二（èr）。

地和天是多年的朋友。一天，地去拜访天，不巧天出门了。地在返家的路上看见了二，惊呼道："天啊，你丢人了？"

二觉得地太不礼貌了，反唇相讥道："你我素不相识，你凭什么说我丢人了呢？"

地使劲用手揉了揉眼睛，这才知道他认错了人，赶快向二道了歉。

An Old Friend or a Perfect Stranger

Characters: 地"earth"; 天"heaven"; 二"two".

One day 地 comes to call on his old friend 天, but 天 happens to be out.

On his way back home, 地 runs across 二.

"Heaven! You've lost the man!" 地 exclaims in astonishment.

"Why do you say that?" 二 answers back, thinking the other downright rude. "I don't believe we've met before."

Rubbing his eyes hard, 地 realizes he has got the wrong person and makes an apology immediately.

Note: 天 consists of 二 and 人"man" in composition; the Chinese expression "lose man" means "lose face".

天上下了一群鱼

出场角色：货（huò）。幕后角色：祸（huò）。

老猫正带着妻子和孩子觅食，突然天色大变，转眼间狂风大作。他们正在寻找避雨的地方，一群鱼居然从天而降。

"这真是货从天降啊！"老猫和几个孩子兴高采烈地喊道。

注释：本文中的"货从天降"是成语"祸从天降"的戏仿。

Fish Falling from Heaven

Onstage Character: 货"goods". Offstage Character: 祸"calamity".
An old cat was out with his family searching for food when suddenly the sky darkened and a fierce gale began to blow.
As they were looking for shelter from the rain, much to their surprise, a school of fish dropped from the sky.
"Goods falling from Heaven!" cheered the cat and his children.

Note: "Goods falling from Heaven" is a parody of the Chinese idiom "Calamity falling from Heaven" which means a disaster strikes unexpectedly. The parody and the original idiom sound the same in Chinese.

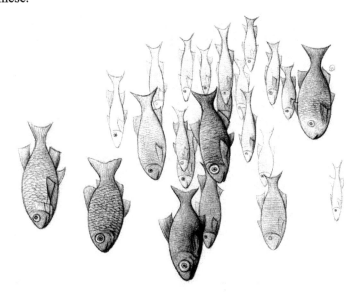

半斤八两

出场角色：呈（chéng）；啻（chì）。
呈对啻说："兄弟，我是王上有嘴！"
啻笑道："太巧了，我是帝下有口！"

注释：啻，但、只、仅的书面语。

Six and Two Threes

Characters: 呈"submit"; 啻"only".
"Hey, buddy. I am a king with a mouth at the top," 呈 says 啻.
"What a coincidence!" smiles the other. "I'm an emperor with a mouth at the bottom."

Note: 呈 is structured top to bottom with 口"mouth" and 王"king"; 啻 is composed top to bottom of 帝"emperor" and 口"mouth".

猴子与松树

出场角色：钉（dīng）。幕后角色：丁（dīng）。
猴子看到一个旅行者手里拿着一颗钉子。他觉得很好玩，于是问旅行者有关钉子的知识。
旅行者一五一十地告诉猴子有关钉子的名称和作用，而且把它送给了猴子。
猴子兴高采烈地拿着钉子向松树炫耀。
"这是什么？"松树不解地问。

"没想到你如此老迈年纪，居然也是目不识钉啊！"猴子大失所望道。

注释：本文中的"目不识钉"是成语"目不识丁"的戏仿。

A Monkey and a Pine Tree

Onstage Character: 钉"nail". Offstage Character: 丁"fourth".

A monkey, noticing a tourist holding a nail, found it interesting and asked about its knowledge.

The sightseer then told the monkey everything about the nail, including its name, usage, and so on, and finally gave it to the monkey.

Delighted, the monkey showed off the nail to a pine tree.

"What's it?" the tree asked in confusion.

"I can't believe you such an oldie don't know a nail!" exclaimed the monkey, greatly disappointed.

Note: "Not knowing a nail" is a parody of the Chinese idiom "not knowing a fourth" which refers to illiteracy or ignorance, as "fourth" is one of the simplest Chinese characters with a few strokes. The send-up and the idiom are phonetically identical in Mandarin.

实至名归

出场角色：毳（cuì）。

在一次朋友聚会上，主人让毳介绍一下自己。

毳自我介绍说："我的自传《三毛流浪记》有人看过吗？"

注释：毳，鸟兽的细毛。

A Name Fitting Well

Character: 毳"fine hair".

At a party, 毳 is asked to introduce himself.

"Has anyone here read the book The Adventures of San Mao?" he says. "Well, that's my autobiography."

Note: 毳 is structured with one 毛"hair" at the top and two others at the bottom, representing "three hairs"; the Chinese "San Mao" literally means "three hairs".

伯仲之间

出场角色：邓（dèng）；取（qǔ）。

邓望着取好大一会儿，突然对取大笑道："我是又在左，耳在右。"

取笑着接茬儿说："我是耳在左，又在右。"

Nip and Tuck

Characters: 邓"a surname"; 取"obtain".

Staring at 取 for quite a while, 邓 bursts out laughing and says, "I have 又 on the left and 耳 on the right."

"But I have 耳 on the left and 又 on the right," adds the other with a smile.

Note: 邓 is composed of 又 on the left and a semantic radical 阝"ear" on the right; 取 is composed of 耳 "ear" on the left and 又 on the right.

臭不可闻

出场角色：殿（diàn）；臀（tún）。

殿呆呆地仰视着臀，无比羡慕地说："我这兄弟都跑月亮上头了，真有高度呀！"

臀叹着气道："我有什么高度啊。整天被裤子捂着，还不时被臭气熏上两下。"

Stinking to High Heaven

Characters: 殿"temple"; 臀"hip".

Looking up at 臀, 殿 says in deep admiration, "Wow, buddy! You reach a great height standing on the moon."

"What a height!" 臀 sighs. "I'm wrapped in the pants all day long and suffocated by the odour from time to time."

Note: 臀 is structured top to bottom with 殿 and 月"moon".

倒霉的狐狸

出场角色：盗（dào）。幕后角色：道（dào）。

狐狸发现一个鸡场。他听见里面公鸡母鸡叽叽咕咕的说话声，顿时口水流了出来。

细心的狐狸仔细侦查着鸡场周围的情况。

一连三天，狐狸都没有发现警犬。

"这个养鸡人太粗心了。今晚我要大展身手了。"狐狸得意地笑了。

令狐狸没有想到的是，他刚刚趁着夜色溜进鸡场的大门，就被一条黄狗捉住了。

"我观察了好几天，怎么一直没发现你呀？"狐狸垂头丧气地问。

"天下有盗则见，无盗则隐。没有小偷，我自然不会出现了。"黄狗笑嘻嘻地答道。

注释：本文中的"天下有盗则见，无盗则隐"是格言"天下有道则见，无道则隐"的戏仿。

An Unlucky Fox

Onstage Character: 盗"theft". Offstage Character: 道"harmony".

A fox found a chicken farm and his mouth began watering as soon as he heard the clucks and crows inside.

The fox was so cautious that he made a thorough check around the farm. For three consecutive days, he had seen no trace of a guard dog.

"What a careless owner!" laughed the fox complacently. "I'm going to show off my skills tonight."

Much to his surprise, no sooner had the fox sneaked into the gate in the dark than he got caught by a yellow dog.

"Having observed for days, how come I never saw you?" asked the fox in depression.

"One is to show when there is theft and hide when there is peace. With no intruder around, I just cover myself," chuckled the dog.

Note: "One is to show when there is theft and hide when there is peace" is a parody of the Chinese maxim "One is to show when there is harmony and hide when there is corruption" which means that one should display his talents when the political system aligns with natural order and live in seclusion when it is decadent. The send-up and its original have the same speech sound in Mandarin.

闻鸡起舞

出场和幕后角色：闻（wén）。

老虎羡慕人类的武术，于是高薪请来一位师傅教他功夫。

师傅十八般武艺样样精通，打起拳来如行云流水，舞起枪来似银蛇翻滚，看得老虎眼花缭乱。

"师傅，你是怎么练就这一身硬功夫的？"老虎谦虚地求教。

"没什么秘诀。我不过是闻鸡起舞罢了。"师傅平静地答道。

"看来学成武艺也不是什么难事。"老虎一边喃喃自语，一边吩咐狐狸端上一盘熏鸡，用鼻子闻了几下，然后便手舞足蹈起来。

师傅看到老虎的怪样子，不禁大笑起来。

"闻鸡起舞不是用鼻子闻熏鸡，而是用耳朵听到活鸡打鸣以后马上起床练习武功。"师傅对老虎说道。

Practice at the Crow of the Rooster

Onstage and Offstage Character: 闻"smell/hear".

A tiger admired human martial arts and hired a master to teach him kung fu with a high salary.

The tutor dazzled the tiger with his complete mastery of martial arts, demonstrating his punching skills like scudding clouds and running rivers, and his spearing skills like a rolling silver snake.

"How did you make it, sir?" asked the tiger humbly.

"It's no secret. Hearing the rooster I rise to practice," replied the master calmly.

"Sounds like easy work," muttered the tiger to himself as he ordered a fox to bring a plate of smoked chicken and took a sniff at it, and then started to dance around.

Seeing his odd behaviour, the master couldn't help laughing out loud.

"Hearing the rooster doesn't mean smelling smoked chicken with the nose, but picking up the crow with the ears, and to practice is not to dance, but to sharpen the skills," said the master to the tiger.

Note: The Chinese idiom "Hearing the rooster one rises to practice" was misunderstood by the tiger as "Smelling the chicken one rises to dance". "practice" and "dance" sound the same and it should be specially noted that "hear" and "smell" are the two definitions of one Chinese character.

爱干净的猫

出场角色：洁（jié）。幕后角色：节（jié）。

猪请猫到他家里做客。

猫进了猪圈以后，主人热情地端来一碗泔水请猫品尝。

猫看见泔水上漂着两片烂菜叶，味道臭不可闻，赶快从猪圈里逃之夭夭。

猫自言自语道："饿死事小，失洁事大呀。"

注释：本文中的"饿死事小，失洁事大"是成语"饿死事小，失节事大"的戏仿。

A Cat's Hygiene

Onstage Character: 洁"hygiene". Offstage Character: 节"chastity".

A pig invited a cat as an honoured guest to his house.

At the pigsty, the host entertained his guest warmly with a bowl of slop.

At the sight of two rotten leaves floating on the stinky swill, the cat took to his heels.

"Better starve to death than lose hygiene," said the cat to himself.

Note: "Better starve to death than lose hygiene" is a parody of the Chinese proverb "Better starve to death than lose chastity" which is an old idea that it is a minor matter for a widow to die of hunger in poverty but a major disgrace to lose her chastity if remarried. The proverb and its imitation sound exactly the same in Mandarin.

破戒

出场角色: 酒 (jiǔ)。幕后角色: 韭 (jiǔ)。

中秋之夜,和尚释空悄悄拿出他从山下偷买的一瓶酒。

"老话说,'八月酒,佛开口'。"释空嘟囔道,"既然佛都要为美酒破戒,何况我这个小和尚呢!"说罢,他打开酒瓶,痛饮起来。

注释: 本文中的"八月酒,佛开口"是谚语"八月韭,佛开口"的戏仿。

Breaking a Precept

Onstage Character: 酒"liquor". Offstage Character: 韭"leek".

One Mid-Autumn night, monk Shi Kong quietly take out a bottle of liquor he had secretly bought down the mountain.

"As the old saying goes, 'Tempted by August liquor, Buddha would break a precept,' " muttered Shi Kong to himself. "Even Buddha couldn't resist the temptation of good liquor, let alone me a monk." Then he opened the bottle of liquor and began to drink it to his heart's content.

Note: "Tempted by August liquor, Buddha would break a precept" is a parody of the Chinese proverb "Tempted by August leeks, Buddha would break a precept" which means the chive in August has such a mellow flavour and exquisite fragrance that even Buddha, who has transcended the Three Realms and the Five Elements, would be lured to have a taste of it. "leek" and "liquor" are homophones in Chinese.

老虎与狐狸

出场角色：衣（yī）。幕后角色：医（yī）。

老虎："狐爱卿，朕今天要出席加冕典礼，你说朕穿哪件礼服合适啊？"

狐狸："大王，古人云，'荐贤不荐衣'。我不便给出我的建议啊。"

注释：本文中的"荐贤不荐衣"是谚语"荐贤不荐医"的戏仿。

King Tiger and Minister Fox

Onstage Character: 衣"clothe". Offstage Character: 医"doctor".

King Tiger: "Dear Minister Fox, which robe do you think I should wear for the coronation ceremony today?"

Minister Fox: "Your Majesty, as the old saying goes, 'Suggest persons of virtue rather than clothes.' So I regret that I cannot give any advice on this matter."

Note: "Suggest persons of virtue rather than clothes" is a parody of the Chinese proverb "Suggest persons of virtue rather than doctors" which means helping introduce someone virtuous is preferable to recommending a medical person. Since the doctor's job is of vital importance, a rash recommendation is liable to invite trouble. In Chinese, "clothes" and "doctors" are phonetically identical.

灾星到了

出场角色：火（huǒ）；灾（zāi）。

冬天来了，火先生觉得头有点冷，于是他走进一家老朋友开的帽店，看看有没有合适的帽子。

"火兄戴帽，灾星高照。"帽店老板一边递给火先生一顶呢子帽，一边跟他开着玩笑。

A Baleful Star

Characters: 火"fire"; 灾"disaster".

Feeling the chill of winter on his head, 火 steps into a hat shop run by an old friend for a right fit.

"A cap on fire makes a baleful star," jokes the shop-owner as he hands 火 a felt hat.

Note: 火 joined by a radical 宀 on top forms the character 灾 "disaster".

自视甚高

出场角色：猴（hóu）；个（gè）。

猴与个是无话不谈的好友。

个问猴："你看我这样子，像不像一棵参天大树啊？"

猴瞄了一眼个,哈哈大笑道:"你见过跟猴子一般高的参天大树吗？"

A Towering Tree

Characters: 猴"monkey"; 个"individual".

猴 and 个 are good buddies who always talk straight to each other.

One day 个 asks 猴, "Do I look like a towering tree?"

Throwing the other a brief glance, 猴 laughs, "Is there a towering tree at a monkey's height?"

Note: 个 resembles a tree.

挂冠而去要不得

出场角色：家（jiā）；豕（shǐ）。

家对豕说："兄弟，没事别轻易摘帽子。"

豕苦笑道："我何尝不想戴帽子，可我这个畜生不配呀！"

A Hatless Wanderer

Characters: 家"house"; 豕"pig".

"Hey, pal," says 家 to 豕. "Don't take off your cap as you please."

"How I wish to have on a hat!" responds 豕 with a bitter smile. "But a beast is not worthy."

Note: 家 is composed of 豕 with a radical 宀 on top representing a hat.

偷菜的兔子

出场角色：哭（kū）。幕后角色：窟（kū）。

兔子因为偷菜又被菜农捉住了。

兔子大哭道："先生，放了我吧。我一家老小还等着我拿回食物呢！我以后再也不会偷你的菜了。"

"你这是第三次偷菜，第三次被捉，第三次向我哭诉求情了吧！好你个狡兔三哭啊。我这次不会饶恕你了。"菜农愤怒地答道。

注释：本文中的"狡兔三哭"是成语"狡兔三窟"的戏仿。

A Rabbit Stealing Vegetables

Onstage Character: 哭"cry". Offstage Character: 窟"burrow".

A rabbit was caught stealing vegetables by a farmer.

"Forgive me, sir! I have a large family to feed. I promise I will not come to steal again," the rabbit cried and said.

"This is the third time you've stolen my vegetables, got caught and cried begging for mercy! 'A sly rabbit has three cries.' Never will I spare you for one more time!" declared the farmer crossly.

Note: "A sly rabbit has three cries" is a parody of the Chinese idiom "A sly rabbit has three burrows" which implies a person has many places to hide or different ways to avoid a crisis. The spoof and the original have the same speech sound in Mandarin.

后悔莫及

出场角色：犬（quǎn）：太（tài）。

犬问太："兄弟，你肩膀上的瘤子呢，割啦？"

太得意地说："我嫌长在肩膀上不雅观，让医生把它移植到裆部了。"

犬大惑不解道："你既然做了手术，直接割了不就完了吗？"

太结结巴巴地说："是啊，我怎么没想到这一点呢？"

Too Late to Repent

Characters: 犬"dog"; 太"too".

"Where's the tumor on your shoulder, chum? " 犬 asks 太. "Removed?"

"It looked inelegant up there, so I got it transplanted to my thigh," replies the other complacently.

"Now that you had surgery, you should have had it cut off once for all, shouldn't you?" says 犬, extremely puzzled.

"Yes," 太 stutters. "Why didn't I think of that?"

Note: The dot stroke in 太 represents a tumor on the thigh.

老虎出征

出场角色：背（bèi, bēi）。

老虎即将带兵出征狮国，欲与狮王决一死战。

老虎问计于狐狸，此战如何获胜。

"我方将士的武艺和装备与敌方相比没有任何优势。大王只有令全军将士背水一战，才能获胜。"狐狸献计道。

老虎点头称是，遂令全军每位士兵各背大桶一个，里面必须盛满了水。

累得苦不堪言的士兵刚刚遇到狮王率领的大军就败下阵来。

注释：本文中的"背水一战"是成语，典故出自汉将军韩信率军攻赵，穿出井陉口，命令将士背靠大河摆开阵势，与敌人交战。韩信以前临大敌，后无退路的处境来坚定将士拼死求胜的决心，结果大破赵军。由于汉语中的"背"还有"背负"之意，所以老虎误解了狐狸的计策。前后两个"背"字音调不同。

King Tiger Going to War

Onstage Character: 背"back/carry".

King Tiger was planning to lead his troops to the Lion Kingdom, determined to fight King Lion to the death.

King Tiger asked Minister Fox for tactics to win the campaign.

"In terms of martial arts and equipment, we have no edge over our enemy. Your Majesty, only by ordering all the commanders and soldiers to fight with their backs against the water can we win," suggested Minister Fox.

King Tiger agreed and ordered every soldier to carry a large bucket filled with water on his back.

As can be imagined, the exhausted soldiers were defeated as soon as they encountered King Lion's army in battle.

Note: "Fighting with back against water" is a Chinese idiom originated from the Han general Han Xin's strategy to attack Zhao Kingdom. Marching out of the Jingxing Pass, he ordered his warriors to lay up in battle array with their backs against a river to fight the enemy. In a dire situation with no way out, Han Xin's strategy inspired his soldiers to battle to the bitter end, resulting in a great victory over the enemy. "Fighting with back against water" metaphorically means fighting to the death when one is in a desperate situation. In this story, King Tiger misunderstood Minister Fox's advice as "carrying water on the back" due to the homophonic character "背 (bèi, bēi) ", which can mean "back" or "carry on one's back".

养鸡还是养鸭?

出场角色: 鸡 (jī) 。幕后角色: 饥 (jī) 。

老虎想养些禽类以供食用。

"鸡和鸭哪个好养?"老虎问狐狸。

"当然是鸡好养。狐狸毫不犹豫地答道,"因为鸡不择食嘛。"

注释: 本文中的"鸡不择食"是成语"饥不择食"的戏仿。

Chickens or Ducks?

Onstage Character: 鸡"chicken". Offstage Character: 饥"hunger".
A tiger was planning to rear some poultry for food.
"Which is easier to raise, a chicken or a duck?" he asked a fox.
"The former, of course," the fox replied without hesitation, "because chickens know no choice."

Note: "Chickens know no choice" is a parody of the Chinese idiom "Hunger knows no choice" which implies when one is hungry, he will eat any food put in front him without qualms, metaphorically meaning that someone in urgent need is in no position to make selections. In Mandarin the spoof and the original are phonetically identical.

爱狗人士

出场角色：伏（fú）。
伏照着镜子自语道："看了我的模样，就知道人狗情未了啊。"

A Dog Lover

Character: 伏"vanquish".
Looking in the mirror, 伏 mummers to his own reflection, "You remind me of the saying 'Man's best friend is his dog.' "

Note: 伏 is structured with a semantic radical 亻"man" on the left and 犬 "dog" on the right.

头上长草

出场角色：果（guǒ）；巢（cháo）。

果聚精会神地看着巢。

果困惑地问巢："兄弟，你头上咋有一团草啊？"

巢笑着答道："是喜鹊放的。它垒了个小高层。"

Hay on Top

Characters: 果"fruit"; 巢"nest".

Fixing his gaze on 巢, 果 asks in confusion, "How come you've got a ball of hay on top, chum?"

"A magpie put it there," replies the other with a smile. "He's built an attic."

Note: 巢 is composed of 果 with a radical 巛 on top resembling a ball of dry grass.

耐人寻味

出场角色：冀（jì）；粪（fèn）。

冀对粪说："我俩长的很像，可有人说闭上眼睛就能把咱俩分出来。"

粪坏笑着答道："是啊，我有味儿，你没味儿啊。"

A Heavy Adour

Characters: 冀"hope"; 粪"manure".

"You and me look like two peas in a pod," says 冀 to 糞. "But some people claim they can tell us apart with their eyes closed."

"Indeed," replies the other with a wicked grin. "I stink while you don't."

Note: 冀 and 糞 are graphically similar, both structured top to middle and bottom with three components only different in top.

空门里面人有声

出场角色：闪（shǎn）；门（mén）。

闪和门是老邻居了，两个性情幽默的人经常串门。

这不，闪老兄又来敲门老弟的门了。

"兄弟，你门里没人呀！"闪开着玩笑说。

"没人。"门知道闪在捉弄他。

"没人咋有声音?"闪一本正经地问。

门开了，两个老邻居彼此哈哈大笑。

A Voice in the Door

Characters: 闪"flash"; 门"door".

As long-time neighbours, the two witty guys 闪 and 门 frequently visit each other's homes. Now 闪 is knocking on the other's door.

"Hey, anybody in?" asks 闪 jokingly.

"Nobody," answers门, aware that his neighbour is pulling his leg.

"Then why is there a voice?" counters 闪, acting serious.

At this point, the door opens and they both burst out laughing.

Note: 闪 is composed of 人"person" enclosed by 门 (from left, top and right sides); compared with 闪, 门 has "nobody in".

不对称之美

出场角色：耶（yē）。

耶照着镜子，遗憾地说："为啥我的俩耳朵长得不一样帅呢？"

Beauty of Asymmetry

Character: 耶"yeah".

Looking at his reflection in the mirror, 耶 sighs with regret, "How come my ears are not equally pretty?"

Note: 耶 has 耳"ear" on the left and a semantic radical 阝"ear" on the right.

童言无忌

出场角色：乙（yǐ）；甲（jiǎ）。

乙站在湖边欣赏美景。

一对母子正好从此处路过。孩子看见了乙，大叫道："妈，一只大鹅。"

母亲笑道："这是乙叔叔，不是鹅。"

"甲太太，您这是带着公子出游啊！"乙向母子二人点头致意，"人家都说我长得像一只鹅呢！"

"原来您是乙叔叔啊！您长得像鹅挺好。我爸爸长得像一只苍蝇拍。恶心死了。"小孩子真是童言无忌。

"哈哈，"乙大笑道，"我可不敢这么说你爸，他是我们的甲大哥呀！"

Children Tell the Truth

Characters: 乙"second"; 甲"first".

乙 stands at a lake, admiring the spectacular view when a mother and her son happen to pass by.

"Look, Mom. A goose!" exclaims the boy.

"It's Uncle 乙, not a goose," smiles the woman.

"Hi, Mrs 甲. You are on an outing with your son!" 乙 greets them with a nod. "They all say I look like a goose."

"You turn out to be Uncle 乙," says the kid innocently. "Good for you to have the look of a goose, but it's disgusting of my dad to be the spitting image of a flyswatter."

"Hah-hah. I wouldn't dare talk about your father that way," laughs 乙. "After all, he is the Big Brother."

Note: 乙 resembles a goose and 甲"first" a flyswatter.

四只猴子

出场角色：申（shēn）；由（yóu）；甲（jiǎ）；电（diàn）。

在猴年新年联欢晚会上，申、由、甲和电一起登场了。

主持人告诉观众，今晚台上的四位演员都与"猴"沾亲带故。

"这位是申先生。"主持人把第一位演员介绍给观众。"十二生肖中的'猴'对应十二地支中的'申'，所以申先生是今晚当之无愧的猴子。"台下掌声雷动，申频频向观众点头致意。

"这位是由先生。"主持人微笑着面向由，"请你自己说说与猴的关系吧！"

"我是断尾猴。"由一边说，一边象征性地摸了摸自己的屁股。引得台下观众哄堂大笑。

主持人又让甲和电自我介绍。

"我是无头猴。"甲边说边把头往衣服里缩。台下又是笑声一片。

轮到电了。他用右手在身后做了一个向上翻卷的手势，大声道："鄙人是一只卷尾猴。"

台下的观众笑得前仰后合。

Four Monkeys

Characters: 申"ninth earthly branch"; 由"from"; 甲"first"; 电"electricity".

At the New Year Gala in the Year of the Monkey, 申, 由, 甲 and 电 take the stage as a group.

The host tells the audience that all the four are related to the monkey.

"This is Mr. 申," the host introduces the first one. " '申' in the Twelve Earthly Branches corresponds to the 'monkey' in the Chinese zodiac, so Mr. 申 well deserves to be the monkey of tonight." Thunderous applause breaks out and 申 nods to the audience over and over.

"This is Mr. 由," The host turns to 由 with a smile. "Please tell us your relationship with the monkey!"

"I'm a monkey without a tail," says 由, touching his butt symbolically. The audience erupts with laughter.

甲 and 电 are then asked to introduce themselves. "I am a monkey without a head," says 甲 as he retracts his head into his coat. The crowd bursts out laughing once again.

It's the turn for Mr. 电. Making a roll-up gesture behind his back with the right hand, 电 says in a loud voice, "I am a capuchin monkey!" The spectators are now rocking with laughter.

Note: Graphically 由 has no tail and 甲 has no head; the middle vertical stroke in 电 turns and hooks, with the turn and hook resembling a curly tail.

只弯一条腿

出场角色：只（zhī）；兄（xiōng）。

只见到了兄，对他打趣道："兄啊，我让你猜个谜语——只弯一条腿。打一字。"

兄低着头想了半天，突然他想出了答案。兄狠狠地打了只一拳："好啊你，敢开哥哥我的玩笑！"

只笑弯了腰。

A Bent Leg

Characters: 只"only"; 兄"elder brother".

只 sees 兄 and teases him, "I have a riddle for you to solve, bro. What's

311

the character for '只 with a bent leg'?"

兄 ponders a while and suddenly comes up with the answer.

"Alright, you dare to pull my leg!" says 兄 as he gives the other a punch.

只 doubles over with laughter.

Note: 只 has a radical 八 at the bottom resembling the legs; the stroke 乚 (vertical curved hook) in 兄 represents a bent leg.

东坡遇才女

出场角色：坡（pō）；土（tǔ）；皮（pí）。

苏东坡穿着皇帝赏赐的漂亮袍子在街上闲逛。一个女子拦住了他。

"姑娘有何见教啊？"苏东坡刚刚喝了不少酒，醉醺醺地问。

"坡公，人人都仰慕你的才华。但是小女子只爱坡公的一半。"姑娘笑盈盈地说。

苏东坡眨了眨眼道："'坡'的一半是'土'啊。莫非你爱上了苏某人身上的灰尘不成？"

"我爱的是另一半。"姑娘狡黠地说。

苏东坡哈哈大笑，毫不犹豫地把袍子脱下来送给了女子。

"'坡'的另一半是'皮'呀。能遇见如此聪明的女子，是我三生有幸啊！"

A Clever Encounter

Characters: 坡"slope"; 土 "soil"; 皮"skin".

In the fine robe awarded by the emperor, 坡 is strolling down the street when a girl stops him.

"What can I do for you, lass?" asks the man, tipsy from his heavy drink.

"I must admit, sir, while everyone admires you for your talent, I only adore half of you," says the girl with a radiant smile.

"Since half of 坡 is soil, can I take it that you love the dust on me?" responds the man, blinking his eyes.

"What I fancy is the other half," says the young lady cunningly.

"Oh, the other half of 坡 is skin," laughs the man as he takes off his robe and hands it to the girl. "It's a great honour to meet such a bright lady!"

Note: 坡 is structured left to right with the radical 土"soil" and 皮"skin"; 坡 (Su Dongpo) was a Chinese scholar-official, active as a poet and essayist in the Song Dynasty.

野猪访猴

出场角色：猴（hóu）。幕后角色：侯（hóu）。

一头野猪扛着一只独木舟吃力地走在路上。

"兄弟，你要下海呀？"豹子看见野猪气喘吁吁的样子，好奇地问。

"不下海。我去拜访猴哥。"野猪疲惫不堪地答道。

"猴子住在山上，你扛着船干什么？"

"我是头一次到猴哥家做客。我听说'猴门深似海'，没有船我怎么进去呀。所以我准备了一只小船啊。"

注释：本文中的"猴门深似海"是谚语"侯门深似海"的戏仿。

A Boar Visiting a Monkey

Onstage Character: 猴"monkey". Offstage Character: 侯"aristocrat".

A boar was labouring his way with a canoe on his back.

"Hey, pal. Are you going to the sea?" asked a leopard curiously when he saw the boar, who was gasping for breath.

"No. I'm going to visit Brother Monkey," replied the weary boar.

"But he lives on the mountain. What are you carrying the boat for?"

"This is my first visit to Brother Monkey. I heard 'A monkey's mansion is deep as the ocean'. Without a vessel, how could I get in? So I bring a boat with me," the boar explained.

Note: "A monkey's mansion is deep as the ocean" is a parody of the Chinese proverb "An aristocrat's mansion is deep as the ocean" which means a dignitary's residence has a large courtyard with the gate heavily guarded. "Monkey" and "aristocrat" are homophones in Chinese.

倒霉的骑手

出场角色：赛（sài）。幕后角色：塞（sài）。

比赛的前一天，有一个骑手把心爱的赛马丢了。他伤心得大哭起来。

"别难过了。"另外一个骑手安慰道，"你没听说过一个故事吗？赛翁失马，焉知非福。说不定从今往后你好运连连呢！"

注释：本文中的"赛翁失马，焉知非福"是成语"塞翁失马，焉知非福"的戏仿。

An Unfortunate Jockey

Onstage Character: 赛"race". Offstage Character: 塞"frontier".

A jockey broke down in sad tears, for his beloved horse was nowhere to be found with his race only one day away.

"Cheer up, pal," another rider comforted him. "Haven't you heard the story? The loss of a race man's horse turned out to be a blessing in disguise. Maybe good fortune will be with you in the days to come."

Note: "The loss of a race man's horse turned out to be a blessing in disguise" is a parody of the idiom "The loss of a frontiersman's horse turned out to be a blessing in disguise" which implies misfortune begets fortune, originating from a Chinese folk story about an old frontiersman whose favourite stallion escaped and after some time came back with several other steeds. The idiom and its imitation sound exactly the same, with the two characters "race" and "frontier" bearing a close resemblance in structure.

断腿狼的绝望

出场角色：羊（yáng）。幕后角色：洋（yáng）。

狼不慎摔断了一条腿。他疼得在草地上痛苦地打滚。

"兄弟，前面来了一群羊。咱们又有香喷喷的午餐了！"狼的一个伙伴兴奋地招呼着他。

"我哪还有力气追羊啊！"断腿狼绝望地呻吟道，"我只能望羊兴叹了。"

注释：本文中的"望羊兴叹"是汉语成语"望洋兴叹"的戏仿。

A Wounded Wolf in Despair

Onstage Character: 羊"sheep". Offstage Character: 洋"ocean".
A wolf accidentally broke one of his legs and was rolling with pain on the grass.

"Hey, buddy! Ahead of us comes a flock of sheep," another wolf called out to him excitedly. "We are going to have a delicious lunch again!"

"I am too weak to chase them," groaned the wounded wolf in despair. "I can only bemoan my inability before the sheep."

Note: "To bemoan one's inability before the sheep" is a parody of the idiom "to bemoan one's inability before the ocean" which means facing the vast ocean one laments his insignificance. "Sheep" and "ocean" are homophones in Mandarin.

直言为佳

出场角色：全（quán）；金（jīn）。

全钦佩地对金说："兄弟，我真佩服你关键时刻能为朋友两肋插刀。你的品格堪比金子。"

金哈哈大笑道："不用比喻了，我就是金子。"

Enough with Similes

Characters: 全"total"; 金"gold".
"Pal, I really admire the way you help a friend in need with each side of your chest pierced by a knife," says 全 to 金 with respect. "You have a

character like gold."

"Save the simile," responds the other with a hearty laugh. "I am gold myself."

Note: With two more dot strokes representing two knives, 金 differs from 全 in composition.

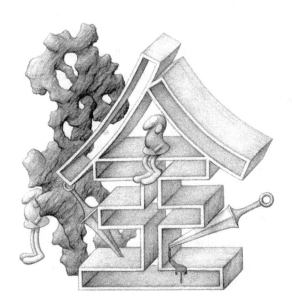

两只老鼠

出场角色：粮（liáng）。幕后角色：梁（liáng）。

夫："老婆，咱俩把家安在粮仓真是太英明了。"

妻："是啊，咱们再也不会吃了上顿没下顿了。"

夫："吃饱了喝足了，我突然想给自己起一个雅号。"

妻："什么雅号？"

夫："粮上君子。怎么样？"

妻："老公，真有你的。这个名字太有绅士派头了。"

注释：本文中的"粮上君子"是汉语成语"梁上君子"的戏仿。"梁上君子"代指小偷。

Two Rats

Onstage Character: 粮"grain". Offstage Character: 梁"beam".

He-rat: "Honey, it's really sensible of us to settle down here in the barn."

She-rat: "Indeed. We feel no more concern for meals."

He-rat: "With a full stomach, I hit upon a fancy nickname for myself."

She-rat: "What is it?"

He-rat: "A noble on the grain. What do you say?"

She-rat: "You never cease to amaze me, darling. It really has a gentlemanly feel."

Note: "A noble on the grain" is a parody of the idiom "a gentleman on the beam" referring to a burglar, originating from a Chinese folk tale. The two expressions have the same phonetic sound in Mandarin.

自卑的仙鹤

出场角色：机（jī）。幕后角色：鸡（jī）。

仙鹤常常感到很自卑。

心理咨询师乌龟建议仙鹤经常到人类的飞机场转转。

"人类常常说'鹤立机群'这个成语，"乌龟对仙鹤道，"他们说，一只仙鹤到了机群里就会有居高临下的感觉。"

仙鹤飞到附近的一座机场。

"我的天，这些家伙可真大呀！"望着比自己高大很多的飞机，仙鹤变得更自卑了。

注释：本文中的"鹤立机群"是汉语成语"鹤立鸡群"的戏仿。

A Crane with a Sense of Inferiority

Onstage Character: 机"plane". Offstage Character: 鸡"chicken".

A crane often felt inferior to others.

Psychiatrist Tortoise suggested that the bird should go on some tours around airports.

"Humans often use the idiom 'A crane stands amidst the planes'," said the tortoise to the feathered creature. "They say a crane would feel like a commander among the aircraft."

So the crane flew over to a nearby airport.

"Oh my!" exclaimed the bird, becoming more self-abased at the sight of the airbuses towering over him. "These guys are huge!"

Note: "A crane stands amidst the planes" is a parody of the Chinese idiom "A crane stands amidst the chickens" implying one's ability or appearance stands out in a crowd. As "plane" is a homophone of "chicken", the tortoise misinterpreted the idiom and gave a lousy piece of advice to the crane beset with a sense of inferiority.

狗大夫的诊断

出场角色：骨（gǔ）。幕后角色：古（gǔ）。

一匹饿狼一口气把一只羊吞进了肚子里。

狼感觉肚子有点疼，不禁呻吟起来。狼父赶忙把他送进了森林医院急诊室。

狗医生给狼做了B超检查。

"狗大夫，我到底怎么啦？"狼痛苦地问狗医生。

"食骨不化。"狗医生答道。

注释：本文中的"食骨不化"是成语"食古不化"的戏仿。

A Diagnosis from Doctor Dog

Onstage Character: 骨"bone". Offstage Character: 古"classics".
A wolf devoured a sheep in one gulp, and was groaning with a dull pain in the stomach. His father hurriedly brought him to the emergency room of the forest hospital.
"What is the matter with me, doc?" asked the patient in agony after Doctor Dog had given him a B-ultrasonic checkup.
"Indigestion caused by swallowing bones," came the reply.

Note: "Indigestion caused by swallowing bones" is a parody of the idiom "indigestion caused by swallowing classics" referring to the learning problem of not acquiring a deep or thorough understanding of the ancient masterpieces. The two expressions sound exactly the same in Mandarin.

长错了脑袋

出场角色：贝（bèi）；负（fù）。
贝与负是两小无猜的好朋友。

长大以后，贝与负进了同一家大公司。贝勤勤恳恳、任劳任怨，总是出色地完成上司交办的任务。他从一个办事员做起，最终成了该公司一个部门的经理。负做事总是毛手毛脚，还自以为很了不起，结果一事无成。

一次聚会上，负一直在唉声叹气。"为什么我的命这么不好啊！"

贝安慰负说："兄弟，谁让你长了个兔子脑袋呢！"

A Wrong Head

Characters: 贝"treasure"; 负"failure".

贝 and 负 go way back, growing up together and trusting each other.
Both employed in a big company, 贝 is such a diligent, obedient,
and efficient worker that he rises all the way from a junior clerk to a
department manager, while 负 is careless and conceited, and thus gets
nowhere. At a reunion, 负 sighs and groans, "Why is fate unkind to me?"
"It's your bunny head that is to blame, pal," says 贝 soothingly.

Note: 负 is composed of 贝 with a component ⺈ (top of 兔"rabbit") on top.

有一手不如没一手

出场角色：出（chū）；拙（zhuō）。

出遇见了陌生的拙。

出徘徊在拙的身边，久久不愿离开。

拙见出欲言又止，于是问道："先生，我能帮你做点什么吗？"

出不好意思地说："我只是好奇，你比我多一只手，怎么看上去那么笨呢？"

More Is Not Better

Characters: 出"appear"; 拙"clumsy".

Meeting 拙 for the first time, 出 wishes to have a word with him but hesitates, hanging around for quite a while until the other comes up breaking the ice.

"Sir, would you like me to give you a hand?" 拙 asks.

"No, thank you," replies 出, embarrassed. "I was just wondering why the hand makes you look so clumsy."

Note: 拙 is structured with a semantic radical 扌"hand" on the left and 出 on the right.

望图生义

出场角色: 春 (chūn) ; 夏 (xià) ; 秋 (qiū) ; 图 (tú) 。

北国雪飘。

冷得受不了的春、夏和秋组团出游，留下冬值班。

春、夏和秋在一个港口见到了图，大惊失色道: "冬弟，你咋被关在这儿啦? 我们解救你。"

三个人上去就扯，把图扯了个稀巴烂。

奄奄一息的图呻吟道: "我就是一张画，哪是你们说的什么'冬'啊!"

A Mere Picture

Characters: 春"spring"; 夏"summer"; 秋"autumn"; 图"picture".

In the snowy North, there live four brothers 春, 夏, 秋 and 冬, the elder three of whom suffer so badly from the cold that they set out on a journey, leaving 冬 behind on duty.

Then at a port, they are shocked to see 图. "Brother 冬, why are you locked up here?" they exclaim. "Let us free you."

In a flash all the three come up, tearing 图 into pieces.

"As a mere picture, how can I possibly be your brother!" moans the dying victim.

Note: 图 is composed of 冬"winter" fully enclosed by the radical 口.

狐狸与蚯蚓

出场角色：兵（bīng）。幕后角色：冰（bīng）。

蚯蚓看见狐狸朝着老虎的洞穴走去，于是上前问候。

"狐公何事如此匆忙？"蚯蚓问。

"大王要我带领一支军队北伐。我要面见君王听取教诲。"狐狸趾高气扬地说。

"何为军队呢？"蚯蚓又问。

狐狸看了看蚯蚓，叹了一口气道："还是古人说得好，夏虫不可语兵呀。"

注释：本文中的"夏虫不可语兵"是谚语"夏虫不可语冰"的戏仿。

A Fox and an Earthworm

Onstage Character: 兵"warrior". Offstage Character: 冰"ice".

An earthworm saw a fox heading for the tiger's cave and went up to greet him.

"Why are you in such a hurry, Mr. Fox?" asked the earthworm.

"The king has assigned me a mission to lead an army for the northern expedition," replied the fox holding his head high. "I'm going to meet His Majesty for instruction."

"What is an army?" the earthworm continued.

Casting a disdainful look at the earthworm, the fox sighed, "As the ancient saying goes, 'A summer worm has no sense of warriors.' "

Note: "A summer worm has no sense of warriors" is a parody of the Chinese proverb "A summer worm has no sense of ice" which means a worm that has never experienced winter cannot understand what ice is, indicating the limitation of one's knowledge and experience.

戒躁之法

出场角色：丁（dīng）；宁（níng）。

丁的同事宁性格平和，无论遇到什么急事，都能有条不紊地处理好。

丁却是坏脾气，像个爆竹，有点火就着。

为了改正自己的毛病，丁向宁请教如何控制自己的情绪。

宁指了指自己的头，笑道："头上有帽，不急不躁。"

A Hat on Top

Characters: 丁"fourth"; 宁"peace".

丁 has a short fuse, liable to blow up like a firecracker, while his colleague 宁 is good-tempered, always having his wits about him to bring order out of chaos.

Wishing to get out of the bad habit, 丁 comes to 宁 for advice on how to cope with his emotions.

"A hat on the dome keeps anxiety at home," smiles 宁, pointing at his own head.

Note: 宁 is composed of 丁 with a radical 宀 on top resembling a hat.

能拉扯的地平线

出场角色：旦（dàn）；旧（jiù）；申（shēn）。

旦见了旧，大为惊奇道："兄弟，你本事可太大了，能让地平线立起来。"

"我这不算什么。你看看申，不但能让地平线立起来，还能让它穿身而过呢！"旧笑着答道。

The Docile Horizon

Characters: 旦"dawn"; 旧"old"; 申"express".

旦 is most surprised to see 旧. "Buddy, you are really something!" he exclaims. "You've raised the horizon upright."

"It's no big deal," smiles 旧. "Look at 申, who not only erects the horizon but also has his body pierced through."

Note: 旦 is composed of 日"sun" with a horizontal stroke below resembling the horizon; 旧 is structured with a vertical stroke on the left and 申 a vertical line through the middle both representing the upright horizon in imagination.

盼望直航

出场角色：二（èr）；工（gōng）。

二对工说："兄弟，一看见你，我就知道两岸直航有盼头啦！"

Around the Corner

Characters: 二"two"; 工"work".

"Hey, buddy," 二 says to 工. "Seeing you, I come to realise the cross-strait direct transport is right around the corner."

Note: 工 is composed of two horizontal strokes or 二 connected in the middle by a top-down vertical line; 二 represents the shores of Taiwan and the mainland with the strait in between and the vertical line represents a cross-strait air route.

中西相撞

出场角色：工（gōng）；H。

工到英国旅游，见到大街上有个H，与自己长相相似，可是站相不对。

工忍了又忍，实在憋不住了，于是问H："兄弟，我猜你也是从中国来的。可你为啥出了国就歪着站呢？"

H看了看工，大笑道："朋友，我是拉丁字母H，是本地生、本地长的呀。我一生下来就是这么站着！"

East or West

Characters: 工"work"; H"a capital letter".

Travelling in Britain, 工 sees H on the street, who bears a striking resemblance to him but stands in a wrong posture.

"Hey, dude! You are also Chinese, I guess," says 工, with his curiosity getting the better of him. "But why do you stand like that on a trip abroad?"

"I am a capital letter, born and raised here," laughs H, gazing at 工. "This is just the way I am."

Note: The letter H resembles the character 工 standing on the side.

不得其解

出场角色: 敢 (gǎn) ; 憨 (hān) 。

敢看了憨老半天，不解地自言自语："都说有心人聪明，可这位兄弟比我多了个心眼儿，怎么是一副傻乎乎的样子呢？"

Paradox of the Heart

Characters: 敢"bold"; 憨"silly".

Gazing at 憨 for quite some time, 敢 says to himself in confusion, "They say a heart is the seat of wisdom, but why does this guy with a heart look so stupid?"

Note: 憨 is structured top to bottom with 敢 and 心"heart".

童心未泯

出场角色：几（jī）；儿（ér）。

几对儿说："兄弟，你啥时候封顶啊？"

儿笑道："我一封顶，就丢掉了儿时的快乐。"

Innocence Preserved

Characters: 几"small table"; 儿"child".

"Hey, pal," says 几 to 儿. "When will you be roofed?"

"Were the top sealed," smiles the other, "I'd lose my happy childhood."

Note: Compared with 儿, the character 几 has an extra horizontal stroke on top resembling a roof.

老土的困惑

出场角色：加（jiā）；减（jiǎn）；土（tǔ）。

加对减说："快看，那边来了一个怪物。"

远处的土不紧不慢地走了过来。

加和减好奇地打量着土，问道："朋友，你到底是要加还是要减啊？"

土不好意思地说："我就是个老土，听不懂二位在说什么。"

A Clodhopper at a Loss

Characters: 加"addition"; 减"subtraction"; 土"clod".

"Look, here comes a monster," says 加 to 减 as they see 土 coming over at a leisurely pace.

With a curious stare, 加 and 减 ask 土, "Man, what on earth are you going to do, addition or subtraction?"

"As a clodhopper, I don't quite understand what you two are talking about," replies 土, embarrassed.

Note: 土 is composed of 十 (a plus sign) at the top and 一 (a minus sign) at the bottom.

身在苦中不知苦

出场角色：苦（kǔ）；若（ruò）。
苦对若说："兄弟，你有点发育不良啊。脖子都长歪了！"
若笑道："我若是长成你的模样，岂不是要苦一辈子！"

Ignorance of Hardship

Characters: 苦"bitter"; 若"if".

"With a crooked neck, you are abnormally developed," says 苦 to 若.

"If I were your spitting image, I'd be in the throes of hardship all my life," grins the other.

Note: The left-falling stroke in 若 represents a crooked neck.

头尾不分

出场角色：空（kōng）；罕（hǎn）。
空对罕说："我的天啊，你脑袋咋长屁股下边儿了？"

罕笑道："不好意思，那是我的尾巴！"

Head or Tail

Characters: 空"air"; 罕"rare".

"Oh my," says 空 to 罕. "Is your head under your butt?"

"I'm sorry, but it's my tail," grins the other.

Note: The dot stoke at the top of 空 resembles the head, and the bottom extended part of the vertical line in 罕 resembles the tail.

啧啧称美

出场角色：口 （kǒu）； 呆 （dāi） 。
口对呆说："兄弟，你在树上的模样简直是帅呆了！"

Honeyed Words

Characters: 口"mouth"; 呆"stupid".

"Wow, buddy," says 口 to 呆. "You look stunning on top of the tree."

Note: 呆 is composed of 呆 at the top and 木 at the bottom.

嘴上长腿

出场角色：口 （kǒu）； 只 （zhǐ） 。
口对只说："兄弟，看见你的模样，我终于相信了，嘴也会长腿。"

A Funny Look

Characters: 口"mouth"; 只"only".

"Hey, guy," says 口 to 只. "Judging by your appearance, I come to believe that a mouth can have legs."

Note: 只 is composed of 口 with 八 at the bottom resembling the legs.

猴子与骡子

出场角色：骡（luó）。幕后角色：锣（luó）。

猴子在夜里从一户人家那里偷了一头骡子。

猴子把骡子往村外牵，骡子不从，拼命挣扎。猴子无奈，拿手上的棍子狠狠地打骡子的屁股。

骡子疼得大叫道："偷的骡儿敲不得！"

注释：本文中的"偷的骡儿敲不得"是谚语"偷的锣儿敲不得"的戏仿。

A Monkey and a Mule

Onstage Character: 骡"mule". Offstage Character: 锣"gong".

One night, a monkey stole a mule from a human household and tried to drag him out of the village, but the mule refused to move and struggled desperately, leaving the monkey with no choice but to hit him hard on the butt with a stick.

"Never beat a stolen mule!" the animal cried out in pain.

Note: "Never beat a stolen mule" is a parody of the Chinese proverb "Never beat a stolen gong" meaning something unrighteous cannot be done in public. "Mule" and "gong" are homophones in Mandarin.

大口吞噬

出场角色：口（kǒu）；固（gù）。

口和固是一对酒友。这不，他俩又一起下馆子啦。

看着固狼吞虎咽的样子，口笑道："看看你这吃相，真是食古不化呀！"

固嘟嘟囔囔地说："我当然还没消化，我还没咽进肚子里呐！"

Eating like a Pig

Characters: 口"mouth"; 固"solid".

口 and and his pot companion 固 are dining in a restaurant.

"Look at the way you eat," 口 laughs as 固 wolfs down the food on his plate. "You haven't digested the ancient learning."

"Certainly not digested, it's still in my mouth," mumbles 固.

Note: 固 is composed of 古"ancient" enclosed by 口.

点子大王

出场角色：木（mù）；术（shù）。

木看着术，不由自主地说："术兄，怪不得大伙都说你心眼多，原来你比我多了个歪点子。"

术哈哈大笑道："可别小看了这个点子，就是因为有了它，我才能捣鬼有术啊！"

The King of Ideas

Characters: 木"tree"; 术"tactics".

Examining 术 closely, 木 blurts, "Chum, no wonder they all say you are full of wicked ideas. It turns out that you have one more slanting dot than me."

"Never think little of the little dot," laughs the other. "It inspires me to play clever tricks."

Note: With an extra dot stroke on the upper right, 术 differs from 木 in composition; the Chinese expression "slanting dot" means "wicked idea".

不戴高帽儿

出场角色：牛（niú）；牟（móu）。

牛问牟："兄弟，咱们老牛戴三角帽不合适吧。把牸角都遮住了。"

An Improper Hat

Characters: 牛"ox"; 牟"seek".

"Hey, man," says 牛 to 牟. "It's not appropriate for an ox to wear a cocked hat covering the horns."

Note: 牟 is composed of 牛 with 厶 on top representing a cocked hat.

快不起来

出场角色：能（néng）；熊（xióng）。

能对熊说："瞧你能的，啥时候开上四个轱辘了？"

熊苦笑道："别讽刺我了。我可是爬着走路啊！"

On All Fours

Characters: 能"capable"; 熊"bear".

"Wow, good for you," says 能 to 熊. "Since when have you been on four wheels?"

"Don't laugh at me," replies the other with a bitter smile. "I walk on all fours."

Note: 熊 is composed of 能 with four dot strokes below representing four limbs.

千金难买囫囵觉

出场角色：宁（níng）。

宁照着镜子，自言自语道："小丁戴帽，睡个好觉。"

Sleep Is the Best Medicine

Character: 宁"peace".

Looking in the mirror, 宁 says to himself, "丁 wears a cap, to have a sound nap."

Note: 宁 is composed of 丁 with a radical 宀 on top resembling a cap.

偷乌鸦的狐狸

出场角色：乌（wū）；屋（wū）。

一个人养了一只乌鸦。他平时都是把乌鸦关在一个笼子里。

一天，狐狸趁这个人午睡之际，悄悄地溜进他的家门，把乌鸦连同笼子一起偷走了。

"我因为太喜欢你，也就喜欢上了这个笼子。我这是爱乌及屋啊！"狐狸笑嘻嘻地对乌鸦说。

注释：本文中的"爱乌及屋"是成语"爱屋及乌"的戏仿。

A Fox Running Off with a Crow

Onstage Characters: 乌"crow"; 屋"house".

A man raised a crow and kept it locked up in a cage most of the time.

One day, while the man was napping, a fox sneaked into his home and ran off with the bird along with its cage.

"I love you so much that I even love this cage. Just as the saying goes, 'Love the crow, love the house,' " chuckled the fox.

Note: "Love the crow, love the house" is a parody of the Chinese idiom "Love the house, love the crow" which means that if you love a house you also love the crow on its roof. The parody and the original idiom sound exactly the same in Mandarin though differ in character sequence, with the original indicating that when you love someone, your care for anyone or anything connected with him or her.

比牛还牛

出场角色：强（qiáng）；犟（jiàng）。

强看见了犟，悄悄对一个路人说："我这兄弟能骑在牛身上作威作福，不是一般人啊。"

Above an Ox

Characters: 强"strong"; 犟"stubborn".

Upon seeing 犟, 强 whispers to a passerby, "Look at that guy. Putting on airs on the back of an ox, he's anything but ordinary."

Note: 犟 is composed of 强 above and 牛"ox" below.

四个儒生一条狗

出场角色：器（qì）。

器照着镜子，自言自语道："我这是狗战群儒啊！"

注释：器字当中的犬被四张嘴（口）围着，儒是古代的读书人，只会动口。所以说"狗战群儒"。

Four Scholars and a Dog

Character: 器 "ware".

Looking at his own image in the mirror, 器 thinks aloud, "A dog challenging four scholars."

Note: 器 is composed of 犬 with two 口 "mouth" representing words on top and another two below; a scholar is known as a man of words but not of deeds.

席地而卧的苦恼

出场角色：日 (rì)；旦 (dàn)。
日对旦说："兄弟，你有床板睡啦？"

A Pang of Envy

Characters: 日 "sun"; 旦 "dawn".

"Wow, buddy," says 日 to 旦. "You've got a board to sleep on, right?"

Note: 旦 is composed of 日 with a horizontal stroke below resembling a bed board.

吃了豹子胆

出场角色：人 (rén)；全 (quán)。

人问全："兄弟，你真是胆大包天，居然骑到王的头上啦？"

A Daring Act

Characters: 人"man"; 全"total".

"Mate, how dare you ride on the king's shoulders!" says 人 to 全.

Note: 全 is composed of 王"king" with 人 on top.

男士也玩高低杠

出场角色：人（rén）；　夫（fū）。

人对夫说："先生，你也会玩儿高低杠啊？"

Athletic Talents

Characters: 人"person"; 夫"man".

"Wow, man," says 人 to 夫. "You can play the asymmetric bars, too?"

Note: 天 consists of 人"person" and 二 resembling two horizontal bars of different height (used in an event in women's gymnastics).

不是一个"师"

出场角色：尸（shī）；　层（céng）。

尸从医院溜出来闲逛。他遇到了层。

尸以为层是他的一个登上了云朵的兄弟。

"尸兄，想不到你上了西天。太平间里不是挺好吗？"

339

层看着尸，不解地问："先生，咱俩不是同门啊！你为何称我'师兄'啊？"

Not Pupils of the Same Master

Characters: 尸"corpse"; 层"tier".

Sneaking out of the hospital, 尸 runs across 层 and mistakes him for a brother lying prone on a cloud.

"Brother corpse, it's quite unexpected you are up in heaven," 尸 exclaims excitedly. "Isn't it nicer to stay in the mortuary?"

"Why do you call me fellow apprentice, sir?" 层 replies with a puzzled stare. "We are not pupils of the same master."

Note: 层 is composed of 尸 at the top and 云"cloud" at the bottom; "brother corpse" and "fellow apprentice" are phonetically identical in Chinese.

有得有失

出场角色：师（shī）；帅（shuài）。

师对帅说："兄弟，咋截肢啦? 是不是为了帅一点，做了手术啦?"

Win Some, Lose Some

Characters: 师"teacher"; 帅"handsome".

"Pal, why did you get amputated?" 师 asks 帅. "You had surgery to make yourself a little more handsome, didn't you?"

Note: Without a horizontal stroke on top of the component 巾, 帅 differs from 师 in composition.

天下山水各不同

出场角色：汕（shàn）；录（lù）。

汕端详了录好一阵，然后说："你我都是山水相连，乍模样差别那么大呢？"

录笑道："你是山在水边，我是山在水上。模样当然不一样啦！"

Contrasts in Nature

Characters: 汕"weir"; 录"record".

Staring at 录 for quite a while, 汕 says finally, "We both have a mountain bordering water, but why do we look so different?"

"Your mountain lies beside the water and mine on the water," laughs 录. "Of course we two are like chalk and cheese."

Note: 汕 is composed of 山 with a semantic radical 氵"water" on the left; 录 graphically has 山 (lying on the side) at the top and 水"water" at the bottom.

人师难遇

出场角色：生（shēng）；筛（shāi）。

生在路上遇见了筛，他觉得筛很像自己的老师，就是头上多了一顶竹编帽子。

生问筛："老师，您的帽子可真不错。"

筛苦笑道："千万别称我为师，我是筛子。"

A Mentor Hard to Meet

Characters: 生"student"; 筛"sieve".

生 comes across 筛 on the road who looks very much like his teacher 师 wearing a bamboo hat.

"Hello, 师. The hat looks good on you," says 生 to 筛.

"Never call me 师," replies the other with a bitter smile. "I am a sieve."

Note: 筛 is composed of 师"teacher" with a semantic radical ⺮"bamboo" representing a bamboo hat.

形似神不似

出场角色：士（shì）；土（tǔ）。

士对土道："兄弟你好。"

土苦笑道："我是个土老帽，怎敢与先生您称兄道弟呀。"

Similar in Look but Not in Spirit

Characters: 士"scholar"; 土"clod".

"It's good to see you, brother," says 士 to 土.

"Don't call me brother, sir," replies the other with a bitter smile. "As a clodhopper, how can I presume to accept that mode of address!"

Note: The top horizontal line in 土 is shorter than the bottom, as opposed

第四章　人兽之间
Chapter 4　Man and Beast

to 士.

目光如炬

出场角色：土（tǔ）；幸（xìng）。
土对幸说："兄弟你的运气真好啊！"
幸对土说："你眼力真不错，连我下半身的钱也看见了。"

注释：幸的下部近似人民币符号"¥"。

A Keen Eye

Characters: 土"clod"; 幸"fortunate".
"You were born with a silver spoon, mate," says 土 to 幸.
"What a sharp eye you have!" replies the other. "You can spot the money on my lower half!"

Note: The lower part of 幸 resembles the Chinese currency sign ¥.

眼神不济

出场角色：王（wáng）；于（yú）；宇（yǔ）。
老王和老于是多年好友。他们经常在一起谈天说地。
后来，老于移居海外，两个朋友天各一方，彼此多年没有联系了。
一天，老王在大街上闲逛。突然他见到一个人，模样很像老于。
只不过原来老于从不戴帽子，这回却戴着一顶上面有个小疙瘩的帽子。
"老于，你一戴帽子我差点没认出你来。"老王抓住对方的手摇个不停。

"对不起，我不姓于，我姓宇。"老宇笑道，"先生你认错人了。"

Chum Chaos

Characters: 王; 于; 宇"all surnames".

Often having idle chats together, 王 and 于 go way back.

Yet they break off contact for years, as 于 has moved overseas.

One day, while strolling down the street, 王 spots a man who looks like 于 in every way except that he wears a knot cap.

"Hello, 于! It's hard to recognise you," exclaims 王, grabbing the other's hand and shaking it vigorously. "You never used to wear a cap."

"Sorry, sir, but you've got the wrong person," grins the man. "My name is 宇, not 于."

Note: 宇 is composed of 于 with a radical 宀 on top resembling a cap.

恍然大悟

出场角色：我（Wǒ）；匕（bǐ）；它（Tā）。

我对匕说："你的模样怪吓人的，戴个帽子遮遮吧！"

匕笑道："戴了帽子就不是我了！"

我恍然大悟："对了，戴上帽子你就是它了。"

A Sudden Realization

Characters: 我"me"; 匕"dagger"; 它"it".

"Your appearance is quite unsettling," 我 comments to 匕. "Perhaps you should consider covering yourself with a cap."

匕 responds with a grin, "If I were to wear a cap, I wouldn't be myself."

Suddenly, it dawns on 我, "Ah, I understand. With a cap on, you would become 它."

Note: 它 is composed of 匕 with a radical 宀 on top resembling a cap.

铁路警察，各管一段

出场角色：泄（xiè）；泻（xiè）。

泄对泻说："Xiè兄，虽说咱俩的名字同音，可是意思却不大相同。"

泻对泄说："是啊，你管泄气，我管泻肚。"

Each Goes His Own Way

Characters: 泄"let out"; 泻"pour out".

"Pal, our names sound the same but differ in meaning," says 泄 to 泻.

"That's right. You serve to release the gas and I to loosen the bowels," comes the reply.

Note: 泄 and 泻 are homophones.

没大没小

出场角色：兄（xiōng）；克（kè）。

兄在大街上见到了克。

"克兄，你好！"

克笑道："羞煞人也。你才是兄啊！"

Sense of Propriety

Characters: 兄"elder brother"; 克"conquer".

兄 bumps into 克 on the street.

"Hello, big brother!" 兄 exclaims.

"I'm dying of shame," laughs the other. "You are the one."

Note: 克 has 兄 at the bottom.

救急的驴粪蛋

出场角色：下（xià）；上（shàng）；卞（biàn）。

下与上捉迷藏。眼看被发现了，下急中生智，往头上搁了一个驴粪蛋。

"我找到你啦！"上兴奋地喊道。

"你找错人了，我是卞，不是下。"下用手指了指头上的驴粪蛋，"我比下多一点。"

A Clever Disguise

Characters: 下"down"; 上"up"; 卞"a surname".

下 and 上 are playing hide-and-seek. On the point of being found, 下 tactfully grabs a ball of dung and places it on top of his head.

"There you are!" exclaims 上 in excitement.

"You've got the wrong person," grins the other as he points at his head. "With an extra dot on top, I'm actually 卞, not 下."

Note: 卞 is composed of 下 with dot stroke on top resembling a dung ball.

得胜之道

出场角色：月（yuè）；　生（shēng）。

月对生说："兄弟，你我若是联袂出战，必胜无疑。"

A Strategy for Victory

Characters: 月"moon"; 生"life".

"Joining forces, we will undoubtedly emerge victorious," says 月 to 生.

Note: 月 joined by 生 on the right forms 胜"win".

无头老幺

出场角色：之（zhī）；　Z。

之对Z说："兄弟，你的脑袋呢？"

Z对之说："我不是汉字。我是排行老末的英文字母Z，不知道你说的脑袋指什么。"

A Letter with No Head

Characters: 之"go"; Z"an English letter".

"Where's your head, pal?" 之 asks Z.

"I am not a Chinese character but the English letter izzard, which comes last in the alphabet. I don't know what you mean by head," comes the reply.

Note: Z is shaped like 之 without the dot (resembling the head) on top.

藏头诗

出场角色: 主 (zhǔ) ; 玉 (yù)

主问玉: "先生, 一看你的相貌, 便知你是某一类文体的高手。"

玉惊讶道: "是吗? 我怎么不知道啊! 什么文体呀? "

主笑着指了指自己的脑袋, 又指了指玉腰间的一点: "藏头诗啊! "

Acrostic Poetry

Characters: 主"lord"; 玉"jade".

"From your appearance I can tell you must be a master at a form of writing," says 主 to 玉.

"Really? I don't have the slightest idea about that," replies 玉 in surprise. "What is it?"

"Acrostic poetry," smiles 主, pointing to his own head and then to the dot on other's waist.

Note: 主 has dot stroke at the top resembling the head; 玉 has a dot on the lower right representing a hidden head; an acrostic, or "hiding-head verse", is a poem in which the first characters of each line make up a name or a message of blessing.

施主饶命

出场角色：屁（pì）；尼（ní）。

屁得意洋洋地对尼说："师太，我比你多一把刀子。咱俩打起来肯定我占上风。"

尼连连摆手道："施主，你可千万别占上风。贫尼受不了你的味儿。"

Too Heavy to Bear

Characters: 屁"fart"; 尼"nun".

"Hey, sister. With one more dagger, I will surely gain the upper hand if involved in a fight with you," says 屁 to 尼 proudly.

"Never can you be in an upper position, sir," replies the other with a refusal hand gesture. "Your odour is too heavy to bear."

Note: Graphically 屁 is structured with one more 匕"dagger" than 尼 at the bottom.

"做人难啊！"

出场角色：人（rén）；贝（bèi）。

人在海滩上见到了贝。

人第一次见到贝，好奇地问："兄弟，你咋顶着一个大盖子呀！"

"那是我的壳。"贝答道。

"那玩意儿有什么用啊！"人上前把贝的壳扯了下来，"丢掉包祆，做一个轻装上阵的人不好吗？"

"我何尝不想做一个人啊！" 贝呻吟道，"可让你这一揪，别说做人了，我现在连贝也做不行了。"贝把话说完就一命呜呼了。

The Tragic Tale of a Conch

Characters: 人"person"; 贝"shellfish".

At the beach, 人 meets 贝 for the first time.

"Hey, buddy. Why do you carry such a big lid on the head?" asks the man in surprise.

"It's my shell," comes the reply.

"What a useless burden!" says 人 as he rips the shell off. "You should throw it away and be a man traveling light."

"How I wish to be a human!" groans 贝. "But now I can't even pull through as a conch."

With these words, the poor creature breathes his last.

Note: 贝 is composed 人"man" with a component on top resembling a lid.

该办就办

出场角色：力（lì）；办（bàn）。

力对办说："兄弟，好样的！一看模样，就知道你能为朋友两肋插刀。"

办憨厚地笑了笑："没什么，不过是为大伙儿办点事儿。"

Ready to Help Others

Characters: 力"force"; 办"do".

"Good for you, pal," says 力 to 办. "Judging by your appearance, I believe you would be willing to have each side of your chest pierced by a knife for the sake of your friends."

"It's nothing really," replies the other with a gentle smile. "I am just ready to do something for others."

Note: 办 is composed of 力 with a dot stroke on each side resembling two knives piercing the chest.

分解不当

出场角色：居（jū）。

居新到一家公司就职。在欢迎他的聚会上，老板请居向同事们做个自我介绍。

"吾乃古尸一具。"居自我介绍说。

同事们赶紧用手捂住了嘴巴和鼻子。

An Unconventional Introduction

Character: 居"house".

Newly employed in a company, 居 is asked to introduce himself at the welcome party held in his honour.

"I am an ancient corpse," he says.

Immediately, all the others cover their mouths and noses with their hands.

Note: 居 is composed of 尸 "corpse" above and 古 "ancient" below.

辨认猪

出场角色：猪（zhū）。幕后角色：珠（zhū）。

猫把豹子和猪都用布蒙住，问狗哪个是猪。

狗上前，一把就将蒙在猪身上的布扯了下来。

"你真是慧眼识猪啊。"猫惊叹道。

"我是用鼻子辨认的。哪个难闻哪个就是猪。"狗大笑道。

注释：本文中的"慧眼识猪"是成语"慧眼识珠"的戏仿。

An Eye for Pigs

Onstage Character: 猪"pig". Offstage Character: 珠"pearl".

A cat covered a leopard and a pig each with a cloth and asked a dog to identify the pig.

The dog immediately came forward and took the cover off the pig.

"Wow! You have an eye for pigs!" the cat exclaimed.

"I sniff, and the pig stinks," the dog laughed.

Note: "To have an eye for pigs" has the same phonetic sound as the idiom "to have an eye for pearls" meaning being good at identifying talent. "An eye" originated from Buddhism referring to one of the Five Eyes, and now generally means a good insight or judgment.

第五章　不是那块料

Chapter 5　Not Up to Snuff

深不可测

出场角色：并（bìng）；井（jǐng）。

并和井是公司同事。有一天，并看见旁边没有别人，好奇地问井："井姐，你的俩辫子咋是直的？"

井笑道："我觉得直辫子挺好。是不是你听到别人议论我啦？"

"是啊，人家都说你深不可测呀！"并直言相告道。

Too Deep to Measure

Characters: 并"union"; 井"water well".

并 and 井 are workmates. One day, with no one else around, 并 asks 井 nosily, "Sis, why do you wear your braids upright?"

"I just think they look good on me," smiles 井. "You've heard someone gossiping about me, haven't you?"

"Actually, yes," replies 并 frankly. "They say you are unfathomable."

Note: 并 is structured with a radical 丷 resembling two braids at the top; the top extended parts of the left-falling stroke and the vertical stroke in 井 represent two upright braids.

避之不及

出场角色：必（bì）；心（xīn）。

在一次同学聚会上，必和心相遇了。

必对心说："兄弟，你的腰刀哪儿去啦？"

心答道："一想到身上插一把凶器，我就心如刀绞啊。你说我能要这个家伙吗？"

Aversion to Weapons

Characters: 必"must"; 心"heart".

At a class reunion , 必 asks 心, "Buddy, why don't you wear a sabre?"

"Whenever thinking of a sharp weapon on me, I feel as if it were piercing my heart," replies 心. "So, do you think I could live with that stuff?"

Note: 必 is composed of 心 with a left-falling stroke resembling a sabre running through.

吹皱一池春水

出场角色：吹（chuī）。

吹自叹道："我不过是喜欢说几句大话，可人家都说我嘴欠。"

注释：嘴欠，方言，意思是一个人说出来的话总让人不爱听。"吹"字由"口"和"欠"组成，"口"即是"嘴"，所以说它"嘴欠"。

A Sharp Tongue

Character: 吹"brag".

"I just enjoy talking big," 吹 laments. "But why do people say that I have a sharp tongue?"

Note: 吹 is structured with a semantic radical 口"mouth" on the left and 欠 dialectally meaning "hurtful" on the right.

没头没脑

出场角色：良（liáng）；艮（gěn）。

良和艮是一对无话不谈的好友。

一天，艮苦恼地对良说："为啥在公司里大伙儿都不待见我呢？"

良对艮说："和我相比，你少了个头。无头必无脑，说话惹人恼。"

注释：艮，性子直。

No Head, No Brain

Characters: 良"good"; 艮"blunt".

良 and 艮 are good buddies who are perfectly frank with each other.

One day, 艮 asks 良 in annoyance, "Why does everybody in the firm frown on me?"

"Different from me, you have no head," replies the other. "Someone headless speaks without a brain, causing others stress and pain."

Note: Without a dot stroke on top resembling the head, 艮 differs from 良 in composition.

鼓励朋友

出场角色：大（dà）；一（yī）。

大和一是多年的好友。

大知道自己的这位朋友很自卑，于是想了一个办法鼓励他。

"你站到我头上来，再看看眼前的水面。"大对一说。

一不知道大的葫芦里卖的什么药，但还是按照朋友的吩咐，小心翼翼地站到了大的头上。

"我看到了水里有一个'天'。"一惊喜地说。

"对呀，"大开导道，"没有你，我不过是个江湖老大。有了你，咱俩成了天啦！你现在知道自己的价值了吧！"

一的眼里闪出了晶莹的泪花。

Words of Encouragement

Characters: 大"big"; 一"one".

大 and 一 have been close friends for many years.

Knowing that his friend lacks self-confidence, 大 thinks of a way to encourage him.

"Stand on top of my head and look out at the water in front of us," 大 says to 一.

Although unsure of what his friend has in mind, 一 still follows his instructions and carefully climbs up onto his head.

"I see a 'heaven' in the water!" 一 exclaims with joy.

"Exactly," 大 comforts him. "Without you, I would merely be a small-time gang leader. With you, we can be heaven together! Do you now realize your worth?"

Tears glisten in the other's eyes.

Note: 大 joined by 一 on top forms the character 天"heaven".

自愧不如

出场角色：允（yǔn）；兄（xiōng）。

允对兄道："我是尖脑袋，你是方脑袋。你说咱俩谁厉害？"

兄谦虚地说："当然是你厉害。尖脑袋能钻营。"

A Superior Head

Characters: 允"fair"; 兄"elder brother".

"You have a square head and I have a conic one," says 允 to 兄. "Who do you think is stronger?"

"Of course you are," replies the other humbly. "A sharp top helps thrust the way to favours."

Note: 允 has ㄙ at the top resembling a conic head and 兄 has 口 resembling a square one.

鱼缸里的泥鳅

出场角色：鱼（yú）。幕后角色：愚（yú）。

正在鱼缸里优哉游哉地戏水的金鱼突然发现一条泥鳅混进了他们群里。

"你是何方神圣？"一条金鱼生气地问。

"主人从池塘里把我捉到的。他本想杀了我吃肉。"泥鳅答道。

"那你为什么能进我们的泳池呢？"另一条金鱼问。

"我告诉主人，我非常聪明，而且简直大智若鱼。如果能放我一条生路，我会回报他的。主人听我能说人言，于是就没杀我，而是把我放在你们中间了。"泥鳅笑答。

注释：本文中的"大智若鱼"是成语"大智若愚"的戏仿。

A Loach in the Tank

Onstage Character: 鱼"fish". Offstage Character: 愚"fool".

A school of goldfish was swimming leisurely in their tank when suddenly a loach broke in.

"Hey! Where did you come from?" asked one of the goldfish in annoyance.

"I was caught by the owner from the pond. He meant to cook me for dinner," came the reply.

"Then how come you are here in our swimming pool?" another goldfish asked.

"I told him 'A sage looks like a fish' and that I would repay him if I could be spared alive. Hearing me speak human words, he did not kill me but put me among you instead," replied the loach with a smile.

Note: "A sage looks like a fish" is a parody of the Chinese idiom "A sage looks like a fool" which is similar to the English proverb "Still waters run deep" meaning a man of great wisdom appears slow-witted. In Chinese the idiom and the spoof sound the same.

就餐以后

出场和幕后角色：费（fèi）。

老虎请狐狸到餐馆就餐。餐后，老虎付了款，准备与狐狸离开。

"先生，您还没给小费呢！"伺者猴子向老虎伸出了毛茸茸的爪子。老虎犹豫了一下，不太想给。

"大王，古人云，'成大事者，不惜小费'。"狐狸道，"您既有统一山头的雄心，何必在乎这点钱呢。我看您还是给他点儿吧！"

老虎很不情愿地丢给猴子两个硬币。

After Dinner

Onstage Character: 费"tip". Offstage Character: 费"expense".

A tiger invited a fox to dine at a restaurant.

Soon they finished the meal, and the tiger paid the bill and was about to leave with the fox.

"Excuse me, sir. May I have a tip, please?" the waiter monkey requested the tiger, extending his furry hand.

The tiger hesitated, not so willing to pay anything extra. "Your Majesty, as the old saying goes, 'Great achievers spare no small tips,' " said the fox. "Now that you have the ambition to unify all the mountains, why do you care about such a modest sum? A small change would do."

Reluctantly, the tiger dropped two coins in the monkey's hand.

Note: "Great achievers spare no small tips" has exactly the same speech sound and the same characters as the maxim "Great achievers spare no small expenses" meaning a person with great aims does not grudge expenses or losses.

傻瓜的发财梦

出场角色：币（bì）。幕后角色：毙（bì）。

有一个傻瓜一直想发大财。

有一天，他突然来了灵感，于是用绳子把自己紧紧捆住，在院子里的大树下闭目养神。

"你这是要干什么？"一个邻居大惊失色地问。

"等着发财呀！"傻瓜睁开双眼，笑嘻嘻地说，"你没听说过'束手待币'这个成语吗？"

注释：本文中的"束手待币"是成语"束手待毙"的戏仿。

An Idiot's Fortune Dream

Onstage Character: 币"money". Offstage Character: 毙"death".
There was once a fool who was always dreaming about striking it rich.
One day, the fool suddenly had an inspiration. He tied himself tightly with a rope, and sat under a tree in his yard meditating with his eyes closed.
"What are you doing?" asked a neighbour in shock.
"I'm waiting for a fortune!" the idiot opened his eyes and chuckled.
"Haven't you heard of the idiom 'waiting with tied hands for money'?"

Note: "Waiting with tied hands for money" is a parody of the Chinese idiom "waiting with tied hands for death" which means being tied up and waiting to die, metaphorically referring to not actively solving a problem and waiting for failure. In Mandarin, the idiom and the parody sound exactly the same.

以裸为美

出场角色：公（gōng）；衮（gǔn）。

公对衮说："兄弟你真行啊，居然穿上衣服了。"

衮笑道："像你这样赤条条来、赤条条去也不错嘛！"

注释：衮，古代君王等的礼服。

Good to Be in the Nude

Characters: 公"sir"; 衮"robe".

"Hey, pal," says 公 to 衮. "Good for you to get dressed!"

"It's not bad to come naked and depart naked as you do," smiles the other.

Note: 衮 is structured like 公 in the middle of 衣 "a garment".

从头说起

出场角色：急（jí）；慧（huì）。

急问慧："为啥我办事总是毛手毛脚，你却那么胸有成竹呢？"

慧看了一眼急，不禁笑道："你顶着一颗兔子脑袋，办事能不是急性子吗。你看看我的头上，两根天线，每天接收不尽的信息。所以我是个万事通啊！"

The Head Makes the Man

Characters: 急"rash"; 慧"wise".

"I always act rashly, but you are confident and composed, " 急 says 慧. "Why is that?"

Casting a glance at the other, 慧 cannot help but laugh. "Your bunny head explains why you are out of patience with everything," he says. "Look at me. With two antenna arrays at the top, I receive endless information every day, thus becoming a jack of all trades."

Note: 急 and 慧 are both structured top to middle and bottom with three components different only in top; the top of 急 is ⺈(top of 兔"rabbit") and the top of 慧 resembles two antenna arrays.

哥哥出谜弟弟猜

出场角色：兄（xiōng）；弟（dì）；阅（yuè）。

兄和弟成年以后分别在两个不同的城市工作和娶妻生子。

他们已经好几年没有见面了。

有一天，兄打电话给弟，说他近期要来看弟，但是时间尚未确定。

几天以后的一个周末上午，弟正在家里看书，快递员按响了弟家的门铃。

兄寄来一个快件。包裹里面只有一张纸，纸上只有一个字："阅"。

弟看着这个"阅"字，哈哈大笑道："太好了，两点迎兄进门！"

下午两点，兄果然如约而至。

A Riddle

Characters: 兄"elder brother"; 弟"younger brother"; 阅"read".

兄 and 弟 settle down in different cities after they come of age, and they haven't seen each other for years.

One day, 兄 calls 弟 and says that he is coming to see him soon, but the exact time is not fixed.

One weekend morning a few days later, while 弟 is reading a book at home, a courier rings his doorbell and hands him an express package from 兄, in which is a mere piece of paper with only one character "阅".

"Excellent!" laughs 弟 as he reads it. "Welcome him in at two."

At exactly two o'clock in the afternoon, 兄 arrives as scheduled.

Note: 阅 is composed of 兄 with two dots on top enclosed by 门"door", representing "elder brother getting in the door at two".

个中之人

出场角色: 丕 (pī) ; 个 (gè) 。

丕对个道: "兄弟, 你看看我, 上有天, 下有地。你怎么上不着天, 下不着地呀? "

个笑道: "没办法, 这就是个性。"

The Way I Am

Characters: 丕"big"; 个"individual".

"Hey guy. Look at me," says 丕 to 个. "I have heaven above and earth

below. How come you neither reach for the sky nor touch the ground?"
"That's just how I am," grins the other.

Note: 丕 is shaped like 个 with a horizontal line above and another one below.

自惭形秽

出场角色：齐（qí）。

齐对着镜子，自言自语地说："我两条腿都站不直，还敢自称为齐吗？"

A Pang of Shame

Character: 齐"symmetry".

"Unable to stand up straight on both legs, how dare I call myself symmetry?" mutters 齐 to his reflection in the mirror.

Note: 齐 has a left-falling stroke and a vertical stroke at the bottom resembling the legs with the left one bent.

称王的代价

出场角色：全（quán）；王（wáng）。

全："王兄，你也该像我这样安个大屋顶，晴天遮阳，雨天防水，岂不一举两得。"

王笑道："全兄所言极是，只是那样一来，我的王者风范也就荡然无存了。"

The Price to Pay for Being a King

Characters: 全"complete"; 王"king".

"Hey man. Why not put up a large roof overhead as I have done?" says 全 to 王. "You could stay sheltered from sun and rain, killing two birds with one stone."

"You make a good point, buddy," grins the other. "But if I were to do that, my regal style would be all gone."

Note: 全 is composed 王 with 人 on top resembling a roof.

懒猫

出场角色：鸡（jī）。幕后角色：机（jī）。

从前有一只懒猫，做什么事情都是无精打采的，一有空就躺在草地上晒太阳。

有一天，懒猫已经多半天没吃东西了，正饿得发慌。忽然，他看见河边走过一只小鸡。他很想扑上去美餐一顿。可是又懒得动身子。

"再等等，等小鸡走近点儿我再捉他，岂不是手拿把掐吗？"

正当懒猫做着美梦时，一只狐狸不知从何方窜了出来，一口叼住了小鸡。

"就要到嘴边的美味跑了。"懒猫失望地说，"这真是鸡不可失，失不再来呀。"

注释：本文中的"鸡不可失，失不再来"是谚语"机不可失，失不再来"的戏仿。

A Lazy Cat

Onstage Character: 鸡"chicken". Offstage Character: 机"opportunity".

There was once a lazy cat who was listless to everything and took every chance to lie in the grass soaking up the sun.

One day, not having taken in anything since the morning, the cat started to panic from hunger. Suddenly, he saw a chick walking by the river, and he had a strong desire to pounce on it for a square meal, but he was too lazy to move.

"I'll wait till the little chicken comes closer, and then it's going to be a breeze to catch it," thought the lazy cat.

While he was dreaming, a fox jumped out of nowhere and snatched the chick away.

"What a shame I messed up a sure thing!" said the cat regretfully. "Chicken comes but once."

Note: "Chicken comes but once." is a parody of the proverb "Opportunity knocks but once" meaning that when a good opportunity comes one should seize it without hesitation, or it will be lost forever. The parody and the original proverb have the same phonetic sound in Mandarin.

羞煞人也

出场角色：公（gōng）；么（me）。

公在一次聚会上见到了么。

公钦佩地对么说："我猜公乃南宋名士王佐，为了拯救百姓、造福社稷，甘愿自折一臂。让我等凡人自愧不如啊！"

么不好意思地对公说：“羞煞人也，鄙人非公，更不是名士王佐，哪有什么‘自折一臂’之事啊。”

注释：此句从“公”字认为“么”字是自己同类，但是断了一条胳膊引申出“王佐断臂”的故事。典故出自《说岳全传》，岳飞部下王佐为策反金军猛将陆文龙自断右臂，获取了对方信任，最终取得成功。

Dying of Shame

Characters: 公"mister"; 么"the youngest".

公 meets 么 at a gathering.

"You must be the great hero of the Southern Song Dynasty, Mr. Wang Zuo," says 公 to 么 admiringly, "who readily cut off the right arm in the interest of the people and the country, putting me and other ordinary persons to shame."

"I'm dying of shame, sir," replies the other, embarrassed. "I'm not the hero at all, having nothing to do with the act of bravery."

Note: Compared with 公, the character 么 lacks a left-falling stroke (resembling an arm) on the upper right.

一加一等于几

出场角色：个（gè）；竹（zhú）。

个对竹说：“看见你，我明白了一个道理——一个加一个，未必是两个。”

Unexpected Sum

Characters: 个"individual"; 竹"bamboo".

个 says to 竹, "Seeing you, I come to realize that one plus one doesn't necessarily make two."

Note: 竹 is shaped like two 个 joined together.

个中滋味

出场角色：古（gǔ）；苦（kǔ）。

古对苦说："兄弟，头上顶草是啥滋味儿啊？"

苦垂泪道："苦啊！"

The Weight of Misery

Characters: 古"ancient"; 苦"miserable".

"Hey, buddy, how are you doing with that heavy load of straw on your head?" 古 asks 苦 with concern.

"I feel absolutely miserable," 苦 replies, tears streaming down his face.

Note: 苦 is composed of 古 with a semantic radical 艹"grass" on top.

小虫子，大用途

出场角色：工（gōng）；虹（hóng）。

工对虹说："兄弟，你身边有只虫子，快碾死它。"

虹摇头道："使不得，没有了这只虫子，我还怎么气势如虹啊！"

Small Bug, Big Part

Characters: 工"work"; 虹"rainbow".

"Bro, there is a bug on your side," says 工 to 虹. "Squish it to death!"

"Forget it," replies the other, shaking his head. "Without the bug, how could I be imposing as a rainbow?"

Note: 虹 is composed of a semantic radical 虫"bug" on the left and 工 on the right.

高高在上

出场角色：高（gāo）；膏（gāo）。

高仰着头看了膏好大一会儿，赞叹道："我这兄弟真厉害，竟然爬到月亮上头了。"

Up on the Moon

Characters: 高"high"; 膏"paste".

Looking up at 膏 for quite a while, 高 gasps in admiration, "It's simply incredible of my brother to have climbed onto the moon!"

Note: 膏 is structured top to bottom with 高 and 月"moon".

373

主在何处？

出场角色：古（gǔ）；田（tián）。

德国科隆大教堂里，两个中国旅行团的基督徒古和田刚刚做完礼拜。

步出教堂时，古问田："兄弟，你为什么不把主顶在头上呢？"

田答道："因为我把主放在心里了。"

Faith in the Heart

Characters: 古"ancient"; 田"field".

At Cologne Cathedral in Germany, 古 and 田, two Christians from a Chinese tourist group, have just finished the worship.

"Brother, why don't you place the Lord on top of your head?" 古 asks 田 as they step out of the hall.

"Because I carry Him in my heart," comes the reply.

Note: 古 is structured top to bottom with 十 and 口, while 田 is composed of 十 enclosed by 口, with the radical 十 in each resembling a Christian cross.

听天由命

出场角色：叩（kòu）；命（mìng）。

叩羡慕命的运气好，有个漂亮的大屋顶。

一天，叩愤愤不平地问命："凭啥你头上严严实实，我头上却是光秃秃的？”

　　命笑答：“命里有时终须有，命里无时莫强求。”

The Divine Will

Characters: 叩"ask"; 命"fate".

叩 feels envious of 命 for his beautiful large rooftop.

One day, 叩 asks 命 indignantly, "Why the hell is your top tightly covered while I am left bareheaded?"

"Fate decrees what we have and what we lack," smiles the other.

Note: 命 is composed of 叩 with a component on top representing a roof.

原来是摆设

　　出场角色：龙（lóng）；聋（lóng）。

　　龙对着聋说了好大一阵的话，聋只是一言不发。

　　龙大惑不解地问一个路人：“我这兄弟的尾巴上吊着一只大耳朵，可咋什么也听不见呢？”

　　路人看了看聋的模样，沉吟道：“看来耳朵再大，长不对位置也不行。”

Merely for Show

Characters: 龙"dragon"; 聋"deaf".

Talking to 聋 for quite a while, 龙 finds the other giving no response at all.

Extremely puzzled, 龙 asks a passerby, "This guy has a large ear hanging from his tail, but how come he is as deaf as a post?"

Casting a look at 聋, the passerby mutters, "However big it is, an ear never works once it grows in the wrong place."

Note: 聋 is composed of 龙 at the top and 耳 "ear" at the bottom.

一叶障目

出场角色：目 (mù)；自 (zì)。

目对自说："兄弟，我一看见你的样子，就想起了一句成语。"

自好奇地问："什么成语呀？"

目笑道："'一叶障目，不见泰山'啊！"

自愁眉苦脸地说："怪不得人家都说我眼里只有自己呢。"

A Leaf before the Eye

Characters: 目"eye"; 自"self".

"Your appearance reminds me of a saying, chum," says 目 to 自.

"What is it?" asks the other curiously.

"A leaf before the eye shuts out Mount Tai," smiles 目.

"No wonder they say I only have myself in the eye," says 自 with a gloomy expression.

Note: 自 is composed of 目 with a left-falling stroke on top representing a leaf.

众人皆醉我独醒

出场角色：入（rù）。

入望着镜子里的自己，喃喃自语道："大伙儿都骂我'不是人'。我明明是人啊！看来是众人皆醉我独醒啊！"

No One Is Sober but Me

Character: 入"enter".

Staring at his own mirror image, 入 mutters to himself, "They all say I'm not a human, but obviously I am one. It seems that no one is sober but me."

Note: 入 reflects in the mirror as 人"person".

以身试险要不得

出场角色：食（shí）；良（liáng）。

食对良说："兄弟，搭个帐篷吧？"

良想了想，说："我可不想让人吃掉。"

Better Safe Than Sorry

Characters: 食"food"; 良"good".

"Set up a tent for yourself, pal," says 食 to 良.

After pondering for a moment, 良 replies, "I'd prefer not to be devoured."

Note: 食 is composed of 良 with 人 on top resembling a tent.

逸趣横生

出场角色：舌（shé）；适（shì）。

舌问适："兄弟，坐上躺椅啦！怪不得你一副悠哉悠哉的样子。"

A Life of Ease

Characters: 舌"tongue"; 适"comfortable".

"Wow, buddy. You are seated in a sling chair," says 舌 to 适. "No wonder you look free and easy."

Note: 适 is composed of 舌 enclosed (from left and bottom sides) by a radical 辶 resembling a sling chair.

名实相符

出场角色：士（shì）；土（tǔ）。

士对土说："先生，我刚刚给你相了面，上窄下宽，模样寒酸啊。要想摆脱土气，就要像我这样，上面宽一些。"

土大笑道："感谢赐教，我就是土，有点土气名副其实嘛！"

A Matter of Course

Characters: 士"scholar"; 土"clod".

"Sir, I've just read your facial features and found that you look rather countrified with the top narrower than the bottom," says 士 to 土. "A wider top like mine may help you get rid of that air."

"Thank you for your advice," chuckles the other. "But I am just a clodhopper, countrified by nature."

Note: The top horizontal line in 土 is shorter than the bottom, as opposed to 士.

丢了西瓜捡芝麻

出场角色：实（shí）；头（tóu）。

实问头："兄弟，为了把头护好，出门一定要戴上帽子。"

头笑道："我也知道戴上帽子暖和，可我不能因为戴了帽子丢了身份啊。"

Penny Wise and Pound Foolish

Characters: 实"truth"; 头"head".

"To shield your head from the hash elements, remember to wear a cap when you go out," advises 实 to 头.

"I know a cap helps keep warm," grins the other. "But I won't allow anything on top to strip me of my identity."

Note: 实 is composed of 头 with a radical 宀 on top resembling a cap.

不是那块料

出场角色：网（wǎng）；肉（ròu）。

网正要下河捕鱼，肉走了过来。

"网兄，带上我吧！逮鱼一定很好玩吧！"肉想跟着网一起下河。

网看了看肉，笑着说："一看你这副长相，就知道不是捕鱼的料。"

"那我给你打打下手总可以吧？"

"实话跟你说吧，"网叹了一口气说，"你跟我下河捕鱼，只能当饵料了。"

Not Up to Snuff

Characters: 网"net"; 肉"meat".

网 is going fishing on the river when 肉 comes over.

"Take me with you, bro," says the latter, wishing to join the former. "It must be lots of fun."

Throwing the other a glance, 网 smiles, "Judging by your appearance, I know you are not cut out for catching fish."

"Then can I at least be your assistant?"

"To tell the truth, you can be nothing but the bait if I bring you along," says 网 with a sigh.

Note: 网 and 肉 are graphically made up of the same components but look quite different.

轻功

出场角色：公（gōng）；翁（wēng）。

公对翁道："我在大地行走，君是羽上飘忽。您的轻功远胜于我呀！"

翁叹息道："先生过奖了。在下乃白头老汉一个，哪敢要什么轻功啊！"

Lightweight Kung Fu

Characters: 公"public"; 翁"old man".

"You float on the plume while I walk on the ground," says 公 to 翁. "So you are far superior to me in lightweight kung fu."

"I am flattered, sir," responds the other with a sigh. "As a white-haired old fellow, how dare I show off martial skills!"

Note: 翁 has 公 above and 羽"feather" below.

抱怨爹妈

出场角色：兀（wù）。

兀照着镜子叹道："我爹妈也太粗心了，把我养得两条腿不一般齐。"

A Compliant against Parents

Character: 兀"bare".

Looking in the mirror, 兀 sighs, "It was so careless of my parents to leave my legs off balance."

Note: 兀 is composed of a semantic radical 儿"legs" with a horizontal stroke on top.

巨大的代价

出场角色：折（zhé）；逝（shì）。

折见到了逝，十分嫉妒地说：想不到你在躺椅上悠然自得啊!

逝叹了一口气，悲伤地答道："这舒适可是以生命为代价换的呀！"

A Heavy Price

Characters: 折"break"; 逝"die".

折 comes across 逝. "I can't imagine you are at leisure in the lounge chair!" says 折, green with envy.

"I've given my life for this comfort," responds 逝 with a sigh of sadness.

Note: 逝 is composed of 折 enclosed from lower and left sides by a radical 辶 resembling a lounge chair.

越呆越傻

出场角色：于（yú）；迂（yū）。

于对迂说："整天在躺椅上呆着，越呆越傻。"

The Lazier, the Duller

Characters: 于"a surname"; 迂"pedantic".

"Slumped in the sling chair all day long, you become more and more fatheaded," says 于 to 迂.

Note: 迂 is composed of 于 enclosed (from lower and left sides) by a radical 辶 resembling a sling chair.

业无止境

出场角色: 亚 (yà) ; 业 (yè) 。

亚对业说: "兄弟, 还是安个顶子踏实。"

业对亚说: "要想建功立业和出人头地, 顶上不能有天花板啊! "

No Ceiling to Great Feats

Characters: 亚"second"; 业"trade".

"Bro, having a ceiling above gives one a sense of security," says 亚 to 业. "But you'll have to tear it down if you wish to pull off great feats and rise high in life," comes the response.

Note: Compared with 业, 亚 has one more horizontal line at the top resembling a roof.

再穷不能当裤子

出场角色：子（zǐ）；了（liǎo）。

子对了说："兄弟，你的裤腰带呢？咱再穷也不能把这家伙当了啊！"

A Waistband Put in Hock

Characters: 子"son"; 了"end".

"Mate, where is your belt?" says 子 to 了. "We cannot pawn it, however poor we are."

Note: Compared with 了, 子 has an extra horizontal stroke resembling a waistband.

我的行头我做主

出场角色：庄（zhuāng）；主（zhǔ）。

庄对主说："主啊，最近天气不好，你也像我一样弄个披风吧！"

主笑道："我若是披了这玩意，谁还把我当作主来崇拜呢？"

Wardrobe Sovereignty

Characters: 庄"village"; 主"lord".

"Lord, the weather has been terrible these days. Why not cover yourself with a cloak as I do?" 庄 says to 主.

"If I were to don something like that, who'd worship me as the Lord?" the other says, smiling.

Note: 庄 is graphically similar to 主 with an additional left-falling stroke on the left resembling a cloak.

急不择路

出场角色: 火（huǒ）; 灭（miè）。

火被消防员追击，走投无路之际，他急中生"智"，抓住一块石板盖在身上。

"哈哈，我现在成了灭，看你们还能不能认出我。"火得意地说。

没有想到的是，火的呼吸越来越困难，最后竟然被憋死了。

Hasty Strategy

Characters: 火"fire"; 灭"die".

Cornered by some firemen, 火 tactfully grabs a slab of stone and covers himself with it.

"You guys will never recognise me now as I've turned into 灭," he says to himself with delight.

However, finding it more and more difficult to breathe, 火 is soon suffocated.

Note: Compared with 火, 灭 had one more horizontal line at the top resembling a slab.

心眼儿不可缺

出场角色：刃（rèn）；忍（rěn）。

刃问忍："为啥我遇到事情爱冲动，不像你那么能忍呢？"

"缺心眼儿。"忍答道。

Cool as a Cucumber

Characters: 刃"blade"; 忍"tolerate".

"Why is it that I always act on impulse while you are cool as a cucumber all the time?" 刃 asks 忍.

"Because you are mindless," comes the reply.

Note: 忍 is composed of 刃 at the top and 心"heart" at the bottom.

不丢本色

出场角色：笨（bèn）；本（běn）。

笨和本是多年的邻居。他们住在一个阳光明媚的小岛上。

笨百思不得其解的是，他的邻居本即使在阳光很强的时候也不晓得遮挡一下自己。

"兄弟，跟我学学，搭个遮阳的竹棚子吧！"笨实在憋不住了，向本提了一个建议。

本笑道："我有那么笨吗？为了图一时的凉快，却丢了自己的本色！"

True Self

Characters: 笨"stupid"; 本"true self".

笨 and 本 have been neighbours for years, living on a sunny island. 笨 is totally perplexed that 本 never shades himself, even in the blazing sunshine.

"Follow my example, dude. Build a bamboo shade to shield yourself from the scorching sun," 笨 finally suggests, unable to contain his sympathy for his neighbour.

"Do you think I am so stupid?" 本 smiles. "I will never sacrifice my true self for the cool."

Note: 笨 is composed of 本 with a semantic radical ⺮"bamboo" on top.

出头之日

出场角色：昌（chāng）。

昌照着镜子，自语道："一日复一日，终有出头日。"

Every Dog Has His Day

Character: 昌"prosperity".

"Day after day, every dog has his day," 昌 murmurs as he looks at his own reflection in the mirror.

Note: 昌 is graphically structured top to bottom with two 日"day", representing "day after day".

心态决定命运

出场角色：困（kùn）；田（tián）。

困问田："朋友，为啥我一生总是这么困惑呢？"

田看了看困，笑道："因为我心中是主，你心中是木头疙瘩啊！"

A Knot in Heart

Characters: 困"confusion"; 田"field".

困 asks 田, "Why is my life filled with confusion, buddy?"

"Because in your heart is a wood knot while in mine is Lord," grins 田 as he throws a glance at the other.

Note: 困 is composed of 木"wood" enclosed by 口, and 田 is composed of 十 resembling a Christian cross enclosed by 口; the Chinese expression "a knot in one's heart" means "a knotty problem".

处境尴尬

出场角色：卡（kǎ）。

卡照着镜子，自言自语道："为什么我总是不上不下呀！"

A Tight Spot

Character: 卡"block".

Looking in the mirror, 卡 thinks aloud, "How is it that I'm neither up nor down?"

Note: 卡 is graphically structured with 上"up" at the top and 下"down" at the bottom.

心死了，全死了

出场角色：忘（wàng）；亡（wáng）。

忘对亡道："哀莫大于心死啊！"

A Dead Heart, a Dead Man

Characters: 忘"forget"; 亡"dead".

"Nothing is more lamentable than a dead heart," 忘 sighs to 亡.

Note: 忘 is composed of 亡"dead" at the top and 心"heart" at the bottom.

砌墙丢命

出场角色：回（huí）；匹（pǒ）。

回对匹说："兄弟，你那堵墙啥时候砌好啊？"

匹笑答："万万不可。要是把那堵墙砌上了，我的命也就没了。"

A Matter of Life and Death

Characters: 回"chapter"; 匹"impossible".

"Buddy, when will you complete the wall on your side?" says 回 to 匹.

"Never!" smiles the other. "Were the side sealed off, I'd cease to exist."

Note: 巨 is composed similar to 回, without the vertical stroke on the right.

赤手空拳岂能上战场？

出场角色：伐（fá）；代（dài）。
伐对代说："壮士不佩剑，四海莫征战！"

A Warrior Not Armed

Characters: 伐"attack"; 代"replace".
"Not armed with a sword, a warrior fights no war," 伐 says to 代 with a sigh.

Note: With an extra left-falling stroke on the lower right resembling a sword, 伐 differs from 代 in composition.

做个男子汉

出场角色：丰（fēng）；卅（sà）。
丰对卅说："兄弟，站直了，别趴下。"

Be a Man

Characters: 丰"plentiful"; 卅"thirty".

"Buddy, stand up straight," 丰 calls out to 卅. "Don't lie down."

Note: 卅 is shaped like 丰 lying on the side.

前景堪忧

出场角色：焚（fén）。

焚照着镜子，暗自泣道："火上之木，唯有死路一条啊。"

A Gloomy Future

Character: 焚"burn".

Looking in the mirror, 焚 says to himself with a sob, "A forest on fire, my doom is sealed."

Note: 焚 is structured top to bottom with 林"forest" and 火"fire".

穷根究底

出场角色：穷（qióng）；力（lì）。

穷问力："兄弟，我也有的是力气啊，可为啥这么穷啊？"

力笑道："因为你把一身力气藏起来不用啊！"

The Root of Poverty

Characters: 穷"poverty"; 力"strength"

"Listen, pal," says 穷 to 力. "I am strong as an ox, yet why am I as poor as a church mouse?"

"Because all your strength is hidden in the hole," replies 力 with a playful grin.

Note: 穷 is composed of 力 with a semantic radical 穴"cave" on top.

工欲善其事，必先利其器

出场角色：干（gàn）；于（yú）。

干与于一起到河边钓鱼。

傍晚时分，两个人准备打道回府。

"为啥你能钓上来鱼呢？"望着好友装满了鱼的水桶，干羡慕地问。他自己连一条鱼也没钓上来。

"因为我有钩子啊！"于笑嘻嘻地说。

A Sharp Hook Catches More Fish

Characters: 干"work"; 于"a surname".

干 and 于 have been fishing by the riverside.

Dusk is falling and they are about to go back home.

"What makes you so capable of fishing?"

干 asks 于 admiringly as he looks at his mate's pail full of fish, not having caught a single thing himself.

"It's simply because I have a hook," responds 于 with a playful grin.

Note: With its vertical line hooking, 于 differs from 干 in composition.

早不忙，晚必慌

出场角色：尺（chǐ）；迟（chí）。

尺对迟说："朋友，别总是在躺椅上悠哉悠哉了。上班要迟到了。"

Leisure at Dawn, Panic at Dusk

Characters: 尺"ruler"; 迟"late".

"Hey, mate. Don't just relax on the lounge chair all the time," 尺 says to 迟. "You are going to be late for work."

Note: 迟 is composed of 尺 enclosed from lower and left sides by a radical 辶 resembling a lounge chair.

看穿用心

出场角色：儿（ér）；充（chōng）。

儿对充说："兄弟，我看你已经让乌云遮顶了，紧跑两步啊。"

充笑道："你想让我丢弃上半身啊。那我不是变成你的复制品了吗？"

Not Taken In

Characters: 儿"son"; 充"fill".

"Hey, buddy. Notice the looming cloud above your head?" 儿 calls out to 充. "Hasten your pace!"

"You'd like me to part with my upper half?" quips 充 with a smile. "If I did, I'd turn into a replica of you."

Note: 充 is shaped like 儿 with 云 "cloud" on top.

小当益壮

出场角色：虫（chóng）蚕（cán）
虫佩服地对蚕说："好样的，兄弟，咱们小虫也能抵住天。"

One of a Kind

Characters: 虫"worm"; 蚕"silkworm".
"You are one of a kind, pal," 虫 says to 蚕 in admiration. "A worm can hold the sky."

Note: 蚕 is composed of 虫 with 天"sky" on top.

心慈手软

出场角色：心（xīn）；必（bì）。
心做事优柔寡断，在人生的几次重大关口错失良机。心的朋友必却是处事干脆利索，只要自己下了决心的事情就志在必得。
心问必："兄弟，你帮我诊断一下，为啥我做事爱思前想后，总也拿不定主意呢？"必看了心一眼，笑道："因为你不敢往自己身上插刀子啊！"

Soft-Hearted Syndrome

Characters: 心"heart"; 必"must".

心, irresolute and hesitant, has unfortunately missed out on some critical opportunities in life. Meanwhile, his friend 必 approaches everything neatly and efficiently and never gives up once he makes up his mind to do something.

"Buddy, please help me analyze my problem," 心 says to 必. "Why am I always so indecisive?"

Taking a look at the other, 必 smiles, "Because you don't have the guts to pierce yourself with a sabre."

Note: 必 is composed of 心 with a left-falling stroke running through resembling a sabre.

居安要思危

出场角色: 艮 (gěn) ; 退 (tuì) 。

艮见到了退。叹道:"贪图安逸,躺在安乐椅上,焉有不退步之理!"

Ease Goes before a Fall

Characters: 艮"blunt"; 退"retreat".

As 艮 bumps into 退, he lets out a deep sigh and remarks, "Seeking only ease and comfort in the armchair, you are sure to fall behind."

Note: 退 is composed of 艮 surrounded from the lower left by the radical 辶 resembling an armchair.

有腿与无腿

出场角色：兵（bīng）；丘（qiū）。

在一次聚会上，兵认识了丘。

兵同情地对丘说："先生，没有腿你咋走路呢？"

丘不动声色地答道："与其无所事事地四处溜达，不如脚踏实地地屹立千年！"

With and without Legs

Characters: 兵"soldier"; 丘"hill".

兵 meets 丘 at a gathering.

"How do you manage to walk without legs, sir?" 兵 asks 丘 sympathetically.

"I'd rather stand tall and stable for a thousand years than loaf around all day," replies 丘 calmly.

Note: 兵 is structured top to bottom with 丘 and a radical 八 resembling the legs.

没用的烂鱼头

出场角色你：角（jiǎo）；用（yòng）。

角对用道："兄弟，我好羡慕你呀！大伙都夸你是个有用之才。如何才能像你那样呢？请多指点。"

用端详了角一阵，笑道："把你那没用的烂鱼头脑袋拧下来就可以了。"

A Junky Fish Head

Characters: 角"horn"; 用"use".

"Hey, dude. How I envy you! People praise you as someone talented and useful," says 角 to 用. "Could you offer me some advice on how to become as accomplished as you?"

Sizing up 角, 用 grins, "Just wrench off your junky fish head."

Note: 角 is composed of 用 with ⺈ (the top of 鱼"fish") on top.

顶不能歪

出场角色：干 (gān)；千 (qiān)。

干对千说："兄弟，这儿歪那儿歪，顶不能歪。"

Ceilings Cannot Lean

Characters: 干"do"; 千"thousand".

"Listen, bro," says 干 to 千. "Anything can lean except the ceiling."

Note: The horizontal stroke at the top of 干 resembles a ceiling, so does the left-falling stroke at the top of 千, the former flat the latter sloping.

自命不凡

出场角色：工 (gōng)。

工照着镜子，自言自语道："我是一木撑天地呀。"

A Self Admirer

Character: 工 "work".

"I am a pillar supporting both earth and sky," 工 murmurs to his mirror reflection.

Note: 工 is composed of two horizontal strokes or 二 representing the earth and the sky connected by a top-down vertical line resembling a pillar.

语重心长

出场角色：本（běn）；木（mù）。

本和木是无话不谈的莫逆之交。

近日，本听说木不安心工作，经常出入风月场所。本觉得应该跟他好好聊聊了。

本邀请木来到一家酒馆。三杯下肚之后，本对木道："兄弟，千可解，万可解，腰带不可随意解。管不住下半身可不行啊！"

A Friendly Word of Advice

Characters: 本 "self"; 木 "wood".

As close friends, 本 and 木 always speak candidly to each other. When 本 hears that these days 木 is not focused on work and frequents houses with red doors, 本 feels obliged to have a talk with his friend.

"One can afford to loosen everything but the belt, bro," 本 says to 木,

having soaked up three drinks at a tavern. "Never lose your grip on your lower body."

Note: 本 is composed of 木 with a horizontal stroke crossing the vertical line on the lower resembling a belt on the waist.

快乐的秘诀

出场角色：闷（mèn）；门（mén）。

闷问门："为啥我活得这么累呀！老兄能不能告诉我一个快乐的秘诀呀？"

门看了看闷，笑答："没心没肺，活着不累。"

No Core, No Care

Characters: 闷"depressed"; 门"door".

"Am I destined to live a life filled with stress?" 闷 asks 门. "Could you share with me the secret to happiness?"

"No core, no care," smiles 门 as he throws a glance at the other.

Note: 闷 is composed of 心"core" enclosed by 门 from left, top and right sides.

成名之路

出场角色：各（gè）；名（míng）。

各对名说："兄弟，看见你名扬四海，我好生美慕。我奋斗了一辈子，至今在江湖上默默无闻。我该如何成名，请多赐教。"

名打量了一下各，不紧不慢地说："若想成名并非难事，去掉身上影响你成名的东西就行了。"

The Way to Fame

Characters: 各"each"; 名"name".

"How I envy you, buddy," says 各 to 名. "You have gained fame far and wide while I remain unknown in spite of my lifelong efforts. Please offer me some tips on how I could make a name for myself." After sizing up the other, 名 replies in a flat tone, "It's no sweat for you to rise to fame, as long as you tear off the stuff that gets in your way."

Note: 名 is shaped like 各 without the extended part of the right-falling stroke.

惟自重者人方重之

出场角色：三（sān）；丰（fēng）。

三见到了闺蜜丰以后，伤心地说："不管我走到哪儿，人家都叫我'小三儿'。"

丰对三语重心长地说："自己没有脊梁骨，谁会看得起你呢？"

People Respect Her Who Respects Herself

Characters: 三"three"; 丰"abundant".

三 runs into her close buddy 丰. "Wherever I go, they call me 'the third party,'" says 三 with a desolate expression.

"Who'd admire someone who lacks a backbone?" responds the other earnestly.

Note: Without a vertical stroke resembling a backbone running through, 三 differs from 丰 in composition; the Chinese expression "the third party" means "a mistress" or "a home wrecker".

为啥不砌这堵墙？

出场角色: 四 (sì) ; 匹 (pǐ) 。

四对匹说: "兄弟，你还差一堵墙没盖好呢! "

匹看了看四，笑道: "正因为没砌这堵墙，才有了世间独一无二的我呀! "

In the Rough

Characters: 四"four"; 匹"match".

"Pal, I cannot help but notice that one of your walls is not built yet," remarks 四 to 匹.

Glancing briefly at the other, 匹 replies with a grin, "Just because it's left incomplete, there exists in this world an exceptional individual."

Note: The two vertical lines in 四 resemble two walls.

走好人生第一步

出场角色：天（tiān）；夭（yāo）。

天对夭说："你第一笔就不正，下场怎么会好呢？"

A Good Beginning Makes a Good Ending

Characters: 天"day"; 夭"die young".

"Your initial stroke is not level," observes 天 to 夭. "How can you come to a good end?"

Note: 夭 begins with the top left-falling stroke when written.

成才路上

出场角色：木（mù）；才（cái）。

木对才说："兄弟，你为啥要截肢啊？"

才痛苦地答道："为了成才呀！"

The Way to Become Talented

Characters: 木"wood"; 才"talent".

"Hey man, may I ask why you underwent an amputation?" 木 asks 才.

"To become talented," replies the other painfully.

Note: 才 is shaped like 木 without the right-falling stroke.

不要天花板

出场角色：再（zài）；冉（rǎn）。

再对冉说："兄弟，你的顶棚呢？"

冉笑道："我要是有了那玩意儿，还怎么冉冉升起呀！"

A Ceiling Out of Place

Characters: 再"again"; 冉"slowly".

"Where's your ceiling, pal?" 再 asks 冉.

"How could I rise high steadily when there is something weighing me down from above?" replies the other with a playful smile.

Note: 再 is composed of 冉 with a horizontal line on top resembling a ceiling.

士的难处

出场角色：志（zhì）；士（shì）。

志对士说："兄弟，你咋成了无心之士啊！"

士苦笑道："我一安上心就不是'士'了。"

A Warrior's Problem

Characters: 志"will"; 士"warrior".

"Pal, why have you become someone heartless?" 志 asks 士.

"With a heart full of pity, I would not be a true warrior," replies 士 with a bitter smile.

Note: 志 consists of 士 at the top and 心"heart" at the bottom.

昂头挺胸

出场角色：玉（yù）；主（zhǔ）。

玉对主说："凡事莫出头。你总是挺着脑袋招摇，早晚要出事的。"

主说："你想让我学你，把脑袋藏胯骨下边？对不起，我的事情我做主。"

Head Up and Chest Out

Characters: 玉"jade"; 主"master".

"Man, never stick out your head!" 玉 advises 主. "Swaggering around with your head held up, you'll find yourself in trouble sometime or other."

"You expect me to live a life with my head buried under the hipbone as you do?" replies the other. "Sorry, but I am the master of own destiny."

Note: 主 has a dot stroke at the top resembling the head; the Chinese expression "stick out the head" figuratively means "push oneself forward."

失足的懊恼

出场角色：夭（yāo）；跃（yuè）。

夭看着跃生龙活虎的样子，伤心地说："我真是一失足成千古恨啊！"

A Lifelong Regret

Characters: 夭"die young"; 跃"jump".

"A lost foot becomes a lifelong regret!" says 夭 sadly as he watches 跃 leaping with vigour.

Note: 跃 is composed a semantic radical 𧾷"foot" on the left and 夭 on the right.

少了一样东西

出场角色：万（wàn）；方（fāng）。

自打认识了方以后，万便开始闷闷不乐。

方看到朋友一直都郁郁寡欢，于是安慰道："阁下在数字国里的地位远高于个十百千，可以傲视群雄了。难道你还有什么不满意的事吗？"

万道："我虽家财万贯，可和你相比，却少了一个头啊！"

The Missing Piece

Characters: 万"ten thousand"; 方"square".

万 has been in low spirits ever since getting acquainted with 方.

Sensing the other's constant melancholy, 方 says, "Sir, you are far superior to one, ten, hundred and thousand in the world of numbers, in a status that lets you turn your nose up at them. Is there anything you feel unhappy with?"

"Even with ten thousand strings of cash to my name, I still lack the head that you possess," comes the reply.

Note: With an extra dot stroke on top resembling the head, 方 differs from 万.

出头之日

出场角色：刀（dāo）；力（lì）。

刀对力说："兄弟你终于出头了。"

Time to Shine

Characters: 刀"knife"; 力"force".

"Wow, buddy," 刀 says to 力. "You've stuck out your head finally."

Note: The left-falling stroke in 刀 only touches the top horizontal line while the one in 力 runs across the top with the extended part resembling the head; the Chinese "stick out one's head" figuratively means becoming prominent or noticeable.

有的感叹

出场角色：有（yǒu）；宥（yòu）；贿（huì）。

有对着宥和贿感叹道："你们俩一个有乌纱，一个有银子。可怜我是一无所有啊！"

宥和贿安慰道："你就是有啊！你怎么说自己一无所有呢？千万不要妄自菲薄呀！"

Money and Post

Characters: 有"have"; 宥"forgive"; 贿"bribe".

"Look at both of you," 有 laments to 宥 and 贿. "One owns a black hat and the other keeps the green stuff. What a shame I have nothing to my name!"

Being 'have', how can you see yourself as a have-not?" 宥 and 贿 reassures. "Never look down on yourself!"

Note: 宥 is composed of 有 with a radical 宀 on top resenting a black hat which figuratively refers to an official post; 贿 is composed of 贝"money" on the left and 有 on the right.

天然本色不可丢

出场角色：果（guǒ）；裹（guǒ）。

果问裹："裹得这么严实，不舒服吧？咱们是自然之子，还是听从上苍的安排为好。"

Let Nature Take Its Course

Characters: 果"fruit"; 裹"wrap".

"Bundled up so tightly, you're not feeling all that comfortable, are you?" says 果 to 裹. "As fruits of nature, it's best to let nature take its course."

Note: 裹 is structured like 果 in the middle of 衣"garment".

不成器

出场角色：噩（è）；器（qì）。

"器兄，咱俩都有四扇窗，个头、模样也差不多，为啥大伙都愿意跟你交朋友，而对我敬而远之呢？"噩委屈地问器。

器打量了一下噩，笑道："因为你是个不成器的东西呀！"

Not a Ware

Characters: 噩"startling"; 器"utensil".

"You and I have much in common — four windows, similar height and appearance," 噩 complains to 器. "How is it that you are popular while I am unwelcome?"

Casting the other a look, 器 smiles, "It's because you are someone who has not become a ware!"

Note: 噩 and 器 are structured graphically similar; the Chinese expression "become a ware" means "become a success".

平地生波

出场角色：伞（sǎn）；平（píng）。

变天了，倾盆大雨从天而降。

伞和平顶着雨在路上艰难地行走。

伞看见平有点坚持不住了："你这顶子挡雨不行啊，雨水全积在上面了！"

"我以前总是嘲笑你的顶子不正，今天才明白我错在哪里了！"平感慨地说。

A Waterlogged Roof

Characters: 伞"umbrella"; 平"flat".

As the weather deteriorates with rain pouring down, 伞 and 平 trudge through the tempest.

Noticing that the other is struggling to keep up, 伞 says, "Your roof is such a drag, gathering rainwater!"

"I used to mock your slanted top," says 平 with a deep sigh. "But today I realize that I was mistaken!"

Note: 平 has a horizontal stroke at the top resembling a flat roof.

译者后记

李国斌　赵金基

　　华夏汉字源远流长，不仅孕育着国之文化之美，更为艺术创作提供具有挑战却令人兴奋的机会。这些汉字中蕴含着无穷的创意，名家们得以巧妙地运用它们，创作出充满幽默的笑话、精妙戏谑的双关语以及有趣的文字游戏。才华横溢的作家将语言和文学技巧与机智和幽默相融合，在汉字世界中开启了全新的喜剧创作。通过理解语音和语义的奥秘，捕捉构成汉字的视觉元素，作家创作出让人惊叹的笑话和新奇有趣的双关语。将马先生的机智之作翻译出来，不仅具有巨大的挑战性，更是充实满足的过程。译者需要理解汉字的奥秘，抓住作品中所蕴含的幽默精髓。在浏览这些内涵丰富的笑话、双关语和文字游戏时，作者表现出来的机智幽默让译者时常不禁捧腹大笑。因此，我们呼吁读者与我们一起开怀大笑，欣赏华夏汉字和文化的独特之美，而不是嘲笑我们的语言技能之有限。

Translators' Reflection

Li Guobin　Zhao Jinji

The intricate Chinese characters not only embody the beauty and richness of Chinese culture but also present a challenging and exciting outlet for artistic endeavors. These characters contain a wealth of creative potential that can be utilized by skilled minds to create delightful jokes, puns, and wordplays. By merging their linguistic and literary mastery with their wit and humor, experts in Chinese culture and language can unlock a whole new level of comedic expression. With their understanding of the characters' homophonic and semantic meanings, as well as their adeptness at recognizing the visual elements that constitute these characters, they can craft innovative and captivating jokes that are unique to the Chinese language. Translating these witty pieces by Mr. Ma has been a challenging yet enriching process, which requires an understanding of the complexities of Chinese characters and the ability to capture the humor and playfulness that make these works unusual. Navigating the intricacies of these jokes, puns and wordplays, we often find ourselves laughing out loud at the cleverness and wit of the original text. Therefore, we encourage readers to laugh along with us instead of laughing at our limited language skills and to appreciate the beauty and uniqueness of Chinese characters and culture.